T0237720

Construction, Operation and Maintenance of Network System(Junior Level)

Huawei Technologies Co., Ltd.

Construction, Operation and Maintenance of Network System(Junior Level)

 Springer

人民邮电出版社
POSTS & TELECOM PRESS

Huawei Technologies Co., Ltd.
Hangzhou, China

ISBN 978-981-19-3068-3   ISBN 978-981-19-3069-0   (eBook)
https://doi.org/10.1007/978-981-19-3069-0

Jointly published with Posts & Telecom Press, Beijing, China
The print edition is not for sale in China (Mainland). Customers from China (Mainland) please order the
print book from: Posts & Telecom Press.

This Springer imprint is published by the registered company Springer Nature Singapore Pte Ltd.
The registered company address is: 152 Beach Road, #21-01/04 Gateway East, Singapore 189721,
Singapore

Preface

The "1 + X" certificate system is an important reform initiative identified in the National Implementation Plan of Vocational Education Reform and an important innovation in the design of the vocational education system. The pilot project of "1 + X" certificate system for vocational colleges and applied undergraduate colleges is one of the important tasks to implement the National Implementation Plan. In order to help promote the smooth implementation of the vocational skill level standard for network system construction and operation and maintenance and help students pass the network system construction and operation and maintenance certification exam, Huawei Technologies Co., Ltd. (Huawei) organized the compilation of the textbooks (junior level, medium level, and advanced level) of network system construction and operation and maintenance. The preparation of the whole set of textbooks follows the rules of training and accumulation of specialized skills for professionals engaged in network system construction and operation and maintenance and incorporates professional competence, professionalism, and craftsmanship into the design of the books.

As a leading global information and communications technology (ICT) infrastructure and intelligent terminal provider, Huawei is known for developing products covering many fields such as data communication, security, wireless, storage, cloud computing, intelligent computing, and artificial intelligence. Based on the vocational skill standard (junior level) for network system construction and operation and maintenance established by the Ministry of Education, this book is complied with Huawei network product portfolio (routers, switches, wireless controllers, and wireless access points) as a platform, orienting the actual needs of network engineering projects in the industry. Hence, the features of this book are the following:

1. In compilation, this book follows the development law of skillful network talents, with equal emphasis on network knowledge transfer, network skill accumulation, and professionalism enhancement, in order to enable readers to fully prepare for the "1 + X" certification exam, while ensuring the accumulation of project

experience as well as knowledge learning and ability development, laying a solid foundation for adapting to future work positions.

2. In the target design, this book is practical, oriented to the "1 + X" certificate exam and the actual needs of enterprise networks, aiming to cultivate students' abilities to design network, to configure and debug network equipment, to analyze and solve problems, and to innovate.

3. In the selection of content, this book is based on the vocational skill level standard for network system construction and operation and maintenance and adheres to the principle of integrating advancement, scientificity, and practicality, covering the latest and most practical network technologies as far as possible.

4. In the form of content presentation, the book explains the theoretical knowledge of network technology in the simplest and most concise language, expounds network technologies in layers and steps based on detailed laboratory manuals, combines practical operations to help readers consolidate and deepen the principles of network technology learned, and summarizes and annotates the experimental results and phenomena.

As a teaching book, this book is recommended to take 46–66 h for study, with the reference study hours of each chapter as follows:

Theme	Reference hours
Chapter 1 General Operation Safety of Network System	4
Chapter 2 Cabling Engineering	6–8
Chapter 3 Hardware Installation in Network Systems	10–14
Chapter 4 Basic Knowledge of Network Systems	4–8
Chapter 5 Basic Operation of Network Systems	10–14
Chapter 6 Basic Operation and Maintenance of Network System	10–14
Course assessment	2–4
Total hours	46–66

This book is organized by Huawei Technologies Co., Ltd. and written by Ye Libing, Wu Yuexiang, Wang Sunan, and Dong Yueqiu from Shenzhen Polytechnic, with Ye Libing in charge of the final compilation, and it is technically supported and proofread by Changlong Yuan, Yueyue Lu, and Peng Liu of Huawei.

Due to the limited level and experience of the editors, inaccuracies and omissions in the book are inevitable, and readers are invited to criticize and correct them. For resources related to this book, readers can download at www.ryjiaoyu.com.

Hangzhou, China   Huawei Technologies Co., Ltd.
December 2021

Contents

About the Author

Huawei Technologies Co., Ltd. Founded in 1987, Huawei is a leading global provider of information and communications technology (ICT) infrastructure and smart devices. We have approximately 197,000 employees and we operate in over 170 countries and regions, serving more than three billion people around the world.

Huawei's mission is to bring digital to every person, home and organization for a fully connected, intelligent world. To this end, we will: drive ubiquitous connectivity and promote equal access to networks to lay the foundation for the intelligent world; provide the ultimate computing power to deliver ubiquitous cloud and intelligence; build powerful digital platforms to help all industries and organizations become more agile, efficient, and dynamic; redefine user experience with AI, offering consumers more personalized and intelligent experiences across all scenarios, including home, travel, office, entertainment, and fitness & health.

Chapter 1
General Operation Safety of Network System

Work safety refers to the compliance of safety regulations in the production process. The purpose is to ensure the safety and health of individuals, as well as the normal and orderly production of enterprises, and to prevent casualties and property losses. Safety can never be trivial. The occurrence of safety accidents is always accompanied by heavy harm to individuals and their families, which also damages the operation and production of enterprises, and even drags the development of society and the country down in serious cases. Therefore, work safety is a critical policy in China, and also the primary consideration in pre-production.

The safety in installation, operation and maintenance of network equipment are also covered in the scope of work safety. The operation of network equipment should comply with both the general rules of work safety and the safety rules specific to network equipment. This chapter will start with the introduction of general safety norms, including the safety awareness and operation safety knowledge required of operators, and then introduce the operation safety knowledge specific to network equipment, involving electrical safety, battery safety, radiation safety and other safety knowledge.

By the end of this chapter, you will

(1) Comprehend general safety norms (2) Grape the knowledge of electrical safety norms for network equipment operation (3) Grape the knowledge of battery safety norms for network equipment operation	(4) Grape the knowledge of radiation safety norms for network equipment operation (5) Grape other relevant knowledge of safety norm

© The Author(s) 2023
Huawei Technologies Co., Ltd., *Construction, Operation and Maintenance of Network System(Junior Level)*, https://doi.org/10.1007/978-981-19-3069-0_1

1.1 General Safety Norms

The installation, operation and maintenance of network equipment must be carried out in accordance with certain rules and precautions, otherwise the equipment may be damaged to the point that it cannot work properly, or even cause personal casualties. In order to achieve work safety, the operator should first have safety awareness, and then master the corresponding knowledge of operation safety. For this purpose, this chapter will introduce the relevant knowledge.

1.1.1 Safety Awareness

Personnel involved in the construction, operation and maintenance of the network system should study and follow the *Work Safety Law of the People's Republic of China*. They should adhere to the policy of "Safety First, Prevention First" and the awareness of "Safety Is of Paramount Importance", and prevent and reduce the occurrence of engineering accidents and personal casualties by conscientiously learning the relevant operation safety knowledge and abiding by the relevant operation safety norms.

1.1.2 Operation Safety Knowledge

In the actual work and operation, safety is always the top priority, so the relevant norms must be strictly abided. The following is a general introduction to the necessary operation safety knowledge.

1. The personnel responsible for installation, operation and maintenance of the equipment must receive strict training, and should not take his/her post without corresponding qualifications for the post or comprehension of all safety precautions and correct operation methods.
2. During the installation, operation and maintenance of the equipment, the following requirements should be complied with in conjunction with the observance of local laws and regulations.

   (a) Only qualified professionals and trained personnel are authorized to perform equipment installation, operation and maintenance.
   (b) Only qualified professionals and trained personnel are authorized to remove safety facilities and repair equipment.
   (c) Operators should promptly report to the responsible person any failure or error that may cause safety problems.
   (d) The personnel who operate the equipment, including the operators, trained personnel and professionals, should have the special operation qualification

required by the local authorities, such as the qualifications for high pressure operation, high altitude operation, special equipment operation qualification, etc.

3. The personnel operating the equipment should immediately terminate the operation once they detect the possibility of personal injury or equipment damage, and should report to the project leader, and take feasible and effective protective measures.
4. It is strictly prohibited to install, use and operate outdoor equipment (including but not limited to handling equipment, installing cabinets, installing cables, etc.) and connect the equipment to outdoor cables in bad weather such as thunder, rain, snow and strong wind.
5. It is strictly prohibited to wear watches, bracelets, rings, necklaces and other conductive objects when installing, operating and maintaining equipment.
6. During equipment installation, operation and maintenance, personnel operating the equipment must ensure that safety protection measures are in place, such as wearing insulating gloves, protective clothing, safety helmet and safety shoes, as shown in Fig. 1.1.
7. Installation, operation and maintenance must be carried out in accordance with the steps in the instructions in order.
8. Before the contact with any conductor surface or terminal, the shock hazard should be eliminated by measuring the voltage at the contact using a voltmeter.
9. All slots should be ensured to have a board or filler panel in place. The board should be prevent from dangerous voltage leakage,the normal air duct and control of electromagnetic interference should be ensured, and the backplanes, mother boards and boards should be kept free from dust and other foreign matters.
10. The user should carry out routine inspection and maintenance of the installed equipment according to the requirements of the instructions to ensure the timely replacement of the faulty parts and the safe operation of the equipment.
11. After the installation of the equipment, the packaging materials scattering in the equipment area should be removed, such as cartons, foam materials, plastic materials, binding straps, etc.
12. In case of fire, relevant personnel should press the fire alarm bell, and then evacuate the building or equipment area and call the fire alarm. In any case, never re-enter the burning building after evacuation.

Relevant concepts involved in the above introduction are explained as follows.

1. Professionals: Personnel who have the ability to train others or rich experience in operating equipment, while being clear about potential sources and levels of danger in the process of equipment installation, operation and maintenance.
2. Trained personnel: personnel who have received required technical training and accumulated necessary experience, are aware of the possible risks associated with

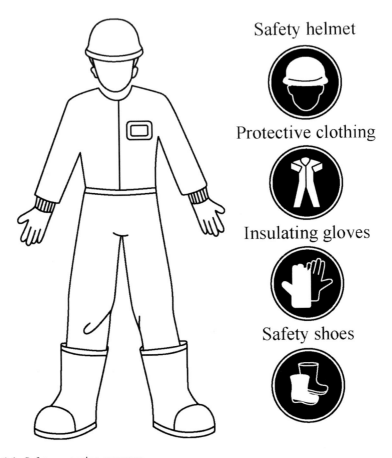

Safety helmet

Protective clothing

Insulating gloves

Safety shoes

Fig. 1.1 Safety protection measures

a certain operation and are capable to take measures to minimize the risks to themselves and other personnel.

3. Users/Operators: All people other than trained personnel and professionals, including operators, customers, ordinary people who may come into contact with the equipment, etc.

1.2   Operation Safety of Network Equipment

In view of the characteristics of network equipment, even technicians with general safety knowledge will inevitably encounter some specific operational problems during the installation, operation and maintenance of network equipment, including problems related to electrical safety, battery safety, radiation safety, mechanical safety and maintenance safety. Therefore, technical personnel need to master the detailed rules to ensure operation safety in any situation.

1.2.1 Electrical Safety

Electrical safety is a key to operation safety of network equipment system. In electrical operation, even a slightly improper operation may lead to casualties, equipment damage and other serious accidents, causing serious consequences. Therefore, the relevant electrical safety rules must be strictly observed during the equipment installation.

1. Grounding

The so-called grounding includes working grounding and protective grounding. Working grounding refers to the grounding of the power supply neutral point (transformer or generator) of an electrical device, which functions as follows.

(a) To relieve the damage to electrical device insulation caused by the increase in the voltage to grounding of the two phases due to transient over-voltage or due to the other phase's connection to ground in the electrical system.
(b) When the electrical device runs into a grounding fault, to provide a path for grounding fault current, in order to immediately start the protective device and cut off the fault circuit.

Protective grounding refers to the grounding of the exposed current-carrying part of an electrical device, which functions as follows.

(a) To reduce the voltage to ground of the exposed conductive part in case of a grounding fault, that is, to reduce the contact voltage.
(b) To provide a path for grounding fault current, in order to immediately start the protective device and cut off the fault circuit.

The network equipment should be installed, operated and maintained with guarantee that the protective ground wire is reliably grounded in accordance with the local power distribution norms for buildings. Installation of equipment to be grounded must begin with the installation of a permanently connected protective ground wire; for dismantling the equipment, the protective ground wire must be removed at the end. If the equipment employs a three-pin socket, you must ensure that the grounding terminal in the three-pin socket is connected to the protective ground wire.

2. Operation requirements for AC and DC power supply

The supply voltage of a power supply system is classified as a hazardous voltage, which may lead to electric shock by direct contact or indirect contact through a wet object. Even, an improper or incorrect operation may cause accidents such as fire or electric shock. Such being the cases, the operation of a power supply system must comply with the relevant safety norms, including the following precautions.

(a) Before installing the equipment, confirm whether the upper-level equipment is matched with the over-current protection device.

(b) The equipment using a permanently connected power entry module should be externally equipped with an accessible disconnecting device.

(c) AC-powered equipment can be applied to TN and TT power supply system.

(d) For DC-powered equipment, it is necessary to ensure enhanced insulation or double insulation between DC power supply and AC power supply.

(e) If there is a possibility of touching a energized part during the electrical connection of the equipment, the corresponding breaking device for the upper-level equipment must be disconnected first.

(f) Before connecting a loaded (electrical equipment) cable or battery cable, it is necessary to confirm whether the input voltage is within the rated voltage range of the equipment.

(g) Before connecting a load (electrical equipment) cable or battery cable, it is necessary to confirm the polarities of the cable and terminal to prevent reversed connection.

(h) Ensure the correct electrical connection of the equipment before switching on the power.

(i) If the equipment receives multiple inputs, all inputs should be disconnected before operation.

3. Cabling requirements

Proper cabling is beneficial to reduce the maintenance cost and prolong the service life of equipment. The following points need to be noted when cabling.

(a) In the case of making the power cable on site, the insulating cover of the power cable in other positions except the wiring part should not be cut, otherwise it may lead to short circuit, and then cause personal injury, fire or other accidents.

(b) The use in high temperature environment may cause aging or damage of the insulating cover of the cable. A sufficient distance should be kept between the cable and the power copper bar, current divider, fuse, heat sink and other heating devices.

(c) Signal cables and high-current or high-voltage cables should be bound separately.

(d) The cables provided by users should conform to local standards.

(e) No cable should pass through the air exhaust vent in the cabinet.

(f) The cables stored below zero temperature should be moved to and stored at room temperature for more than 24 h before laying or cabling.

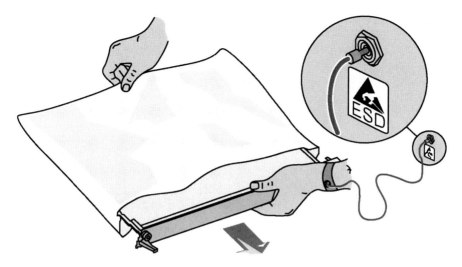

Fig. 1.2 How to wear an ESD wrist strap

4. TNV circuit

A telecommunication network voltage (TNV) circuit is one that carries communication signals, which is defined as suitable for devices with restricted access areas. With proper design and protection, the voltage of this circuit will not exceed the specified limit under either normal operation or single fault. For TNV circuits, there are following general requirements.

(a) To avoid electric shock, never connect a safety extra-low voltage (SELV) circuit to a TNV circuit.
(b) In lightning weather, never plug or unplug the signal interface connected to the outdoor.
(c) To lower the fire risk, be sure to use 26 AWG telephone wires or bigger ones. AWG is short for American Wire Gauge, a standard for specifying wire diameters. The higher number before "AWG" refers to the thinner wire. Please refer to the corresponding manual for details.

5. Antistatic requirement

When the human body moves, clothes rub, shoes rub against the floor, or you get an ordinary plastic product with your hands, the human body generates a static electric field that is prone to persist until discharge. Therefore, before touching a device or holding a plugboard or board, or an application specific integrated circuit (ASIC) chip with your hand, you must wear an ESD wrist strap, with the other end of it being well grounded, to prevent ESD-sensitive components from being damaged by static electricity on human body (see Fig. 1.2). At the same time, attention should be paid to the following two points.

(a) When holding a board, you must hold the edge area without a component, and never touch the chip by hand.

(b) A dismantled board must be packed with anti-static packaging materials before storage or transportation.

1.2.2 Battery Safety

Batteries are commonly used in network equipment. The installation, operation and maintenance of the battery should meet the following requirements.

1. Never expose a battery to high temperatures or to heating devices, such as sunlight, heaters, microwaves, ovens and water heaters, as an overheating battery may explode.
2. To avoid battery leakage, overheating, fire or explosion, never disassemble or modify a battery, insert a foreign matter into it, or immerse it in water or other liquids.
3. In case of discoloration, deformation, abnormal heating or other anomalies happen to the battery in use or stored, it should be replaced immediately.
4. Before installing or maintaining a battery or performing other operations on the battery, you should wear goggles, rubber gloves and protective clothing to avoid the harm caused by electrolyte spills. If the battery leaks, avoid the leaked liquid from contact with skin or eyes. In case of contact, rinse the contact area with plenty of water immediately and go to the hospital for treatment.
5. When handling batteries, they should be placed in the required direction. Never turn the batteries upside down or tilt them.
6. In the installation, maintenance and other operations, the battery circuit should be kept disconnected.
7. A battery may only be replaced with one of the same type or equivalent type. Improper replacement may lead to battery explosion.
8. Never connect a metallic conductor with the battery poles or contact the battery ends, so as to avoid battery short circuit or body injury such as burns caused by battery overheating.
9. Disposal of batteries should comply with local laws and regulations, and it is not allowed to dispose them as household waste Improper disposal may lead to battery explosion.
10. Never squeeze or pierce a battery or make it fall, So as to avoid battery short circuit and overheating caused by the strong external pressure on it.
11. Damaged batteries should not be kept in service.
12. Prevent children or pets from swallowing and biting a battery, so as not to cause damage to them or cause battery explosion.

In view of the differences between batteries from different manufacturers, please read the instruction manual from the manufacturer before installing, operating and maintaining the battery. In addition, safety requirements differ for rechargeable and non-rechargeable batteries used in devices.

1. Safety requirements for rechargeable batteries

Rechargeable batteries need to be protected against battery short circuits, flammable gases, battery leaks, and capacity loss.

(a) Protection against battery short circuit

When the battery short-circuits, the instantaneous large current and the large amount of energy released may cause personal injury and property damage. Therefore, if possible, disconnect the working battery charging connection before performing the job, and avoid battery short circuit caused by conductive objects such as metal.

(b) Protection against flammable gases

Lead-acid batteries will release flammable gases when working abnormally, so they should be placed where is ventilated, with fire prevention in place. Never use a lead-acid battery unsealed. Lead-acid batteries should be placed horizontally and fixed to ensure that hydrogen discharge measures are normal to avoid combustion or corrosion of equipment.

(c) Protection against battery leakage

The battery may deform, damage or leak electrolyte at an excess temperature. When the battery temperature exceeds 60 °C, the electrolyte should be checked for leakage. Once electrolyte spills are discovered, possible damage from the electrolyte should be avoided when moving the leaky battery. Sodium bicarbonate ($NaHCO_3$) or sodium carbonate (Na_2CO_3) can be used for neutralizing and absorbing the spilled electrolyte.

(d) Protection against capacity loss

After the battery connection is completed and before the power supply system is energized, the battery fuse or air switch should be confirmed to be disconnected, so as to avoid the battery capacity loss caused by long-term outage of the system as well as further damage to the battery.

In addition to the above 4 requirements, it is also necessary to tighten the battery cable or copper bar by exerting the torque specified in the battery instructions, otherwise the virtual access of battery bolt may result in unaccessible connection voltage drop, or even heat the battery when the current is high to the extent of burning the battery.

2. Safety requirements for non-rechargeable batteries

There are some safety requirements for devices that use dry batteries or non-rechargeable lithium batteries.

(a) For devices that use non-removable built-in batteries, the batteries should not be replaced by the user to avoid damage to the batteries themselves or the devices. If you need to replace the battery, you can find the manufacturer's after-sales service personnel for replacement.

(b) In order to avoid battery burning and explosion, do not throw the battery into the fire.

1.2.3 Radiation Safety

Radiation here generally refers to electromagnetic radiation, that is, the emission of energy into a space from a source of radiation in the form of electromagnetic wave, or the transmission of energy within the space in this form. Electromagnetic radiation is divided into ionizing radiation and non-ionizing radiation. Electromagnetic waves with very short wavelengths or very high frequencies have great energy in each of its photons, which can break chemical bonds between molecules. This kind of radiation is called ionizing radiation, including gamma rays, cosmic rays and x-rays produced by radioactive materials. Electromagnetic waves with low frequency, whose photons can not damage the chemical bonds between molecules, are called non-ionizing radiation, such as visible light, laser, microwaves, radio waves, etc. The electromagnetic radiation studied here refers to non-ionizing radiation. Electromagnetic radiation is almost everywhere in our daily life. The electromagnetic radiation that is restrained within certain energy limit does not exert impact on people's health until the energy exceeds the limit to gradually produce some negative effects. Next is some safety knowledge of electromagnetic radiation.

1. Electromagnetic field (EMF) exposure

    For wireless transmitting equipment, equipment with wireless transmitting function, and high voltage equipment and facilities, hazards exposure to their power frequency EMF should not be ignored. The operator must comply with relevant local laws and regulations when erecting some specialized equipment or facilities. Any changes to equipment structures or antennas, or RF output specifications or parameters, or to the site environment of specialized erection equipment or facilities will require reassessment of EMF exposure.

    (a) EMF exposure zone

        An EMF exposure zone (over-limited zone) refers to an area that is at a certain distance from electromagnetic equipment or facilities. The forbidden zone is designated according to the exposure limits prescribed by relevant regulations for the purpose of controlling the exposure of the public or operators to the EMF. Appropriate measures to ensure a safe distance from EMF exposure include but are not limited to the following.

        (i) Sites where specialized equipment or facilities are deployed should not be open to the public and should be planned in areas inaccessible to the public.
        (ii) Only professionals and trained personnel should be allowed to enter the site of specialized equipment or facilities.

(iii) Before entering the forbidden zone of EMF exposure, professionals should know the location of the areas of excess radiation in advance, and close the emission source before entering.

(iv) The site should be clearly marked to alert professionals that they are or may be in the EMF exposure zone.

(v) After the installation in the site, it should be monitored and checked regularly.

(vi) Effective physical barriers and striking warning signs should be set up in each EMF exposure zone.

(vii) Isolating devices should be installed in the outside of the equipment structure.

(b) Security precautions for installation and use of BTS

The RF electromagnetic radiation of Base Transceiver Station (BTS) is reasonably designed to be below the limits of relevant standards. Therefore, the BTS under normal working conditions will not endanger the public or relevant personnel. However, some defective BTS antennas or other defects in the BTS may cause the RF electromagnetic radiation to exceed the limits.

Professionals should keep to the following principles when installing and operating the BTS or its antennas.

(i) Read the Work Safety Proposal before installing and operating the BTS or its antenna and comply with local laws and regulations.

(ii) Before installing or maintaining an antenna near a tower, mast, etc. where a BTS and its antennas are installed, request the relevant personnel to turn off the antenna transmission source.

(iii) When necessary, field operators should wear radiation monitoring and alarm instruments.

(iv) Raise the antenna mounted on the roof to exceed the height of persons who may work and live on the roof.

(v) The transmitting antennas installed on the roof should be far away from areas where people are most likely to tread, such as roof access points, telephone service points and heating, ventilation and air conditioning equipment.

(vi) The directional antenna installed on the roof should be placed outside, without facing the building.

(vii) Try to balance the choice between large- and small-aperture antennas, as the former provide better signal coverage, while the latter is able to reduce visual impact.

(viii) Be prudent to install antennas provided by multiple companies in the same place. It may be a good idea for a community or building management organization to install antennas provided by all companies in the same location, but this is prone to safety risks, so installation personnel should be very careful.

(ix) Special security measures should be put in place at antenna stations near hospitals and schools.

(c) Guidance for the use of other wireless equipment

  (i) The safe distance from EMF exposure specified in the relevant manuals of wireless equipment shall be followed, if any.
  (ii) If the RF emission power of some equipment is low enough to meet the safety requirements for EMF exposure, there is no need to limit the service distance.
  (iii) For some equipment specially designed to meet the safety requirements for EMF exposure at the time of operating close to the human body, there is no need to limit the service distance.

(d) Guidance for the use of high-voltage equipment or facilities

   Only the power frequency EMF generated by equipment or facilities with higher voltage (for example, more than 100 kV) will have adverse effects on human body, so it is necessary to conduct EMF exposure assessment according to relevant requirements.

2. Laser radiation

   Laser is also widely used in today's social production and life. Laser transceivers are often configured in network equipment, which are mainly used in optical fiber transmission systems and related test tools. Infrared lasers are used to provide the light for optical fiber communications systems, thus optical fibers or connector ports emit lasers that are invisible to the naked eyes but have very high power density. Therefore, looking at the laser output terminal with naked eyes will burn your eyes. In order to avoid damage caused by laser radiation, the following operation rules should be observed when laser related operations are carried out.

(a) Non-authorized personnel who have received relevant training shall not carry out relevant operations.
(b) Always wear goggles properly in laser or optical fiber related operations.
(c) Make sure to turn off the light source before disconnecting the fiber optic connector.
(d) After disconnecting the optical fiber connectors, install the optical fiber caps to protect all the optical fiber connectors.
(e) Before making sure that the light source has been closed, never gaze at the bare optical fiber or connector terminal with naked eyes, but immediately install a dust cap for the optical fiber connector.
(f) Ensure that the optical fiber is disconnected with the light source before cutting or welding the fiber.
(g) Use an optical power meter to measure the optical power to ensure that the light source is turned off.
(h) Take care to avoid laser radiation when opening the front door of the optical fiber transmission system.
(i) It is strictly prohibited to use optical instruments such as microscopes, magnifying glasses and loupes to watch optical fiber connectors or optical fiber terminals.

1.2.4   Other Safety Knowledge

Operational safety knowledge not only covers the aspects introduced above. Other safety knowledge such as mechanical safety, maintenance safety and safety signs will be introduced below.

1. Mechanical safety

   (a) Safety in lifting installation
      Lifting installation shall meet the following requirements.

      (i) Personnel carrying out lifting installation must receive relevant training and get qualified for the operations before the taking up the post.
     (ii) Lifting apparatuses must be all in readiness and be verified before use.
    (iii) The lifting apparatuses must be firmly fixed on load-bearing fixtures or walls before lifting operations.
    (iv) During the lifting, the included angle between the two cables should not exceed 90°, as shown in Fig. 1.3.

Fig. 1.3 Lifting a
heavy load

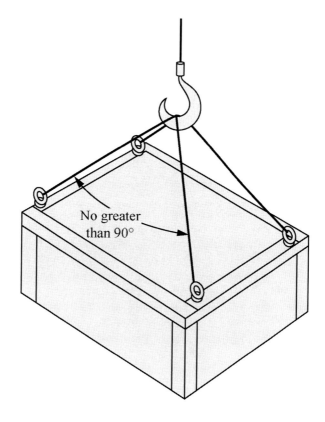

No greater
than 90°

(b) Safety with ladders

The following requirements should be satisfied before using the ladder.

  (i) First confirm that the ladder is intact, and then check that it is in line with the load-bearing restrictions stipulated for the ladder. Overweight use is strictly prohibited.
  (ii) The slope of the ladder is best set to $75°$, which can be measured with an angle square. When using a ladder, the wider ladder butt should be adown or the ladder bottom should be protected against slipping. The ladder should be placed in a stable place.

The following requirements should be satisfied during using the ladder.

  (i) Do not deviate the center of your body weight from the edge of the ladder.
  (ii) Keep your body steady before operation to reduce risks and ensure safety.
  (iii) Do not climb above the fourth step from the top of the ladder
  (iv) If you need to climb the roof, the vertical height of the ladder above the eaves should reach at least 1 meter.

(c) Safety in drilling

Drilling on the cabinet is strictly prohibited. Drilling operations that fail to meet the requirements will damage the electromagnetic shielding performance of the cabinet or damage the cables inside. The metal filings produced by drilling, if any, will cause short circuit to the circuit board if they swoop in the cabinet. The following requirements shall be satisfied when drilling on the wall or ground.

  (i) Always wear goggles and protective gloves when drilling.
  (ii) During drilling, the equipment should be shielded from the metal filings swooping in. After drilling, the metal filings should be cleared up in time.

(d) Safety in heavy load handling

  (i) Before handling heavy objects, get ready for load bearing to avoid the operation personnel being crushed by heavy objects. When handling a shelf, keep your back straight and move steadily to avoid sprain.
  (ii) Wear protective gloves when handling equipment by hand, so as not to cut your hands by sharp corners.
  (iii) When handling a shelf, hold the handles or the bottom edge of the shelf, instead of the handles of the installed modules (e.g. power module, fan module and board) in it.

2. Maintenance safety

   The following requirements are generally required for maintenance on equipment.

   (a) When replacing any accessories or components in the equipment, wear the ESD wrist strap, and ensure that one end of the wrist strap is well grounded, and the other end is in good contact with the your skin.
   (b) When replacing parts, properly place the parts, screws, tools and other objects, so as to prevent them from falling into the running fan and damaging the fan or equipment.
   (c) When pulling out the shelf or parts to be replaced from the cabinet, pay attention not to be crushed or smashed by the unstable or heavy equipment installed in the cabinet.

   Here are a few things need to be noticed in maintenance.

   (a) Replacement of replaceable fuse

       (i) To replace the fuse, the fuse with the same specification as the original one should be selected for the replacement.
       (ii) Before replacing the fuse at the panel, be sure to disconnect the power supply of the equipment, otherwise there may be electric shock hazard.
       (iii) The replaceable fuse is generally located at the panel near the input or output port of the AC or DC power supply for the equipment.
       (iv) To determine the specification of the fuse for replacement, refer to the specification of the backup fuse, or the specification of the standard fuse on the panel. A non-conforming fuse may result in equipment damage, personal injury or property damage.

   (b) Replacement of soldered fuse

       (i) For the fuse with screen-printed rating on the board, it should be replaced only by authorized personnel according to the screen-printed rating.
       (ii) For the fuse without screen-printed rating on the board, it must be returned to the factory for repair, instead of being maintained on site. If replacement is needed, it shall be replaced only by authorized personnel according to the model and rating provided by the manufacturer for the corresponding item number in the Bill of Material of the product.

   (c) Replacement of distribution box and board

       (i) Before replacing the distribution box, ensure that the front protective air switch is disconnected, and wear insulating gloves properly.
       (ii) When replacing the board, never contact the components on the board directly by hand, so as not to damage the board.
       (iii) The unoccupied slot should be installed with a filler panel.

Fig. 1.4 Signs for Laser
Hazard Class 1

Fig. 1.5 Signs for Laser Hazard Class 1 M

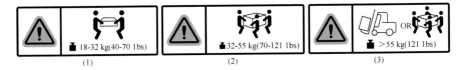

Fig. 1.6 Signs of equipment weight

(d) Replacement of fan

When replacing the fan, wait until the fan stops completely and pull out part of the fan by palling the handle on the fan module. Then, pull the entire fan module out of the frame, otherwise the blades may injure your fingers.

3. Description of safety signs

(a) Signs of laser hazard classes

Laser danger level signs are shown in Figs. 1.4 and 1.5. When optical fiber related operations are carried out, it is strictly prohibited to approach or look at the optical fiber outlet with naked eyes. For other considerations for laser-related operations, please refer to Sect. 1.2.3.

(b) Signs of equipment weight

Equipment weight signs is shown in Fig. 1.6. Figure 1.6 (1) indicates that the weight of replaceable/pluggable part or equipment exceeds 18 kg, that it needs to be lifted by two people jointly; Fig. 1.6 (2) indicates that the replaceable/pluggable parts or equipment weigh more than 32 kg and need

Fig. 1.7 Sign of periodic
cleaning of dustproof net

Clean periodically

Fig. 1.8 Warning sign of
interlocking device

Lift, then close the door.

Fig. 1.9 Danger sign of
high voltage

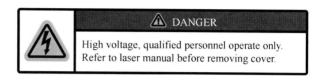

⚠ DANGER

High voltage, qualified personnel operate only.
Refer to laser manual before removing cover.

to be lifted by three people; Fig. 1.6 (3) indicates that the part or equipment
weighs more than 55 kg and needs to be moved by a forklift or by four people.
(c) Sign of regular cleaning of dustproof net
      The sign of periodic cleaning of dustproof net is shown in Fig. 1.7,
indicating that the dustproof net should be cleaned and replaced periodically.
(d) Warning sign of interlocking device
      In general, the door of outdoor equipment is fixed by a metal rod after
opening to prevent accidental closing of the door. To close the door, you
should lift the support rod. The warning sign of the interlocking device is
shown in Fig. 1.8, indicating that the metal rod supporting the door should be
lifted before closing the door.
(e) Danger sign of high voltage
      Danger sign of high voltage is shown in Fig. 1.9. When this sign is
displayed, please read the safety manual completely before operation to
ensure that you have understood the precautions in the manual.

1.3   Summary

This chapter starts with the introduction of general safety norms, including the safety
awareness and operation safety knowledge required of operators, and then introduce
the operation safety knowledge specific to network equipment, involving electrical
safety, battery safety, radiation safety and other safety knowledge.
      Upon the study of this chapter, the reader should master the general safety norms
and operation safety knowledge.

1.4 Exercise

1. During the lifting, the included angle between the two cables should ().

   A. <60°
   B. <90°
   C. >60°
   D. >90°

2. Among the following statements about electrical cabling, the false one is ().

   A. Signal cables and high-current or high-voltage cables should be bound together for space saving.
   B. The cables provided by users should conform to local standards.
   C. No cable should pass through the air exhaust vent in the cabinet.
   D. The cables stored below zero temperature should be moved to and stored at room temperature for more than 24 h before laying or cabling.

3. Among the following statements about laser-related operations, the false one is ().

   A. Non-authorized personnel who have received relevant training shall not carry out relevant operations.
   B. Always wear goggles properly in laser or optical fiber related operations.
   C. Make sure to turn off the light source before disconnecting the fiber optic connector.
   D. It is recommended to use optical instruments such as microscopes and magnifying glasses to watch optical fiber connectors or optical fiber terminals for a close-up view.

4. [Multi-choice] It is strictly prohibited to () in bad weather such as thunder, rain, snow and strong wind.

   A. Install, use and operate outdoor equipment
   B. Connect the equipment to outdoor cables
   C. Install, use and operate indoor equipment
   D. Conduct indoor operations

5. [Multi-choice] Among the following statements about operations related to rechargeable batteries, the correct ones are ().

   A. Short circuits should be avoided.
   B. Sodium bicarbonate can be used for neutralizing and absorbing the spilled electrolyte.
   C. The batteries can be turned upside down during handling.
   D. In the installation and maintenance, the battery circuit should be kept disconnected.

Chapter 2
Cabling Engineering

Generic cabling is a highly flexible modular information transmission pipeline within or between buildings, which can not only connect voice, data, image equipment or switching equipment with other information management systems, but also connect these equipment with the outside. It also covers all cables and associated connection components between connection points of network or telecommunication lines outside the buildings and application system equipment. Generic cabling systems can accommodate components of different series and specifications, including transmission mediums, connection hardware (such as distribution frames, connectors, sockets, plugs, adapters, etc.) and electrical protection equipment, etc. Although they work together to build various subsystems, they undertake different specific tasks. Therefore, the generic cabling system is not only easy to implement, but also can be upgraded smoothly as the demand changes.

Generic cabling schemes were first introduced in China in the 1990s. With China's continued efforts in infrastructure construction, the market demand continues to expand, which has contributed to the rapid development of the generic cabling industry. In particular, the GB 50311 - 2016 "Code for Engineering Design of Generic Cabling System" and GB/T 50312 - 2016 "Code for Engineering Acceptance of Generic Cabling System", which were implemented on April 1, 2017, have greatly driven the application and development of generic cabling system in China, which, as two national standards, put forward specific requirements and provisions for the design, construction, acceptance and management of the genetic cabling systems.

In order to endow readers with intuitive and quick understanding of genetic cabling, this chapter will follow the working process of cabling projects, first of all, taking the reader to know network cabinets from scratch, then looking into all kinds of communication cables and common connecting devices, cabling tools and instruments, and mastering their methods of use, and finally exploring the engineering technical standards of equipment room subsystems and acceptance of works.

© The Author(s) 2023
Huawei Technologies Co., Ltd., *Construction, Operation and Maintenance of Network System(Junior Level)*, https://doi.org/10.1007/978-981-19-3069-0_2

By the end of this chapter, you will

(1) Get familiar with various network cabinets	(4) Understand tools and instruments commonly used in cabling engineering
(2) Master the characteristics and identification methods of communication cables	(5) Understand the engineering standards, technical requirements for installation and acceptance content of equipment room subsystems
(3) Get familiar with common connecting devices of communication systems	

2.1 Network Cabinet

Network cabinet is used to assemble panels, plug-ins, subracks, electronic components and mechanical parts and components into an integrated cabinet.

1. Classification by installation location: indoor cabinet and outdoor cabinet.
2. Classification by purpose: network cabinet, server cabinet, power cabinet, and passive cabinet (used to carry optical fiber distribution frame, main distribution frame, etc.).
3. Classification by installation method: ground mounting, wall mounting, pole installation.

We know network cabinets different styles are operating in various sites. With the continuous development of the ICT industry, network cabinets are taking in more and more powerful functions. These network cabinets are generally installed in cable distribution rooms, central equipment rooms, monitoring centers, shelters, outdoor stations and other places, as shown in Fig. 2.1.

Network cabinets are usually available in white, black and gray, They are classified by material as aluminum profile cabinet, cold-rolled steel cabinet or hot-rolled steel cabinet or other types; and by processing technology as ninefold profile cabinet or 16-fold profile cabinet or other types.

The basic structure of the network cabinet includes the top cover, fan, mounting beam, removable side door, aluminum alloy frame, etc., as shown in Fig. 2.2.

2.1.1 Network Cabinet with "U" as Unit

1. What does the unit "U" mean

   Before introducing various network cabinets, we need to understand the commonly used unit "U" that describes the size of a cabinet.

   "U" is an abbreviation for "Unit" that represents the external dimension (to measure the height or thickness of the cabinet) of the server. The specific dimension representation rules are determined by the Electronic Industries Association (EIA). In terms of thickness, 1 U is equal to the thickness of 4.445 cm, and

Fig. 2.1   Network cabinet

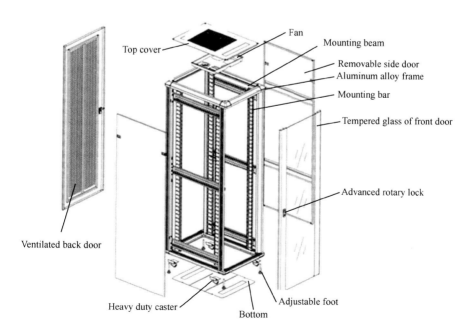

Fig. 2.2   Basic structure of network cabinet

Fig. 2.3 A 1 U server

2 U is 8.89 cm. The so-called "1 U server" refers to the server with the shape conforming to EIA standard and the thickness of 4.445 cm, as shown in Fig. 2.3.

2. Standard U-sized cabinet

Standard U-sized cabinet is widely used in computer network facilities, wired communications equipment, wireless communications equipment, electronic equipment, passive material stack, which features strengthened electromagnetic shielding, ability to block the working noise of the equipment to a certain extent, and reduced floor area occupied by equipment. Some high-end cabinets are equipped with air filtration function to improve the working environment for precision equipment.

Engineering equipment mostly employs panels that are 19 inches (about 48 cm), 21 inches (about 53 cm), 23 inches (about 58 cm), etc. in width, so there are 19-inch (about 48 cm), 21-inches (about 53 cm) and 23-inches (about 58 cm) standard cabinets and things like that. Among them, 19-inch standard cabinet ("19-inch cabinet" for short) is more common. For some equipment in non-standard dimensions, most can be installed and fixed in the standard shelf through the additional adaptive baffle.

The dimension of the cabinet is indicated by three general indicators, namely width, height and depth.

(a) Width: The standard width of a network cabinet is 600 mm or 800 mm. The server cabinet is mostly 600 mm wide; while the network cabinet is mainly 800 mm wide, because it carries more cables inside that the method of cabling on both sides should be facilitated. The 19-inch cabinet allows to install equipment with a width of 482.6 mm.

(b) Height: The cabinet height is generally in shown as "nU" ("n" for quantity) between 2 U and 42 U. In order to ensure heat dissipation, servers need to keep a certain distance between each other, so a cabinet cannot be fully loaded. For example, a 42 U cabinet typically hold 10 to 20 standard 1 U servers. The standard cabinet is 0.7–2.4 m in height, depending on the quantity and unified style of the equipment in the cabinet. Cabinets in special height are usually be customized by manufacturers. 19-inch cabinets are usually 1.6 m or 2 m high.

The mounting dimensions of the rack should meet the standard mounting requirements. The 1 U rack should has three holes, with the middle hole as the center and the distance between the two distal holes being 31.75 mm. The

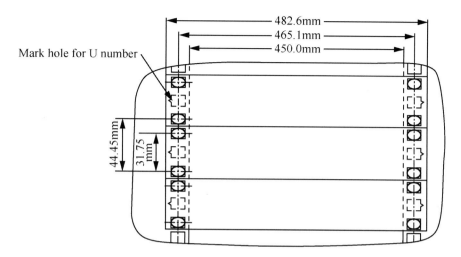

Fig. 2.4   The mounting dimensions of the 19-inch rack

mounting columns on both sides should be 465.1 mm apart, as shown in Fig. 2.4.

(c) The standard U-sized cabinet is 400–800 mm in depth, depending on the dimensions of the equipment in the cabinet. Cabinets in special depth are usually be customized by manufacturers. 19-inch cabinets are usually 500 mm, 600 mm or 800 mm high.

   The standard U-sized cabinet is 600 mm in width, providing a width of 19 inches (about 48 cm) for internal mounting. In general, the depth of the server cabinet is no less than 800 mm, while that of the network cabinet is no more than 800 mm. The dimensions of 19-inch cabinet are shown in Table 2.1.

3. Server cabinet

   Server cabinets are typically manufactured according to the rack-mounted server and following specific industrial standards and specifications. The following will introduce the server cabinet by comparing it with the network cabinet.

(a) Functions and internal composition

   (i) Equipment installation in the network cabinet is generally carried out by the user, that is, the installation of panels, subracks, plug-ins, devices, electronic components, mechanical parts, etc., so that they constitute an entire shelf. At present, the capacity of network cabinet is generally 2–42 U.

   (ii) The cabinets in the IDC machine room are collectively referred to as server cabinets, generally referring to the special cabinet used for carrying 19-inch (about 48 cm) standard equipment such as server, UPS and

Table 2.1 Dimensions of 19-inch cabinet

Type	Model	Height × Width × Depth (mm)
Standard Cabinet	18 U	1000 × 600 × 600
	24 U	1200 × 600 × 600
	27 U	1400 × 600 × 600
	32 U	1600 × 600 × 600
Standard Cabinet	37 U	1800 × 600 × 600
	42 U	2000 × 600 × 600
Server Cabinet	42 U	2000 × 800 × 800
	37 U	1800 × 800 × 800
	24 U	1200 × 600 × 800
	27 U	1400 × 600 × 800
	32 U	1600 × 600 × 800
	37 U	1800 × 600 × 800
	42 U	2000 × 600 × 800
Wall-mounted Cabinet	6 U	350 × 600 × 450
	9 U	500 × 600 × 450
	12 U	650 × 600 × 450
	15 U	800 × 600 × 450
	18 U	1000 × 600 × 450

display. It carries plug-ins, panels, electronic components and so on in the form of combination, so that they constitute an entire cabinet. The server cabinet provides the environment and safety protection necessary for the normal operation of electronic equipment.

(b) Conventional dimensions of the cabinet

(i) The network cabinet is generally 800 mm wide. In order to facilitate in-cabinet cabling, cabling devices are required on the mounting columns on both sides, such as vertical and horizontal cable troughs, cable panel, etc.

(ii) The width of the server cabinet is generally 600 mm or 800 mm, the height is 18 U, 22 U, 27 U, 32 U, 37 U, 42 U, or 47 U, and the depth is 800 mm, 900 mm, 960 mm, 1000 mm, 1100 mm or 1200 mm, as shown in Fig. 2.5.

(c) Requirements for load-bearing and heat dissipation

(i) The equipment in the network cabinet dissipates less heat and weighs less, so the requirements for heat dissipation and load-bearing are not high. For example, a load-bearing capacity of 850 kg and a through-hole rate of 60% are sufficient.

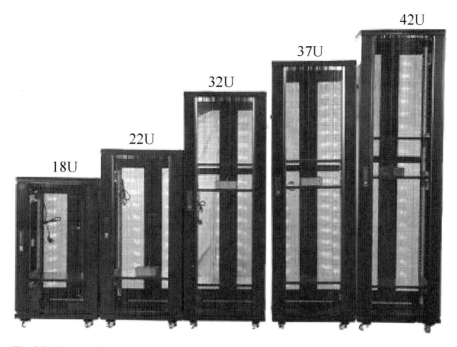

Fig. 2.5 Server cabinet

(ii) The server required enhanced heat dissipation capacity from the server cabinet as it dissipates more heat. For example, the front and back doors require 65–75% through-hole rate, and additional heat dissipation units were appreciated. The server cabinet is required to meet higher load-bearing requirement, such as the load-bearing capacity of 1300 kg.

The server cabinet can be installed along with the special fixing pallet, special sliding pallet, power socket, caster, base anchor, cabling unit, cable manager, L-style bracket, horizontal beam, vertical beam and fan unit. The frame, upper ledge, lower ledge, front door, back door and left and right side doors of the cabinet can be quickly disassembled and installed. The common internal layout of the server cabinet is shown in Fig. 2.6.

4. Fitted Screws

When installing network equipment in the cabinet, it is often necessary to use M6 × 16 screws specially designed for cabinet, including cross recessed pan head machine screws, buckle nuts and gaskets, as shown in Fig. 2.7.

Fig. 2.6 Common internal
layout of the server cabinet

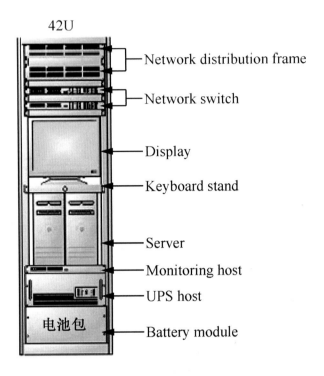

42U

Network distribution frame

Network switch

Display

Keyboard stand

Server

Monitoring host

UPS host

Battery module

电池包

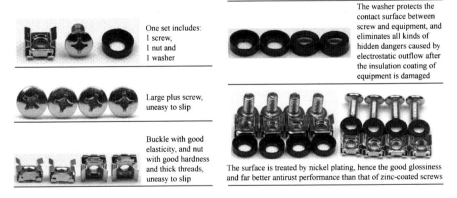

One set includes:
1 screw,
1 nut and
1 washer

The washer protects the
contact surface between
screw and equipment, and
eliminates all kinds of
hidden dangers caused by
electrostatic outflow after
the insulation coating of
equipment is damaged

Large plus screw,
uneasy to slip

Buckle with good
elasticity, and nut
with good hardness
and thick threads,
uneasy to slip

The surface is treated by nickel plating, hence the good glossiness
and far better antirust performance than that of zinc-coated screws

Fig. 2.7 M6 × 16 screws for cabinet

2.1.2 Cable Distribution Cabinet

The cable distribution cabinet is customized for the generic cabling system, which is
special in that it adds some accessories peculiarly needed by the cabling system. The
common cable distribution cabinet is shown in Fig. 2.8.

Fig. 2.8   Cable distribution cabinet in common use

Digital cable distribution unit, optical fiber cable distribution unit, power distri-bution unit, generic cabling unit and other active/passive equipment and accessories can be flexibly installed inside an generic cabling cabinet as needed. The common internal layout is shown in Fig. 2.9.

The cable distribution unit is the most important component in the management subsystem, which serves as the hub for cross-connecting the vertical subsystem and the horizontal subsystem, and also bridges the gap between the cables and the equipment. It features the advantages of convenience for cable management, less occurrence of fault, and neat and aesthetic cabling environment.

The following are some common distribution frames.

1. Twisted-Pair Distribution Frame

    Twisted-pair distribution frame, namely standard RJ-45 distribution frame, is the most commonly used distribution frame in network generic cabling engineer-ing. The distribution frame is primarily used in modular devices that manage front-end information points from the local side. The cable for the front-end information point (Cat 5e or Cat 6 cable) enters the equipment room by first approaching the Copper Wire Distribution Frame B, after which it binds the wire to the Copper Wire Distribution Frame B, and then the Copper Wire Distribution Frame A is connected with the switch with a patch cord (with RJ-45 splice), as shown in Fig. 2.10.

    At present, the common twisted-pair distribution frame is compatible with Cat 5e or Cat 6 cable, or even the next-generation Cat 7. The physical appearance of the twisted-pair distribution frame is shown in Fig. 2.11.

2. Optical fiber distribution frame

    Optical fiber distribution frames are classified into unit type, drawer type and module type. An optical fiber distribution frame generally is used for proper and convenient patch cord connection, fixing and protection of optical fibers, which is composed of the identifiers, optical fiber coupler, optical fiber fixing device,

Fig. 2.9 Common internal layout of an integrated cable distribution cabinet

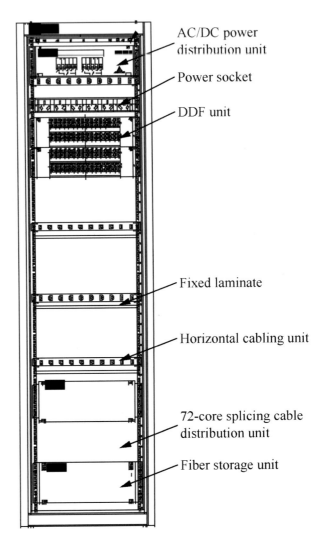

AC/DC power distribution unit

Power socket

DDF unit

Fixed laminate

Horizontal cabling unit

72-core splicing cable distribution unit

Fiber storage unit

welding unit, etc. The physical appearance of the optical fiber distribution frame is shown in Fig. 2.12.

3. Digital distribution frame

The digital distribution frame (DDF), also known as high-frequency distribution frame, is available with 8-system, 10-system, 16-system, 20-system frames, etc. A DDF is used to connect the digital code stream of the digital communication equipment as a whole, presenting increasing importance and superiority in digital communication. The signal input and output with transmission rate of 2 to 155 Mbit/s can be connected to the DDF, which brings great flexibility and convenience for cabling, patching, reconnection and capacity expansion. The physical appearance of the DDF is shown in Fig. 2.13.

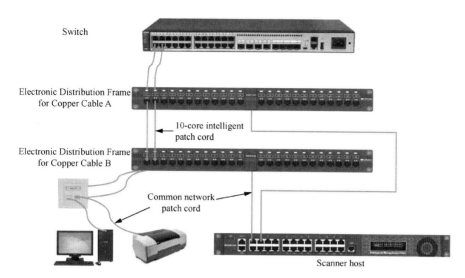

Fig. 2.10 Systematic connection of the twisted-pair distribution frame

Fig. 2.11 Physical appearance of the twisted-pair distribution frame

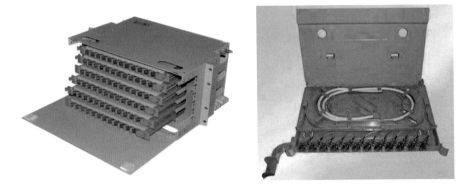

Fig. 2.12 Physical appearance of the optical fiber distribution frame

Fig. 2.13 Physical appearance of the DDF

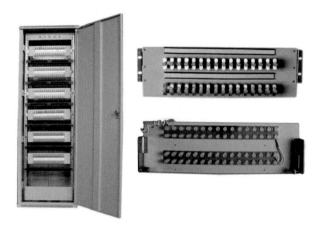

4. Main distribution frame

The main distribution frame (MDF) is an internal cable distribution frame that connects the cable from the outside of the switch on one side and the internal cables at the entrance and exit of the switch on the other side. The physical appearance of the MDF is shown in Fig. 2.14. The main distribution frame is designed to connect ordinary cables and transmit and test low-frequency audio signals or XDSL signals, while protecting the switch from over voltage and over current, and notifying the watchman through acoustics and optical alarm.

5. Intermediate distribution frame

Intermediate distribution frame (IDF) is a secondary communication room in a building that uses a star network topology. The IDF relies on the MDF, where the latter stands for the main equipment room, and the IDF stands for the remote auxiliary equipment rooms serving as cable distribution rooms. IDF and MDF are both distribution frames, the only difference between whom is the position.

Fig. 2.14 Physical appearance of the MDF

Fig. 2.15 Wall-mounted cabinet

2.1.3 Wall-Mounted Cabinet

The wall-mounted cabinet can be fixed on the wall through different installation methods, and is widely used in cable distribution rooms and corridors with small space, thanks to their small profile, convenient installation and disassembly, easy management and anti-theft characteristics. When installing a wall-mounted cabinet, the installer will generally open 2 to 4 holes for wall mounting at the back of the cabinet, and then fix it on the wall or directly embed them into the wall with expansion screws, as shown in Fig. 2.15.

The wall-mounted cabinet is divided into standard model, non-standard model, and embedded model, with the common specifications including 6 U, 9 U, 12 U, and 15 U in height, 530 mm and 600 mm in width, and 450 mm and 600 mm in depth.

2.2 Communication Cables

The most important links in the communication network is the communication line and transmission. Communication is divided into wired communication and wireless communication. The signal sent and received in wired communication is mainly electrical signal and optical signal, the cables responsible for which are collectively referred to as communication cables. At present, the commonly used transmission media in communication lines are twisted pair (TP) and optical fiber.

2.2.1 TP

TP is the most commonly used transmission medium in network generic cabling, which is composed of several pairs of copper conductors with insulating protective layer. Compared with other transmission medium, TP has more restrictions in transmission distance, channel width and data transmission rate, etc., but is relatively low in price, as shown in Fig. 2.16.

1. Classification of TP

   (a) By availability of shielding

      (i) Shielded twisted pair (STP): A metal shielding layer is provided between the TP and the outer insulation sleeve, with the structure shown in Fig. 2.17. The shielding layer reduces radiation, prevents information from being eavesdropped, and also prevents the intrusion of external electromagnetic interference, so the STP, though at a higher cost, has higher transmission rates than comparable unshielded twisted-pair.

      (ii) Unshielded twisted pair (UTP): Unlike the STP, the UTP is not provided with a metal shielding layer, with the structure shown in Fig. 2.18. UTP is widely used because it is low in cost, light weight, easy to bend and easy to install.

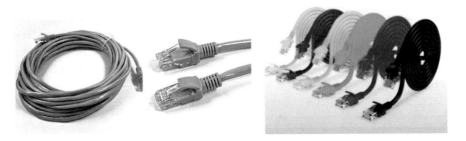

Fig. 2.16 TP

Fig. 2.17 STP Structure

Fig. 2.18 UTP Structure

(b) By performance of transmission

    (i) Cat 5: The cable provides a bandwidth up to 100 MHz and a maximum transmission rate of 100 Mbit/s, suitable for use in voice transmission and data transmission where the maximum transmission rate needs to reach 100 Mbit/s. Cat 5 is mainly used in 100Base-T and 1000Base-T Ethernet, with the maximum network segment length of 100 m, and adopts the RJ connector. Cat 5 is the most commonly used Ethernet cable.

    (ii) Cat 5e: Cat 5e presents low attenuation and less crosstalk. Compared with Cat 5, Cat 5e has higher signal noise ratio (SNR) and smaller delay error, hence the greatly improved performance. The Cat 5e is primarily used in Gigabit Ethernet (GbE) applications. Its structure is shown in Fig. 2.19.

    (iii) Cat 6: Cat 6 is far superior to Cat 5e in transmission performance and is most suitable for applications with transmission rates higher than 1 Gbit/s. Cat 6 differs from the Cat 5e mainly in its improved performance in terms of crosstalk and return loss, because Cat 6 has a cross skeleton structure, Its structure is shown in Fig. 2.20.

        The larger the number indicating the category of cable, the later the version of the cable, the more advanced the technology adopted, and correspondingly the wider the bandwidth and the more expensive the

Fig. 2.19 Cat 5e Structure

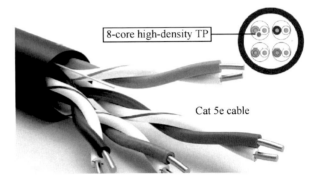

8-core high-density TP

Cat 5e cable

Fig. 2.20 Cat 6 Structure

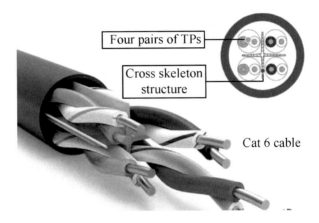

Four pairs of TPs

Cross skeleton
structure

Cat 6 cable

cable. The following is a description of the marking methods for different categories of TPs. For the standard TPs, the format "Cat x" is adopted, for example, the word "Cat 5" or "Cat 6" on the sheath of the cable; the cables of advanced version is marked with "Cat xe", such as "Cat 5e", as shown in Fig. 2.21.

Cat 5 and Cat 5e cables were mainly used by 2005. Since 2006, Cat 5e and Cat 6 took over the dominant position, while Cat 6e and 7 began to serve in some critical projects.

2. Wire sequence standards

The three most influential generic cabling standard organizations in the world are the American National Standards Institute (ANSI), the Telecommunication Industry Association (TIA), and the Electronic Industries Alliance (EIA). The most widely used TP standards are ANSI/EIA/TIA-568A (T568A) and ANSI/EIA/TIA-568B (T568B), with the biggest difference in wire sequence.

The wire sequence of T568A is defined as the order of white green, green, white orange, blue, white blue, orange, white brown, brown; while that of T568b

Fig. 2.21 Marking examples of different cable categories

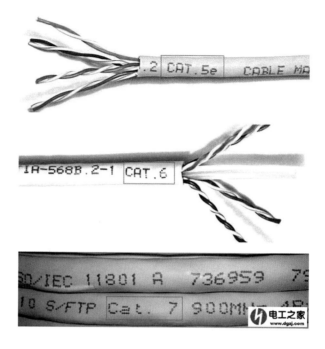

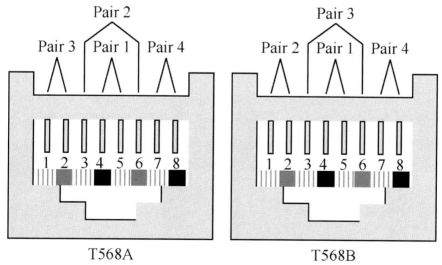

Fig. 2.22 Color labels and wire sequence of the TP

is in the order of white orange, orange, white green, blue, white blue, green, white brown and brown, as shown in Fig. 2.22.

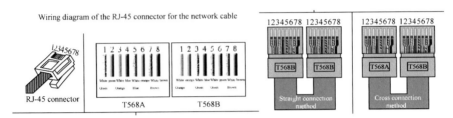

Fig. 2.23 Wiring diagram of the RJ-45 connector for the network cable

3. Connection methods of TPs

    TPs can be connected by straight connection method or cross connection method, so when used as a network cable, a TP is usually called a straight-through cable or a crossover cable according to the connection method. The wiring of the RJ-45 connector for the network cable is shown in Fig. 2.23.

    (a) Straight-through cable

        (i) The registered jacks (RJs) at both ends of the cable are made in accordance with the T568B.
        (ii) It is used for the connection between equipment at different levels, for example, the connection between the switch and the router, and between the switch and the computer.

    (b) Crossover cable

        (i) The RJs of the cable adopt the T568B standard at one end and T568A at the other end.
        (ii) It is used for the connection between equipment at the same level, for example, the connection between computers, and between switches.

            Nowadays, the RJ-45 connectors for communication equipment are mostly self-adaptive. When the cable does not match, the receiving port and transmitting ports can be automatically reversed to solve the problem. So now in the general application scenario, the straight-through cable is sufficient to meet the demand.

2.2.2   Cable

1. Structure and guiding principle of optical fiber

    Optical fiber is short for optical waveguide fiber, a kind of fiber made of glass or plastic that can be used for optical conduction. The optical fiber used for communication is a kind of glass fiber slightly thicker than a human hair, with an outer diameter of 125 to 140 µm, as shown in Fig. 2.24.

Fig. 2.24 Physical appearance of the optical fiber

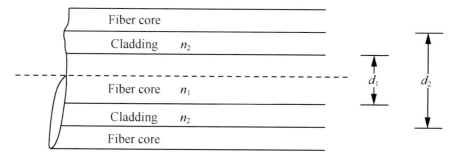

Fig. 2.25 Basic structure of the optical fiber

The basic structure model of optical fiber refers to the layered structure of optical fiber, consisting of fiber core, cladding and coating layer, which appears as a concentric cylinder, as shown in Fig. 2.25.

(a) Fiber core: located in the center of the optical fiber, mainly composed of high purity silicon dioxide (SiO_2), mixed with a small amount of dopant. The optical signal can be transmitted by increasing the optical refractive index n_1 of the fiber core. The diameter d_1 of the fiber core is generally 2 to 50 μm.

(b) Cladding layer: located in the middle layer, also composed of high purity silicon dioxide (SiO2), and mixed with some dopant. By reducing the optical refractive index n_2 of the cladding to less than n_1 to satisfy the total reflection condition, it achieves the purpose of confining the optical signal in the fiber core for transmission. The outer diameter d_2 of the cladding is generally 125 μm.

(c) Coating layer: located in the outermost layer, composed of acrylate, silicone rubber and nylon to protect the optical fiber from water vapor erosion and mechanical abrasion. It also enhances the mechanical strength and bendability of the fiber, playing the role of prolonging the service life of the fiber. The outer diameter of the coated fiber is generally 1.5 mm.

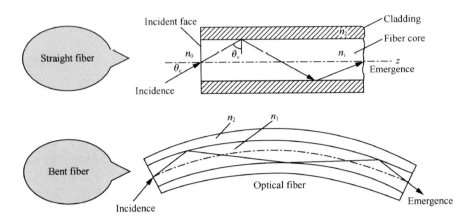

Fig. 2.26 Principle of optical fiber transmission

   Optical fiber transmission is based on the principle of "total reflection of light", as shown in Fig. 2.26. According to the principle of geometric optical total reflection, when the angle of incidence is larger than the critical angle of total reflection, the total reflection will be generated at the interface between the fiber core and the cladding. So, in view of the premise of $n_1 > n_2$, as light travels from the fiber core to the cladding, the light is confined inside the fiber and propagates forward. This ensures that the light travels all the way through the fiber, even through a slightly curved route.

2. Classification of optical fibers

   (a) By transmission mode

      (i) Single-mode fiber: supports transmission in a single mode. The core diameter is 8 to 10 μm, the cladding diameter is 125 μm, and the commonly used diameter combination is 9/125 μm. This type of optical fiber achieves a transmission distance of more than 5 km, and the light is sourced from laser, which is suitable for long-distance transmission. It adopts a yellow outer sheath.

      (ii) Multi-mode fiber: supports transmission in multiple modes. The core diameter is 50 μm or 62.5 μm, and the cladding diameter is 125 μm. The light is sourced from LED, which is suitable for short distance transmission, such as the optical fiber patch cord in the equipment room. It adopts an orange or aqua green outer sheath.

      Comparison between single-mode fiber and multi-mode fiber is shown in Fig. 2.27.

   (b) By definition of ITU-T

      (i) G.651 fiber (graded index multi-mode fiber): mainly applied to the wavelength of 8500 nm and 1310 nm.

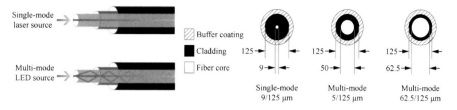

Fig. 2.27 Comparison of single-mode fiber and multi-mode fiber

> (ii) G.652 fiber (conventional single-mode fiber): zero dispersion at the
>   wavelength of 1310 nm, and lowest transmission loss at the wavelength
>   of 1550 nm.
> (iii) G.653 fiber (dispersion-shifted fiber): zero dispersion and lowest trans-
>   mission loss at the wavelength of 1550 nm.
> (iv) G.654 fiber (least attenuation fiber): minimum attenuation at the wave-
>   length of 1550 nm, suitable for long distance submarine transmission.
> (v) G.655 fiber (non-zero dispersion-shift fiber): suitable for long distance
>   transmission.

3. Structure of optical fiber cable

Designed to meet specifications for optical, mechanical, or environmental
performance, the optical fiber cable is a type of communication cable that can
be used individually or in groups. It use one or more optical fibers enclosed in a
sheath as the transmission medium. The appearance is shown in Fig. 2.28.

(a) Classification of optical fiber cables

> (i) By transmission performance, transmission distance and use: long-
>   distance cable, urban cable, submarine cable and household cable.
> (ii) By type of optical fiber: multi-mode optical fiber cable and single-mode
>   optical fiber cable.
> (iii) By optical fiber overlaying method: tight-buffer optical cable, loose-
>   buffer optical cable, beam-tube optical cable and ribbon multi-fiber
>   cable.
> (iv) By optical fiber number: single-fiber cable, dual-fiber cable, 4-fiber
>   cable, 6-fiber cable, 8-fiber cable, 12-fiber cable, 24-fiber cable, etc.
> (v) By laying method: duct optical cable, direct buried optical cable, aerial
>   optical cable and optical cable for lake and river crossing.

(b) Indoor optical cable

The indoor optical cable is laid in the building. Due to the advantages of
the indoor environment over the outdoor environment, which is not affected
by mechanical stress and weather factors from nature, so the dry-type tight-

Fig. 2.28 Appearance of
optical fiber cables

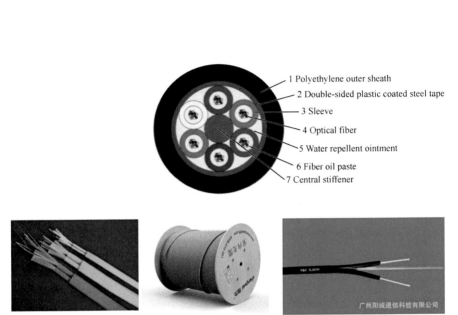

1 Polyethylene outer sheath

2 Double-sided plastic coated steel tape

3 Sleeve

4 Optical fiber

5 Water repellent ointment

6 Fiber oil paste

7 Central stiffener

Fig. 2.29 Appearance of indoor optical cables

buffer optical cable that is flame retardant and flexible is adopted indoor. Its
appearance is shown in Fig. 2.29.

Indoor optical cables are divided into single-fiber, dual-fiber and multi-
fiber cables by fiber number.

They can also be divided into indoor main cable, indoor distribution cable
and indoor trunk cable by service environment and location. The former is
mainly used to provide a passageway between the inside and outside of the
building; the latter two are used to deliver information to a specific location.

The indoor optical cable usually consists of the optical fiber, stiffener and
sheath, with the structure shown in Fig. 2.30.

(c) Outdoor optical cable

The outdoor optical cable needs to expose to the weather, so thicker outer
sheath, pressure resistance, corrosion resistance, tensile strength and other
characteristics are essential. Armored cables (that is, wrapped with a metal
skin) are commonly used for outdoor applications.

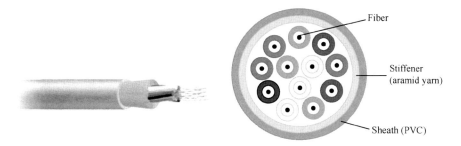

Fig. 2.30 Structure of indoor optical cables

Fig. 2.31 Structure of an
outdoor optical cable

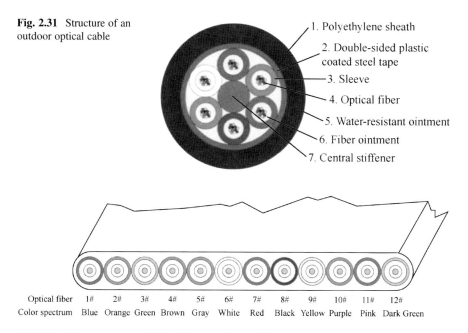

1. Polyethylene sheath

2. Double-sided plastic
   coated steel tape

3. Sleeve

4. Optical fiber

5. Water-resistant ointment

6. Fiber ointment

7. Central stiffener

Optical fiber	1#	2#	3#	4#	5#	6#	7#	8#	9#	10#	11#	12#
Color spectrum	Blue	Orange	Green	Brown	Gray	White	Red	Black	Yellow	Purple	Pink	Dark Green

Fig. 2.32 Color spectrum and identification of optical fiber

The cable consists of cable core, reinforcing steel wire, filling material and sheath. The core is composed of a certain number of optical fibers in a certain way. In addition, the outdoor optical cable is also provided with waterproof layer, buffer layer, insulating metal wire or other components according to the need. Figure 2.31 shows the structure of an outdoor optical cable.

The color of the loose tube and the fiber in it are blue, orange, green, brown, gray, white, red, black, yellow, violet, pink, and dark green in turn. The color spectrum and identification of optical fiber are shown in Fig. 2.32.

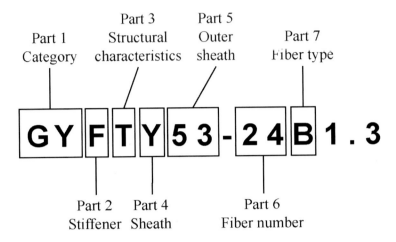

Fig. 2.33 Model of optical fiber cables

4. Identification of optical cable model

The optical cable is varied with the material, structure and use. In order to facilitate the distinction and use of optical cables, the models of optical cables are coded uniformly. The cable model is generally composed of seven parts, that is, category + stiffener + structural characteristics + sheath + outer sheath + fiber number + fiber type, as shown in Fig. 2.33.

(a) The first part represents the code for the category of the optical cable, as shown in Table 2.2.
(b) The second part represents the code for stiffener (reinforced core), as shown in Table 2.3.
(c) The third part refers to the code of structural characteristics of the optical cable. The code should reflect the main type of cable core and the derivative structure of the cable. When there are multiple structural characteristics that need to be reflected, combined codes can be used, as shown in Table 2.4.
(d) The fourth part represents the code for the sheath of the optical cable, as shown in Table 2.5.
(e) The fifth part represents the code for the armor layer of the optical cable, which includes one or more digits, as shown in Table 2.6.
(f) The sixth part represents optical fiber number, such as 2, 4, 6, 8, 12, 24, 36, 48, 72, 96, 144, etc.
(g) The seventh part represents the code for the fiber type, as shown in Table 2.7.

Table 2.2 Code for the category of the optical cable

Code	Optical cable category	Explanation
GY	Outdoor (field) optical cable for communication	The outer sheath is thick, with strong pressure resistance, corrosion resistance and tensile strength. It is suitable for the interconnection between outdoor buildings and between remote networks, and supports long-distance transmission
GJ	Indoor (local) optical cable for communication	Bending resistance, fire retardant, strong flexibility; applicable to communication equipment in buildings; suitable for short-distance transmission
GH	Submarine optical cable for communication	No need for tunnel or support, less investment, fast construction, less interference from the natural environment and human activities, good confidentiality, safety and stability; mostly used for long-distance international transmission
GT	Special optical cable for communication	The types of fiber used are dispersion-shifted fiber, non-zero dispersion-shift fiber, dispersion flattened fiber, etc.; also includes, among other things, all optical cables used for special purposes
GS	Optical cable inside equipment for communication	Adopting metal heavy stiffener and enveloping structure of loose tube; suitable for cabling in equipment
MG	Optical cable for coal mine	Flame retarding and rat proof; suitable for coal, gold, iron and other mining occasions
GW	Metal-free cable for communication	Using non-metallic materials; mainly used in areas with strong electromagnetic influence and lightning prone areas
GR	Soft optical cable for communication	Shorter outer diameter, good flexibility, easy to bend; suitable for indoor or small space; used in optical connectors, FTTH, sensors and other fields

Table 2.3 Code for stiffener (reinforced core)

Code	Stiffener	Explanation
None	Metal stiffener	Metal, non-metallic and metal heavy components are respectively used to strengthen the optical cable, in order to enhance the tensile strength and improve the mechanical properties of optical cables
F	Non-metallic stiffener	
G	Metal heavy stiffener	

2.3 Connection Devices Commonly Used in Communication Systems

In the last section we learned about communication cables. So how to connect the communication equipment with the cable? What we need is the connecting device. Communication connector is the interconnecting device for network transmission medium, whose performance may affect the whole communication system. There

Table 2.4 Code of structural characteristics of the optical cable

Code	Cable structure	Explanation
D	Fiber ribbon structure	Optical fiber units are accommodated into a large tube, offering small volume and high space utilization. The tube can accommodate a large number of optical fibers, and can complete the connection of all units at a time
None	Stranding structure	The bidirectional stranding technology realizes the water resistance for the whole section, and makes the additional attenuation of the fiber close to zero, thus obtaining excellent environmental performance. The structure is suitable for long-distance communication, inter-station communication and the occasions with higher requirements of moisture-proof and rodent-proof
S	Loose tube structure	The structure consists of multiple optical fibers, fiber ointment and PBT loose tube, which is mainly used for outdoor laying. The tube is filled with multiple optical fibers in a free state
J	Tight buffer structure	The structure is composed of the optical fiber and the PVC tight-buffer layer on the fiber surface, forming a soft, easy-to-peel tight-buffer fiber, generally used in indoor optical cable or special optical cable
X	Central tube structure	The structure takes loose tube as the cable core, and the stiffeners are arranged around the loose tube. It has the characteristics of shorter diameter, light weight and easy laying
G	Skeleton structure	The structure can be used for taking out the required optical fiber and butting it with the access cable. With good side compression resistance, it can protect the optical fiber well
B	Flat structure	The flat cable has a soft structure on the core to ensure the softness of the cable. Due to its relative thin depth, small size, and easy connection and disassembly, it is suitable for data transmission or power transmission in electrical equipment
T	Fill-in structure	The structure keeps the round and normal shape of the cable by filling the inside of the optical fiber, playing a role in fire, water, pressure resistance and so on
Z	Flame retardant structure	The structure is low in cost, and can delay the spread of the flame along the cable, And improve the fire protection level of the cable line to avoid the expansion of the fire and the major disaster caused by the cable fire
C	Self-supporting structure	The structure is characterized by low transmission loss, low dispersion, light weight due to non-metallic structure, convenient laying, strong anti-electromagnetic interference, and excellent mechanical and environmental properties, and is suitable for high voltage transmission lines

are various types and standards of communication connectors, mainly including those for power cables and those for optical cables.

Table 2.5 Code for the sheath of the optical cable

Code	Sheath	Explanation
L	Aluminum	The sheath is made of varied materials to protect the cable core from external mechanical action and environmental conditions
G	Steel	
Q	Lead	
Y	Polyethylene sheath	
W	Steel wires reinforced polyethylene sheath	
A	Aluminum-polyethylene sheath	
S	Steel-polyethylene sheath	
V	PVC sheath	
F	Fluoroplastic	
U	PU	
E	Polyester elastomer	

Table 2.6 Code for the armor layer of the optical cable

Code	Armor layer	Explanation
0	Non-armored	A layer of metal protection is added to the outside of the cable to protect the internal utility layer from damage during transportation and installation
2	Double steel strip	
3	Small-gauge round steel wire	
4	Large-gauge round steel wire	
5	Corrugated steel strip	
6	Double-layer round steel wire	
23	Armored polyethylene sheath wrapped with steel strip	
33	Armored polyethylene sheath wrapped with small-gauge steel wire	
53	Armored polyethylene sheath longitudinal-wrapped with corrugated steel strip	
333	Armored polyethylene sheath wrapped with double-layer small-gauge steel wire	
44	Double-layer large-gauge round steel wire	

Table 2.7 Optical fiber type

Code	Fiber type	Explanation
A	Multi-mode fiber	Supporting multi-mode transmission, with high dispersion and loss, suitable for short- and medium-distance transmission and low-capacity optical fiber communication system
B	Single-mode fiber	Only supporting single-mode transmission, with low dispersion, suitable for long-distance transmission

2.3.1 Cable Connection Devices

1. Network jumper

   Jumper is also called patch cord. Jumpers are usually used for patch cord connection between distribution frames, cabling units and switches. The paths are mostly curved and the cables knot easily, so in order to facilitate the cabling of patch cords in the complex path, without damaging the structure, the patch cord itself must be made soft. One of the advantages of a patch cord made from multiple strands of fine copper wire is that it is much softer than a hard patch cord made from a single strand of hard wire. The appearance of a network patch cord is shown in Fig. 2.34.

   The patch cord is mainly composed of cable conductor, RJ and protective sleeve.

2. Network registered jack

   Registered jack (RJ) is a standardized telecommunications network interface that is crystal clear in appearance, for the transmission of voice and data.

   It is suitable for field termination of equipment room subsystem or horizontal cabling subsystem. Its housing is made of high density polyethylene. Each TP is connected to a network card and hub (or switch) via a port made with a RJ.

   In the RJ model number, the letter "RJ"represents the registered jack, and the following number represents the serial number of the interface standard; $xPyC$ means that the RJ has x slot positions and y metal contacts.

   There are two kinds of common network RJs: RJ-45 and RJ-11. They are all composed of PVC shell, shrapnel, chip and other parts, as shown in Fig. 2.35.

   The corresponding interfaces of these two RJ types are RJ-45 interface and RJ-11 interface, as shown in Fig. 2.36.

   (a) RJ-45

   (i) RJ-45 is a type of modular jack or plug following the IEC (60) 603-7 connection standard, with 8 plots defined in accordance with the international standard for connectors. The RJ-45 includes two types: 8P8C and 8P4C, whose structure is shown in Fig. 2.37.

Fig. 2.34 Appearance of a network patch cord

 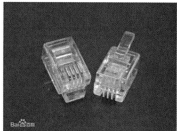

Fig. 2.35 Appearance of the two types of RJs

Fig. 2.36 Appearance of the two types of interfaces

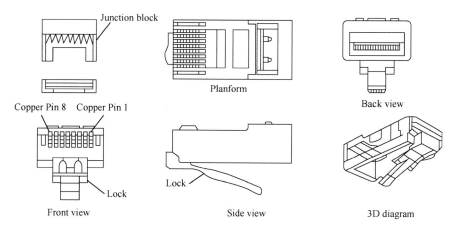

Fig. 2.37 Structure of the RJ-45

(ii) The RJ-45 is often used for data transmission in monitoring projects, generic cabling in equipment rooms and other scenarios. It is an indispensable link in the Ethernet. It is usually installed on both ends of the network cable, used to connect computers, routers, switches and other network equipment.

(iii) The wiring of the RJ-45 is allowed to follow T568A and T568B wire sequence standards. According to the standard adopted, the finished cables can be divided into straight-through cables and crossover cables. However, due to the new generation of switches, network adapters and other devices with automatic reversal function, most network cables are now made in accordance with the T568B standard.

(b) RJ-11

(i) The RJ-11 does not follow the international standard, which is a type of connector usually with only 6 plots and 4 or 2 pins, that is, 6P4C and 6P2C.

(ii) The RJ-11 is often used to connect the telephone with the modem. For example, a telephone cable use the four-core (4C) RJs.

(iii) The RJ-11 is smaller in volume than the RJ-45. These two types of RJs differ in size, wiring standards and application scenarios and are not compatible with each other.

(c) Other types of RJs

The RJ-12 is also commonly used for voice communications. It has 6 pins (6P6C), and is also derived in the types with 6 slots and 4 pins (6P4C) and with 6 slots and 2 pins (6P2C).

(d) Types, appearance and features of commonly used RJs.

The types, appearance and features of the commonly used RJ at present are shown in Table 2.8.

3. Information outlet

Chapter 7 of the GB 50311 - 2016 "Code for Engineering Design of Generic Cabling System" puts forward specific requirements on the installation process of the information outlets in work areas. The information outlet box hidden on the ground should meet the requirements of waterproof and compression. It is advisable for the bottom surface of the information outlet bottom box mounted on the wall or column to be 300 mm away from the ground, as shown in Fig. 2.38. The bottom surface of the information outlet box mounted on the side plate of the workbench and on the adjacent wall is recommended to be 1.0 m away from the ground.

The number of information outlet modules (for power cable or optical cable) in each work area should not be less than two, and should meet the needs of various businesses. Therefore, under normal circumstances, it is appropriate to use the bottom box with 2-port panel, and the number of ports should match the number of ports set on the outlet box panel. The number of information points supported by each bottom box should not be more than twp. The information outlet module in the work area should support the access of different terminal devices. Each 8-position modular outlet should be connected to a cable containing 4 TPs.

Table 2.8 Types, appearance and features of commonly used RJs

Type	Appearance	Feature
Unshielded RJ		Common RJ, without a metal shield
Shielded RJ		With a metal shield and immunity to interference superior to the unshielded RJ
Cat 5e RJ		Widely used, suitable for the Cat 5 TP, but also compatible with the Cat 5e TP
Cat 6 RJ		Suitable for the Cat 6 TP (also compatible with the Cat 5 TP and Cat 5e TP), with the eight wires being arranged into two rows, four in the upper row and the other four in the lower row

The information outlet is usually composed of the bottom box, panel and module, and is generally mounted on the wall, or on the desktop or ground, mainly for the convenience to move the computer or other equipment, and maintain neat cabling.

(a) Bottom box: Classified into metal bottom box and plastic bottom box by material; or classified into open-mounted bottom box and conceal-mounted bottom box by installation method, as shown in Fig. 2.39.
(b) Panel: It must be waterproof, compression resistant and dustproof, in line with the GB 50311 - 2016 "Code for Engineering Design of Generic Cabling System". For the information module, the standard 86 panel should be adopted, as shown in Fig. 2.40.
(c) Module: Information module, also known as information outlet, is an extremely important component in generic cabling. It realizes the physical connection between equipment area and work area through terminal

Seat the wire according to T568B   Install on the panel

Fig. 2.38 Information outlet mounted on the wall

(1) Open-mounted bottom box   (2) Conceal-mounted plastic bottom box   (3) Conceal-mounted metal bottom box

Fig. 2.39 Bottom box

(1) 2-port panel   (2) Ground-mounted metal panel   (3) Multi-functional desktop panel

Fig. 2.40 Panel

Fig. 2.41 Information
module fixed on the back of
the panel

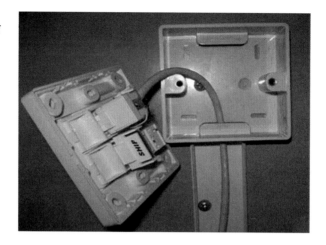

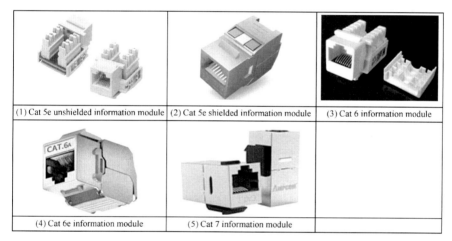

(1) Cat 5e unshielded information module	(2) Cat 5e shielded information module	(3) Cat 6 information module
(4) Cat 6e information module	(5) Cat 7 information module	

Fig. 2.42   Information modules

connection (or clamping). The information module is fixed on the back of the
panel to achieve cable crimping, as shown in Fig. 2.41.

By tested performance, the information modules are classified into Cat 5e
information module, Cat 6 information module and Cat 6e information
module, and are classified into unshielded information module and shielded
information module by occasions of use, as shown in Fig. 2.42.

2.3.2 Optical Cable Connection Devices

Optical cable connection device refers to the connector installed at the end of the optical cables for optical signal transmission between two optical cables. It is responsible for making the optical energy outputted from the transmitting optical fiber coupled to the receiving optical fiber to the maximum extent, and minimizing the impact on the system caused by its access to optical link.

1. Optical fiber splice

   An optical fiber splice connects two optical fibers permanently or detachably together, with a junction can protecting components. As the terminal device of the optical fiber, it serves as the physical interface to connect optical fibers. The common types of optical fiber splices are shown in Table 2.9.

   Splice types include: FC (round threaded style, typically used for distribution frames), ST (round clamping style), SC (square clamping style, typically used for routers and switches), PC (with micro spherical section, employing the grinding and polishing process), APC (with micro spherical section in an angle of 8°, employing the grinding and polishing processes), MT-RJ (square style, featuring two fibers integrated into a single design that supports both single receiving and transmitting), etc.

   Optical fiber splices mainly adopt three section processes (i.e., grinding process): PC section (physical contact), UPC section (ultra physical contact) and APC section (Angled Physical Contact). PC section is flat (actually employs micro-spherical grinding and polishing process). The signal attenuation of the UPC section is smaller than that of the PC section. The APC section is at an 8°, with the micro-spherical grinding and polishing process. The performance of these three sections from high to low is APC, UPC and PC. The APC section is green.

   The splice labeling format is "splice type/section process". For example, "FC/PC" indicates that it is a round threaded splice with a micro-spherical section employing the grinding and polishing process, and the section is flat.

2. Optical fiber patch cord/cable

   Optical fiber patch cord, also known as optical fiber connector, is a patch cord from equipment to optical fiber cabling link, which is applied to optical fiber communication system, optical fiber access network, optical fiber data transmission, local area network, etc. The plugs of the optical fiber patch cord is connected with the connectors installed on both ends of the optical cable, which can realize the active connection of the optical circuit. An optical fiber patch cord with only one end fitted with a plug is called a tail fiber. The core of the optical fiber patch cord is optical fiber, and there is a thin plastic sleeve outside the cable core to protect the sheath. Common optical fiber patch cords are shown in Fig. 2.43.

   (a) Classification of optical fiber patch cords

       (i) Single-mode patch cord: yellow sheath, and relatively longer transmission distance.

Table 2.9 Common types of optical fiber splices

SpliceType	Connection Method	Material	Advantages	Defects	Context of Use	Appearance
SC	Square snap-in splice	Engineering plastics	Easy-plug, and high installation density	Easy to be pulled out, and prone to damage under high temperature	100BASE-FX	SC-APC SC-UPC
LC	Small rectangle plug-in splice	Engineering plastics	Half of the size of the FS and FC, easy-plug, and high installation density	Complex manufacturing process	On the high-density optical interface unit, and for Gigabit interface	LC-UPC
FC	Round-head threaded splice	Metal	Firm and dustproof	When installing, the splice should be aligned before tightening. It is not convenient for high-density installation.	100BASE-FX(phasing out)	FC/APC FC/UPC
ST	Round-head snap-in splice	Metal	Easy to install	Prone to break-off	10BASE-F	ST多模 ST-PC

(continued)

Table 2.9 (continued)

SpliceType	Connection Method	Material	Advantages	Defects	Context of Use	Appearance
MT-RJ	Square clamping splice, equivalent to the telephone wire plug in volume	Engineering plastics	Small profile, featuring two fibers integrated into a single design that supports both single receiving and trans-mitting; lower insertion loss	Not widely used in China	For application from optical fiber to desktop, and for Gigabit interface	E2000/APC
E2000	Slide splice	Engineering plastics	The spring lock protects the pins from wearing and pollution	Not widely used in China	On the high-density Gigabit optical interface unit	

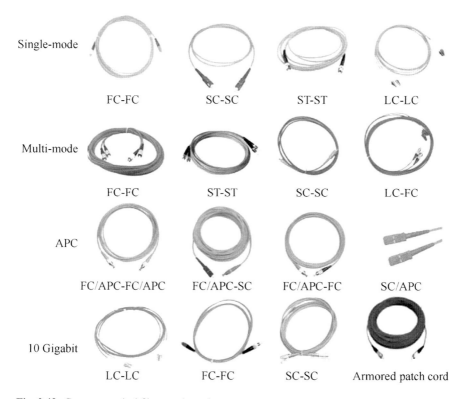

Fig. 2.43 Common optical fiber patch cords

(ii) Multi-mode patch cord: orange or gray sheath, and relatively shorter transmission distance.

(b) Common optical fiber patch cords

   (i) FC patch cord: The patch cord adopts the FC splice, generally used for the optical distribution frame side, most used for the distribution frame. The FC splice is generally used by telecommunications networks, screwed on to the adapter through a nut. It features firmness and dustproof design, but takes more time to install.

  (ii) SC patch cord: The patch cord adopts the SC splice, most used in routers and switches for 100BASE-FX connection. The SC splice is easy-plug and easy to use, but prone to falling off.

 (iii) ST patch cord: The patch cord adopts the ST splice, often used as the 10BASE-F connector for optical fiber distribution frame.

 (iv) LC patch cord: the LC splice is similar to but smaller than the SC splice. The LC splice can be used to connect the SFP optical transceiver, often

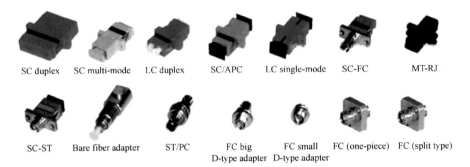

SC duplex   SC multi-mode   LC duplex   SC/APC   LC single-mode   SC-FC   MT-RJ

SC-ST   Bare fiber adapter   ST/PC   FC big   FC small   FC (one-piece) FC (split type)
                                    D-type adapter D-type adapter

Fig. 2.44 Common optical fiber adapters

used in routers, and can increase the density of optical fiber connectors in optical fiber distribution frame to a certain extent.

(v) MT-RJ patch cord: The patch cord adopts the MT-RJ splice that features two fibers integrated into a single design that supports both single receiving and transmitting, which is suitable for indoor applications in telecommunications and data network systems.

3. Fiber optic adapter

The fiber optic adapter, also known as fiber optic connector, fiber coupler and flange, is the most widely used optical passive devices in fiber communication systems, supporting the removable (active) connection between fibers. It precisely mate two end faces of the optical fibers to make the optical energy outputted from the transmitting optical fiber coupled to the receiving optical fiber to the maximum extent, and minimizing the impact on the system caused by its access to optical link. Optical fiber adapters may affect the reliability and performance of optical transmission systems to a certain extent.

Common optical fiber adapters are shown in Fig. 2.44.

4. Fiber optic information outlet

The fiber optic information outlet is a socket for optical fiber splice. The structure is similar to that of TP information outlet, as shown in Fig. 2.45.

2.4 Common Tools for System Cabling

Communication network cabling must be inseparable from the relevant tools. The following examples are Xiyuan generic cabling toolbox (KYGJX-12) and Xiyuan optical fiber toolbox (KYGJX-31).

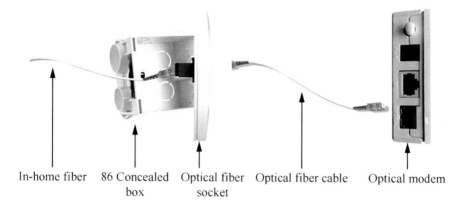

In-home fiber   86 Concealed   Optical fiber   Optical fiber cable   Optical modem
                     box   socket

Fig. 2.45 Fiber optic information outlet

Fig. 2.46 Xiyuan generic cabling toolbox

2.4.1 Communication Cable Toolbox

This section takes the Xiyuan generic cabling toolbox (KYGJX-12) as an example to illustrate the composition of the communication cable toolbox, as shown in Fig. 2.46 and 2.47.

1. RJ-45 crimping pliers: used for clamping the RJ-45 and helping striping wires.
2. Single-port pliers: mainly used for seating wires on the distribution frame. Check the condition of the tool head before seating the wire. If it is in good condition, then align the wire with module and lay it down quickly with appropriate strength. The tool head is consumable that it should be replaced in time once the strokes made by exceed 1000 times.
3. Steel tape measure (2 m): an consumable tool mainly used for measuring consumable materials, cables, etc.

Fig. 2.47 Tools in the Xiyuan generic cabling toolbox

4. Adjustable wrench (150 mm): mainly used for fastening nuts. When using, adjust the jaw to match the nut specification, and exert the appropriate force to prevent the wrench from slipping.
5. Phillips screwdriver (150 mm): mainly used for the disassembly and assembly of cross-slot screws. When using, the cross head of the screwdriver should be tightly clamped into the screw slot with appropriate force.

6. Saw bow and saw blade: mainly used for sawing PVC conduits and troughs.
7. Snap-off knife: mainly used for cutting materials and stripping wire sheaths.
8. Cable conduit cutter: mainly used for cutting PVC cable conduits.
9. Wire pliers (8-inch): mainly used for plugging or unplugging the connecting blocks, clamping cables and other devices, cutting steel wires, etc.
10. Needle-nose pliers (6-inch): mainly used for clamping cables and other objects, cutting steel wires, etc.
11. Tweezers: mainly used to clamp small items. Prevent the sharp end from hurting people when using.
12. Stainless steel angle ruler (300 mm): mainly used for measuring, drawing right-angled lines, etc.
13. Stripe level ruler (400 mm): mainly used for measuring whether the cable conduits, troughs, etc. are level.
14. Pipe bender (Φ20): mainly used for cold-bending PVC pipes.
15. Calculator: mainly used for numerical calculation during operation.
16. Auger bit (Φ10, Φ8, Φ6): mainly used for drilling holes in the material where holes are required. Drill bits of appropriate specifications should be selected according to the size of drilling holes. When drilling, the drill chuck should clamp the drill bit, with the electric drill keeping perpendicular to the drilling surface, and the appropriate force being exerted to prevent the bit from slipping.
17. M6 tap: mainly used to pass the wire through the thread hole.
18. Cross-head screw bit (150 mm): mainly used with the electric screwdriver for the disassembly and assembly of cross-slot screws. Make sure the cross-head screw bit is well installed when using.
19. RJ-45: practical consumable items.
20. M6 × 15 screw: practical consumable items.
21. Cable trough cutter: mainly used for cutting PVC troughs or cords and pull wires. When using, the hand should be away from the edge of the cutter blades. When the material is about to be cut off, the force should be strengthened appropriately.
22. Elbow mold: mainly used for sawing cable conduits and troughs at a certain angle. When in use, place the cable conduits and troughs horizontally into the inner groove of the elbow mold.
23. Rotary stripping pliers for network cables: mainly used for stripping the sheaths of the network cables. When in use, rotate the tool clockwise to strip the sheaths.
24. Tap holder: mainly used with the tap to pass the wire through the thread hole.

2.4.2 Communications Optical Cable Toolbox

This section takes the Xiyuan optical fiber toolbox (KYGJX-31) as an example to illustrate the composition of the communications optical cable toolbox, as shown in Fig. 2.48 and 2.49.

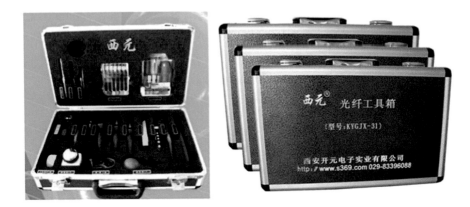

Fig. 2.48 Xiyuan optical fiber toolbox

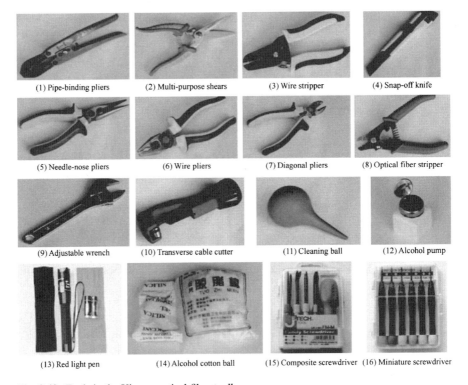

(1) Pipe-binding pliers	(2) Multi-purpose shears	(3) Wire stripper	(4) Snap-off knife
(5) Needle-nose pliers	(6) Wire pliers	(7) Diagonal pliers	(8) Optical fiber stripper
(9) Adjustable wrench	(10) Transverse cable cutter	(11) Cleaning ball	(12) Alcohol pump
(13) Red light pen	(14) Alcohol cotton ball	(15) Composite screwdriver	(16) Miniature screwdriver

Fig. 2.49 Tools in the Xiyuan optical fiber toolbox

1. Pipe-binding pliers: mainly used for cutting the steel wires in the cables.
2. Multi-purpose shears (8-inch): mainly used for cutting relatively soft objects, such as pull wires; not suitable for cutting hard objects.

3. Wire stripper: mainly used for shearing and striping sheaths of optical cables and tail fibers; not suitable for cutting the steel wires in outdoor cables. When in use, choose the jaw of the right specification.
4. Snap-off knife: mainly used for patch cords, pull wires in TPs, etc. Never use it for cutting hard objects.
5. Needle-nose pliers (6-inch): mainly used for stripping cable sheaths and clamping small objects.
6. Wire pliers (6-inch): mainly used for clamping objects and cutting steel wires.
7. Diagonal pliers: mainly used for cutting cable sheaths; not suitable for cutting steel wires.
8. Optical fiber stripper: mainly used for stripping each layer of protective sleeve of optical fibers. Its 3 jaws can shear and strip tail fiber sheaths, middle protective sleeves and resin protective films respectively. When in use, choose the jaw of the right specification.
9. Adjustable wrench (150 mm): mainly used for fastening nuts.
10. Transverse cable cutter: used for cutting the black sheaths of outdoor optical cables.
11. Cleaning ball: used for removing dust.
12. Alcohol pump: used for holding alcohol. To prevent alcohol volatilization, it must not be tilted and the lid must not be removed.
13. Red light pen: used for simply check of the break-make of optical fibers.
14. Alcohol cotton ball: used for dipping in alcohol to wipe the bare fiber, which should be kept dry when idle.
15. Composite screwdriver: combined screwdriver, used for fastening the corresponding screws.
16. Miniature screwdriver: used for fastening the corresponding screws.
17. Steel tape measure (2 m): an consumable tool mainly used for measuring consumable materials, cables, etc. (omitted in Fig. 2.49).
18. Tweezers: mainly used to clamp small items. Prevent the sharp end from hurting people when using (omitted in Fig. 2.49).
19. Straps: for easy carrying of the toolbox (omitted in Fig. 2.49).
20. Marker pen: for marking (omitted in Fig. 2.49).

2.5   Common Instruments for System Cabling

In equipment installation, cabling construction, troubleshooting, inspection and testing, engineering acceptance, etc., dedicated test instruments are essential. This section is a brief introduction some commonly used instruments, such as Nengshou Network Tester, network tester for TPs, optical fiber light pen, optical power meter, optical time-domain reflectometer, and optical fiber fusion splicer.

2.5.1   Nengshou Network Tester

Nengshou Network Tester is a network cable tester, suitable for simple tests of links, such as for 8-core network cables and 4-core telephone cables. It consists of two units: the host as the sending unit, powered by a 9 V laminated battery with a power switch and a green power indicator; the remote terminal as the receiving unit, with indicators displaying the cable connection status. It provides an RJ-45 interface for network cables, and an RJ-11 interface for telephone cables. The appearance of the Nengshou Network Tester is shown in Fig. 2.50.

During measurement, first turn off the power supply of the tester, and then connect one end of a network cable to the network cable interface of the host, and the other end to the network cable interface of the remote terminal. Turn on the host and check whether the numbers above the indicators of the host and the remote terminal are flashing synchronously from 1 to 8. The synchronous display indicates the good condition of the network cable. If they are not displayed synchronously or any indicator does not flash, it means that the cable fails to connect or some wires are wrongly arranged when making the RJ.

2.5.2   Network Tester for TPs

Network tester, also known as network detector, is a type of portable intelligent testing equipment with visual display. It can test the status of the physical layer, data link layer, and network layer defined by the 7-layer model of open system

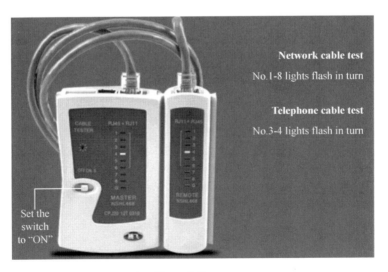

Fig. 2.50 Appearance of the Nengshou Network Tester

Fig. 2.51 Troubleshooting using a network tester

interconnection (OSI), mainly used for fault detection and maintenance of the LAN and generic cabling.

With the popularization and complexity of the network, the rational setting up and normal operation of the network is becoming more and more important. To ensure the normal operation of the network, we must proceed from two aspects. First, the network construction quality which directly affects the subsequent use of the network can not be ignored, so strict requirements and careful inspection must be in place, in order to nip the faults in the bud. Second, troubleshooting of network faults is crucial, because network faults will directly affect the operating efficiency of the network. Therefore, efficient and time-saving investigation must be guaranteed. This is one of the reasons why auxiliary equipment for network detection is increasingly important in network construction and maintenance. With the help of network tester, network administrator can greatly reduce the time of troubleshooting, helping the construction personnel of generic cabling improve work efficiency and quality, and speed up the construction, as shown in Fig. 2.51.

Well-known network tester manufacturers include Fluke, Agilent, Ideal, etc., there are also China's Xinertel, ZCTT, Ntooler, etc. This section will provide a brief introduction with the Fluke DSX2-5000 CableAnalyzer as an example.

Fluke has developed network testers for wired transmission medium, including network testers for optical fibers and network testers for TPs, as shown in Fig. 2.52. The network tester for optical fibers is not commonly used, so the term "network tester" is generally used to refer to the network tester for TPs.

The Fluke Network Tester DSX2-5000 CableAnalyzer (see Fig. 2.53) has been certified by Intertek (ETL). The certification is based on the Level IV accuracy

low voltage line
Generic cabling
Cable test

TP wire
sequence
instrument
(including
audio
generator)

Digital line
checker for
low voltage
line

DTX Series
certification tester
for copper cable
and optical fiber
cable

Certification-level OTDR

Multi-mode fiber certification
tester

Multi-functional optical fiber
testing tools

200-400X cable termination
surface magnifier

Fig. 2.52 Fluke network testers

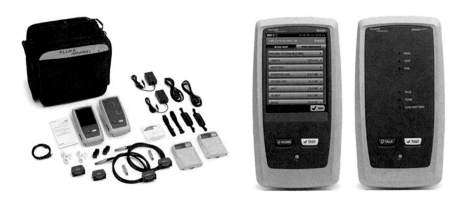

Fig. 2.53 DSX2-5000 CableAnalyzer

specified in the IEC-61935-1 standard and the Level V accuracy in the draft standard, as well as the Level IIIE accuracy specified in the ANSI/TIA-1152. DSX2-5000 CableAnalyzer can test CAT 5E, 6, 6A and Class FA TPs with an accuracy of up to 1000 MHz, helping speed up the copper cable certification tests. For CAT 6A and FA cables, it realizes unmatched test efficiency, meeting even the more stringent accuracy requirements of the Level V in the IEC draft.

With the built-in Projx management system, existing project settings can be invoked on each operation, helping to track the progress from project setup through system acceptance. The Versiv platform, which is easy to upgrade and supports future standards, comes with optical fiber testing (OLTS and OTDR modules), Wi-Fi analysis, and Ethernet troubleshooting. In addition, the Taptive user interface helps speed up troubleshooting by graphically displaying the fault sources, including the exact locations of crosstalk, return loss and shielding fault. Finally, in order to analyze test results, LinkWare management software can be used to generate a professional test report.

The parameters required for testing depend on the testing standard employed, which include the Wire Map, Loop Resistance, Impedance, Length, Propagation Delay, Delay Skew, Insertion loss/Attenuation, the return loss (RL, @host, @remote), near-end crosstalk (NEXT, @host, @remote), Power Sum near-end crosstalk (PS NEXT, @host, @remote), attenuation-to-crosstalk ratio—near-end (ACR-N, @host, @remote), PS ACR-N (@host, @remote), attenuation-to-crosstalk ratio—far-end (ACR-F, @host, @remote), and PS ACR-F (@host, @remote).

2.5.3   Optical Fiber Light Pen

Optical fiber light pen is also called optical fiber fault locater, optical fiber fault detector, visual red light source, light pen, red light pen, optical fiber pen, laser pen, etc. It uses a semiconductor laser with a wavelength of 650 nm as a light-emitting device, driven by a constant current source, and emits stable red light to the multi-mode or single-mode fiber through the optical interface connected with it, so as to realize fiber fault detection, as shown in Fig. 2.54.

The optical fiber light pen is a pen-type red light source specially designed for field construction personnel to perform tasks such as locating optical fiber faults, inspecting optical fiber connectors, optical fiber tracing, etc. As an ideal choice for on-site construction personnel, it features stable output power, long detection distance, solid and reliable structure, longer service time, and multi-functions. The

Fig. 2.54 Optical fiber light pen

optical fiber light pen can be divided into models of 5 km, 10 km, 15 km, 20 km, 25 km, 30 km, 35 km, 40 km, etc. by minimum detection distance. The longer the detection distance, the higher the price.

2.5.4 Optical Power Meter

With the rapid development of optical fiber communication technology, it has become the major way of data transmission in various communication networks. As the most fundamental measurement parameter in optical fiber communication system, optical power is an important indicator to evaluate the performance of optical terminal equipment and the transmission quality of optical fiber. The optical power meter is specially used to measure the absolute optical power or the relative loss of the optical power passing through a segment of optical fiber. It is widely used in the laying of network backbone, equipment maintenance, scientific research and production, as shown in Fig. 2.55.

In optical fiber measurement, the optical power meter is a commonly used instrument that carries a heavy load. An optical power meter can evaluate the performance of an optical device by simply measuring the absolute power of the transmitting terminal or optical network. When used in combination with a stable light source, it can measure joint losses, verify continuity, and help evaluate transmission quality of optical fiber links.

Fig. 2.55 Optical power meter

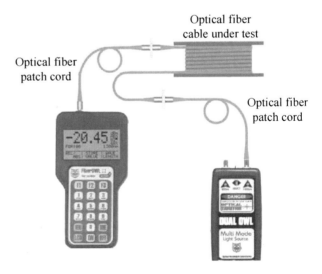

2.5.5 *Optical Time-Domain Reflectometer*

Optical time-domain reflectometer (OTDR) is used to follow the uniformity, defect, fracture, coupling and other properties of optical fiber by analyzing the measured curve. It is designed based on the principle of backscattering of light and Fresnel inversion principle, utilizing the backscattered light generated when the light propagates in the fiber to obtain information about attenuation. As an essential tool in optical cable construction, maintenance and monitoring, it can be used to measure optical fiber attenuation and joint losses, locate optical fiber fault points, and find out the distribution of losses along the fiber, as shown in Fig. 2.56.

The OTDR is an optical fiber tester used to determine the characteristics of optical fiber and optical network, for the purpose of detecting, locating and measuring events at any location of an optical fiber link. One of the main advantages of OTDR is its ability to act as a one-dimensional radar system to learn the characteristics of an entire optical fiber from only one end. The resolution of OTDR is 4 to 40 cm.

OTDR testing is a very effective means of maintaining and repairing optical fiber links. The basic working principle is to measure the distance in accordance with the time difference between the incoming light and the reflected light so as to accurately determine the location of a fault. The OTDR injects probe pulses into the fiber and then estimates the length of the fiber based on the reflected light. OTDR testing is

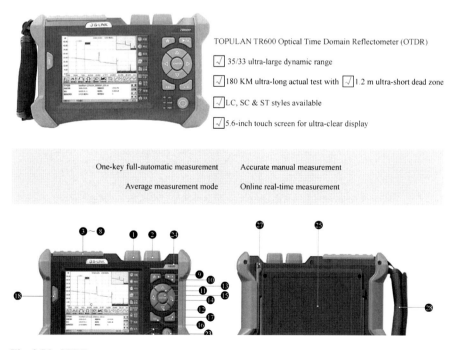

TOPULAN TR600 Optical Time Domain Reflectometer (OTDR)

☑ 35/33 ultra-large dynamic range

☑ 180 KM ultra-long actual test with ☑ 1.2 m ultra-short dead zone

☑ LC, SC & ST styles available

☑ 5.6-inch touch screen for ultra-clear display

One-key full-automatic measurement   Accurate manual measurement

Average measurement mode   Online real-time measurement

Fig. 2.56 OTDR

suitable for fault location, especially for determining the location of a broken or damaged cable. OTDR testing documentation provides technical personnel with a graphical representation of fiber characteristics, as important data for network diagnostics and network expansion.

2.5.6   Optical Fiber Fusion Splicer

The working principle of fiber fusion splicer is that two fiber sections are melted at a high temperature above 2000 °C produced by high-voltage arc discharge. At the same time, the two fibers are gently advanced by a high-precision motion device, so that the two fibers are fused into one, realizing the coupling of fiber mode field. Fiber splicing is one of the most widely used connection methods in fiber engineering. Fiber fusion splicer is mainly used in optical cable line construction, maintenance and emergency repair and production and testing of optical fiber devices by telecom operators, engineering companies and public institutions, as well as research and teaching in scientific research institutes, as shown in Fig. 2.57.

Tools necessary for fiber splicing include the optical fiber fusion splicer, incision knife, optical fiber stripper, alcohol pump (for 99% industrial alcohol), cotton ball, and heat-shrinkable sleeve. From stripping, cleaning, cutting to final welding, these tools can help users complete a qualified fiber splicing. The toolbox of optical fiber fusion splicer is shown in Fig. 2.58.

Well-known brands of fiber fusion splicer include Fujikura, Sumitomo and Furukawa from Japan, Comway from the US, South Korea's Inno, Dark horse,

Fig. 2.57 Optical fiber
fusion splicer

Fig. 2.58 Toolbox of
optical fiber fusion splicer

and Ilshin. There are also China's CETC 41st, Signal Fire, Jilong, Ruiyan, SHINHO, Eloik, etc.

2.6   Engineering Technology of Equipment Room Subsystem

The equipment room subsystem is a centralized equipment area that connects common equipment of the system and connect to the management subsystems (such as LAN, mainframe, and building automation and security systems) through the backbone subsystem.

The equipment room subsystem is the place where the backbone subsystems for data and for voice are connected in the building, the place where the cables from the building complex are connected to the building, and the place where all kinds of mainframes and protection facilities for data and voice are installed. It is generally located in the middle or on the first or second floor of the building; it should not be located in the top floor or basement, nor be far away from the elevator; space should also be reserved for future expansion, as shown in Fig. 2.59. The cables from the building complex should be provided with corresponding over-current and over-voltage protection while entering the building.

Space design of the equipment room subsystem should comply with ANSL/TLA/ELA-569 requirements. This space is used for installation of telecommunication equipment, connection hardware, connector sleeve, etc., providing control environment for grounding and connection facilities and protection devices as a place for

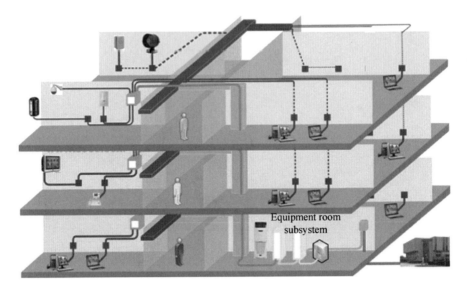

Fig. 2.59 Location of the equipment room subsystem in a building

system management, control and maintenance. In addition, the space should also meet the requirements of doors and windows, ceiling, power supply, lighting, and grounding.

2.6.1 Standard Requirements

1. Standard requirements of equipment room subsystem
   Chapter 7 of the GB 50311 - 2016 "Code for Engineering Design of Generic Cabling System" puts forward specific requirements on the installation processes in equipment rooms.

   (a) Each building should be equipped with not less than one equipment room.
   (b) The equipment room should not be located directly under or adjacent to the toilet, bathroom or other wet and water-prone areas.
   (c) The equipment room should be away from dust, lampblack, harmful gases and places with corrosive, flammable and explosive items.
   (d) The available space in the equipment room should not be less than 10 m^2.
   (e) The net height under the beam in the equipment room should not be less than 2.5 m.
   (f) The room temperature of 10 °C to 35 °C and relative humidity of 20% to 80% should be maintained in the equipment room, and good ventilation should be provided.

Table 2.10 Installation requirements of cabinets for equipment room

Project	Requirements
Installation position	Design requirements should be followed. The cabinet should be 1 m away from the wall for easy installation and construction. All screws installed should not be loose, and the protective rubber pad should be firmly installed
Base	The base should be firmly installed, and the construction should be carried out according to the shockproof requirements of the design drawing
Placement	The cabinet should be placed vertically, with the top keeping level. The vertical deviation should not be more than 1‰, and the horizontal deviation, no more than 3 mm. The gap between the cabinets should be no more than 1 mm
Surface	The surface should be intact, free of damage, and the screws should be tightened. The surface convexity per square meter should be less than 1 mm
Connection	The connection should meet the design requirements and keep in good condition, with complete terminal signs
Distribution Equipment	The grounding body, protective grounding, cross-section of wires, and cable color should meet the design requirements
Grounding	Grounding terminals should be provided and well connected to building grounding terminals
Cable reservation	(1) There should be no visible reserved cable in the cabinet fixed. The cable should be reserved in a place where it can be concealed, with a length of 1 to 1.5 m (2) For all cables connected to the movable cabinet, at least 1 m should be reserved at the entrance of the cabinet, and the length difference of various reserved cables should not exceed 0.5 m
Cabling	The cables in the cabinet should be all fixed and kept horizontal and vertical

(g) The equipment room should be opened with double fire doors with a net height not less than 2.0 m and a net width not be less than 1.5 m.

(h) The cement floor of the equipment room should be no less than 100 mm higher than the ground of the floor where the room is located, or a waterproof threshold should be installed.

(i) No less than two 220 V/10A single-phase AC power socket boxes should be installed in the equipment room, and the distribution lines of each power socket should be equipped with protectors. The power supply of the equipment should be separately configured.

2. Installation requirements of cabinets for equipment room

The installation requirements of cabinets for equipment room are shown in Table 2.10.

3. Distribution requirements

The power supply of the equipment room is provided by the mains electricity of the building, which goes into the special distribution cabinet of the equipment room. The dedicated underfloor socket for UPS should be installed in the equipment room. In order to facilitate maintenance, maintenance sockets should be installed on the wall. Other rooms should be equipped with corresponding maintenance sockets according to the quantity of equipment.

In addition to meeting the power supply demand of the equipment in the equipment room, the distribution cabinet shall also reserve redundant space for future capacity expansion.

4. Requirements for installation of lightning protector in equipment room

According to the relevant provisions of GB 50057-2010 "Design Code for Protection of Structures against Lightning", the power supply system of computer network center equipment room should adopt three-stage lightning protection design.

Lightning protection in the equipment room is especially important. Perfect lightning protection system is not only the basis of protecting expensive and important network exchanges and servers and other important equipment and maintaining the normal operation of the network system, but also can avoid personal injury incidents and protect personal safety.

5. Grounding requirements for equipment room

Equipment grounding in the equipment room cannot be ignored. DC and Ac working grounding resistance should not be greater than 4 Ω commonly, lightning protection grounding resistance should not be greater than 10 Ω. There should be a grounding network set in the building to ensure that an equipotent reference for all equipment is established. In order to achieve a good grounding state, it is recommended to adopt the joint grounding mode, that is, the lightning protection grounding, AC working grounding, DC working grounding, etc. are connected to the common grounding device.

2.6.2 Installation Technology

1. Installation and construction of cabling channel
   The laying of all kinds of cable bridges, pipelines and other cabling channels in the equipment room shall meet the following requirements.

   (a) The cabling should be horizontal and vertical, with lateral deviation no more than 10 mm for the horizontal cabling and vertical deviation no more than 5 mm for the vertical cabling.
   (b) When the cabling channel is installed onto a pipe rack together with other pipes, the cabling channel should be arranged on one side of the pipe rack.
   (c) When the cable is laid vertically in the cabling channel, the upper end of the cable should be fixed on the channel support, and the body of the cable should be fixed on the support at 1.5 m intervals. When laying horizontally, the cable should be fixed at its head, end and turnings and at 3 to 5 m intervals.
   (d) The cable laid on the cable bridge should be bound to the bridge and keep straight and tidy, with even-spaced and moderate-tightened buckles.

(e) AC and DC power cables and signal cables should be laid on their respective bridges; if laid in a metal groove, a metal plate shall be used to separate the cables. If the cables are laid in the same groove, the spacing between them should be ensured.
(f) The cables should keep straight without crossing, and should be bound to be fixed at turnings.
(g) The cables laid in the cabinet should not be tightened, with an appropriate amount of redundancy, and with even-spaced and moderate-tightened buckles. The cables should keep straight and tidy without crossing.
(h) When laying Cat 6e UTP network cables, the filling rate in the cabling channel should not exceed 40%.

2. Cable termination

There are a lot of patch cords and cables need to be connected and terminated in the equipment room. The termination should meet the following basic requirements.

(a) When cross-connecting, the redundancy and length of patch cords should be minimized to keep them tidy and artistic.
(b) The bending radius of the cable shall be met.
(c) The cable shall be connected to the connecting hardware with the same performance level.
(d) The backbone cable and the horizontal cable shall be terminated on different distribution frames.
(e) The outer sheath of the TP should be stripped as shortly as possible.
(f) The length the separated wires of the TP shall not exceed 13 mm.
(g) The Cat 6e network cable should not be bound tightly.

3. Installation and construction of open network bridge

(a) Ground-based installation

The network bridge in the equipment room must be connected to the building's vertical subsystem and the main bridge in the management room. In the equipment room, ground brackets or supports shall be installed at 1.5 m intervals and fixed with bolts and nuts. Common installation methods include bracket-based installation and support-based installation, as shown in Figs. 2.60 and 2.61.

In general, the support-based installation is feasible. The height above ground of the bracket or support may depend on the actual situation of the site, but the bottom of it should be at least 50 mm from the ground.

(b) Ceiling-mounted installation

When installing the bridge on the ceiling, the ceiling-mounted method should be adopted. The bridge can be suspended above the cabinet with U-steel support or reinforcement reinforcing steel suspending lever, combined with the horizontal bracket and M6 bolts. When laying the cables in the

Fig. 2.60 Bracket-based
installation

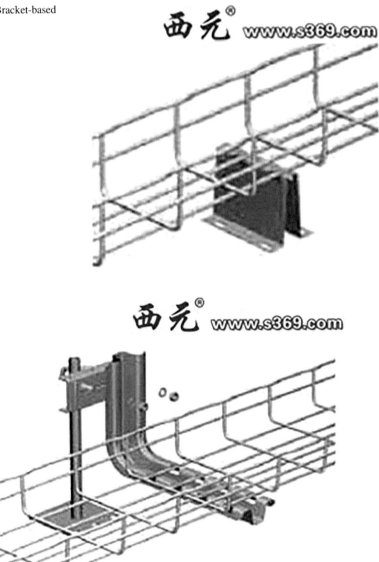

Fig. 2.61 Support-based installation

cabinet, the cables should be arranged and bound with a cabling unit in the
cabinet, as shown in Fig. 2.62.

(c) Special installation methods

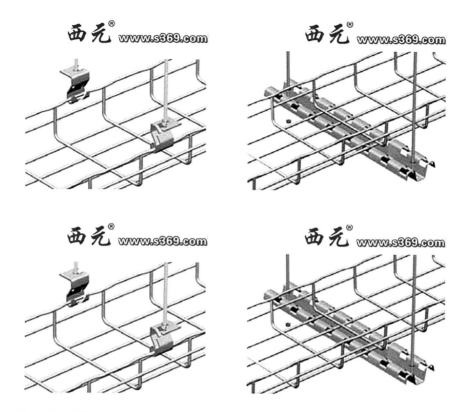

Fig. 2.62 Ceiling-mounted installation

(i) Layered installation: This method allows for laying of more cables, easier maintenance and management, as well as the aesthetically pleasing site, as shown in Fig. 2.63.

(ii) Installation of supporting bridge for rack: With this new installation method, the installer does not need to drill holes into the ceiling or climb high during installation and cabling, which saves time and effort and is very convenient, as shown in Fig. 2.64. This method not only gives the user more intuitive control of the entire installation engineering, but also provides natural ventilation and heat dissipation conditions for the cables, which is convenient for the maintenance and upgrading of the equipment room in the future.

4. Grounding connection in the equipment room

(a) Grounding connection of the cabinet and rack

The cabinet and rack in the equipment room must be grounded reliably, which generally uses self-tapping screws for connection with the steel plate of the cabinet. If the cabinet surface has been painted, the electrical connection

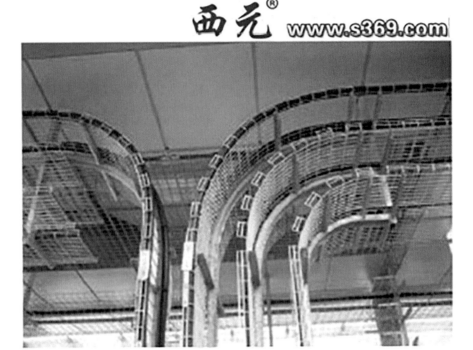

Fig. 2.63 Layered installation of bridges

can be made by using a paint removal solvent or an electric drill to direct the grounding facility to the metal surface of the cabinet.

(b) Grounding connection of the equipment

The server, switch and other equipment installed in the cabinet or on the rack must be reliably grounded through the grounding bar.

(c) Grounding connection of the bridge

The bridge must be grounded reliably, and the open bridge grounding method is often employed, as shown in Fig. 2.65.

5. Design and installation of aisles and channels in the equipment room

(a) Personnel aisles

(i) The width of the aisles for transport equipment shall not be less than 1.5 m.

(ii) The distance between the fronts of the cabinets or racks arranged face to face should not be less than 1.2 m.

(iii) The distance between the backs of the cabinets or racks arranged back to back should not be less than 1 m.

Fig. 2.64 Installation of supporting bridge for rack

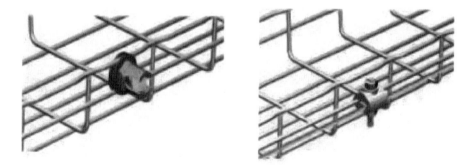

Fig. 2.65 Open bridge grounding method

(iv) When maintenance or testing is performed on the side of the cabinet, the distance between the cabinets, and between the cabinet and the wall should not be less than 1.2 m.

(v) When the total length of a row of cabinets exceeds 6 m, there should be an aisle at both ends. When the distance between two such aisles exceeds 15 m, aisles shall be added between them. The width of each

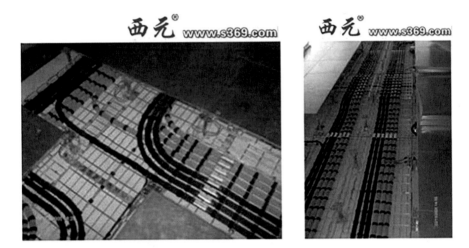

Fig. 2.66 Cabling channels under the raised floor

aisle should not be less than 1 m, but the local width of the aisle may be contracted to 0.8 m.

(b) Cabling channels under the raised floor

The ground of the raised floor plays an anti-static role. The space under the floor can be set with channels for heating, ventilation and cooling, as well as grooves and pipes for laying cables.

When cabling under the raised floor of the equipment room, the cables shall not be placed under the floor at will, but shall be laid in the cabling channels. The channels may be set separately for each category of cable and installed in multiple layers, but the height of the cable bundle should not exceed 150 mm. In architectural design, cabling channels under the floor should be coordinated with other equipment pipelines (such as those for air conditioning, fire protection, electricity, etc.), and corresponding protective measures should be in place.

According to the international standards, if the space under the raised floor is only used for laying communication cables, the net height under the floor should not be less than 250 mm; if the space also serves as a static pressure box for the air conditioning, the net height under the floor should not be less than 400 mm. The cabling channels under the raised floor are shown in Fig. 2.66.

According to the Data Center Design and Implementation Best Practices published by the BICSI, the net height under the raised floor shall be at least 450 mm, and the net height of 900 mm is recommended. The distance between the bottom of the floor plate and the top of the cabling channel should be at least 20 mm. If there is an outlet for cable bundles or pipes or

Table 2.11   Net heights under the ceiling of the equipment rooms

	Tier 1	Tier 2	Tier 3	Tier 4
Net height under the ceiling	At least 2.6 m	At least 2.7 m	At least 3 m; not less than 0.46 m from the ceiling to the top of the highest equipment	At least 3 m; not less than 0.6 m from the ceiling to the top of the highest equipment

grooves, the distance should be increased to 50 mm to meet the needs of cable placement and air distribution of the air conditioning.

(c) Cabling channels under the ceiling

(i) Requirements for net height

Commonly used cabinets are usually 2 m high. In view of the need of air distribution, the top surface of the cabinet and the ceiling are generally 500 to 700 mm apart. This distance should be as close as possible to the net height under the raised floor, so the net height of the equipment room should not be less than 2.6 m.

According to the international standard for data center tier rating, the net heights under the ceiling of the equipment rooms of Tier 1 to 4 data centers are shown in Table 2.11.

(ii) Channel style

The ceiling-mounted cabling channel is composed of open bridges or groove-style closed bridges and corresponding accessories for installation. The open bridge is widely used in new data centers because of its convenience in cable maintenance.

The cabling channel shall be installed in the upper spaces of the aisles in the equipment room and other public areas, above 2.7 m from the floor, otherwise the bottom of the cabling channels installed on the ceiling shall be laid with solid material to prevent personnel from touching it and accidental or intentional damage to the cables. The ceiling-mounted cabling channels are shown in Fig. 2.67.

(iii) Requirements for channel location and dimensions

- The top of a channel should be no less than 300 mm from the ceiling or other obstacles.
- The width of a channel should not be less than 100 mm, and the height should not exceed 150 mm.
- The filling rate in the cross section of a channel should not exceed 50%.
- Multiple ceiling-mounted cabling channels may be installed in layers, if any. The optical cables are preferably laid above the copper cables. In order to facilitate construction and maintenance, the copper cable link and optical fiber link should be laid separately.
- The sprinklers of fire extinguishing devices shall be placed between the cabling channels, instead of being placed directly on the channels.

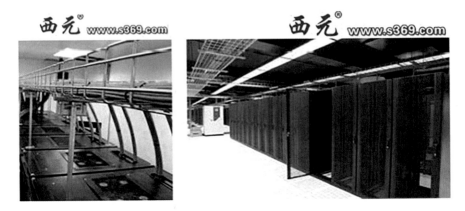

Fig. 2.67 Ceiling-mounted cabling channels

Where the pipe-style gas fire-extinguishing system is adopted in the equipment room, the cable bridge shall be installed above the fire-extinguishing gas pipeline, without blocking the sprinkler or gas.

2.7   Acceptance of Cabling Engineering

Acceptance is the final part of the whole project, which also marks the completion of the project. In order to ensure the quality of the whole project, it is necessary to employ relevant industry experts to participate in the acceptance. The acceptance process generally includes pre-construction inspection, follow-up acceptance, preliminary acceptance and completion acceptance.

2.7.1   Completion Documents

After the completion of the project, the construction organization shall deliver the completion documents to the development organization before the acceptance of the project. The completion documents of the generic cabling system project shall include the installation bill of quantities, project specifications, equipment list, as-built drawings, test records, engineering change records, inspection records, design changes during construction, negotiation records of construction, design and construction units regarding relevant measures, follow-up acceptance records, concealed work confirmation and final project accounts.

2.7.2 Project Contents

Generic cabling system engineering shall be accepted according to Table 2.12. The acceptance conclusion shall be an integral part of the completion documents and serve as a proof in the project acceptance.

2.8 Summary

Based on the demand of primary standards, this chapter guides the reader along the basic workflow of cabling engineering to understand the engineering technical standards and installation specifications for equipment room subsystem, covering network cabinets, communication cables, cable connection devices and optical cable connection devices commonly used in communication systems, common tools and instruments for system cabling, etc., and introduces the completion documents involved in project acceptance and items subject to the acceptance.

Upon the study of this chapter, the reader should get familiar with various network cabinets; master the characteristics and identification methods of TPs and optical fibers; have the ability to skillfully identify and use connection devices commonly used in communication systems; understand common tools and instruments for system cabling; and understand the engineering standards, technical requirements for installation and items subject to the acceptance of the equipment room system.

2.9 Exercise

1. The wire sequence of T568B is ().

   A. White orange, orange, white green, blue, white blue, green, white brown, brown
   B. White orange, orange, white green, green, white blue, blue, white brown, brown
   C. White green, green, white orange, blue, white blue, orange, white brown, brown
   D. White green, green, blue, white blue, white orange, orange, white brown, brown

2. The basic structure of a bare fiber is ().

   A. Fiber core, reinforced layer and sheath
   B. Cladding, sleeve and central stiffener
   C. Fiber core, shielding layer and coating layer
   D. Fiber core, cladding and coating layer.

Table 2.12 Acceptance checklist

Stage	Items for acceptance	Content	Acceptance method
Pre-construction inspection	1. Environmental requirements	(1) Civil construction conditions, floors, walls, doors, power sockets and grounding devices; (2) Civil engineering technology, equipment room area and reserved holes; (3) Construction power supply; (4) Laying of floors; (5) Inspection of facilities at the entrance to the building	Pre-construction inspection
	2. Equipment inspection	(1) Appearance; (2) Model, specification and quantity; (3) Electrical performance test of cables and accessory connecting devices; (4) Performance test of optical fibers and accessory connecting devices; (5) Inspection of test instruments and tools	
	3. Safety and fire protection requirements	(1) Fire equipment; (2) Placement of dangerous materials; (3) Fire prevention measures for reserved holes	
Equipment installation	1. Telecom room, equipment room, equipment cabinet, and rack	(1) Specifications and appearance; (2) Perpendicularity and levelness of installations; (3) Good condition of painted surfaces, and comprehensiveness and completeness of signs; (4) Screw fastening; (5) Reinforcing measures for earthquake resistance; (6) Grounding measures	Follow-up acceptance
	2. Cabling module and 8-position modular outlet	(1) Specification, location and quality; (2) Screw fastening; (3) Comprehensiveness and completeness of signs; (4) Compliance with installation process requirements; (5) Reliable connection of the shielding layer	
Layout of cables and optical cables(in the building)	1. Arrangement of cable bridges and grooves	(1) Correct installation position; (2) Compliance with installation process requirements; (3) Compliance with	Follow-up acceptance

(continued)

Table 2.12 (continued)

Stage	Items for acceptance	Content	Acceptance method
		cabling process requirements; (4) Grounding	
	2. Concealed laying of cables (including hidden pipes, grooves, underfloor cabling, etc.)	(1) Cable specification, routing and location; (2) Compliance with cabling process requirements; (3) Grounding	Concealed work confirmation
Layout of cables and optical cables(between buildings)	1. Aerial cables	(1) Suspension specifications, positions and installation specifications; (2) Perpendicularity of the cables; (3) Cable specifications; (4) Buckle intervals; (5) Compliance of cable introduction process	Follow-up acceptance
	2. Duct cables	(1) Locations of duct holes; (2) Cable specifications; (3) Cable direction; (4) Quality of cable protection measures	Concealed work confirmation
	3. Buried cables	(1) Cable specifications; (2) laying position and depth; (3) Quality of cable protection measures; (4) Quality of cable burial	
	4. Channel cables	(1) Cable specifications; (2) Installation location and routing; (3) Compliance with civil construction requirements	
	5. Others	(1) Distance between communication lines and other facilities; (2) Installation and construction quality of the facilities in the cable entry room	Follow-up acceptance and concealed work confirmation
Cable termination	1. 8-position modular outlet	Compliance with process requirements	Follow-up acceptance
	2. Optical cable connection devices	Compliance with process requirements	
	3. Patch cords/cables	Compliance with process requirements	
	4. Distribution modules	Compliance with process requirements	
System test	1. Electrical performance test	(1) Wire Map; (2) Length; (3) Attenuation; (4) NEXT; (5) PS NEXT; (6) ACR;	Completion acceptance

(continued)

Table 2.12 (continued)

Stage	Items for acceptance	Content	Acceptance method
		(7) PS ACR; (8) FEXT; (9) PS FEXT; (10) RL; (11) Propagation Delay; (12) Delay Skew; (13) Insertion Loss; (14) DC Loop Resistance; (15) Tests specially specified in the design; (16) Conducting of the shielding layer	
	2. Optical fiber characteristic test	(1) Attenuation; (2) Length	
Management system	1. Management system level	Compliance with design requirements	Completion acceptance
	2. Layout of signs and labels	(1) Type and composition of the special signs; (2) Label setting; (3) Label material and color code	
	3. Records and reports	(1) Records; (2) Reports; (3) Engineering drawings	
General acceptance	1. Completion documents	Checking and handover of completion documents	
	2. Project acceptance evaluation	Project quality assessment and acceptance result confirmation	

3. The optical fiber splice () is typically used for distribution frames and shows as a round threaded splice with a micro-spherical section employing the grinding and polishing process.

   A. FC/APC
   B. FC/PC
   C. SC/APC
   D. SC/PC

4. [Multi-choice] An information outlet consists of ().

   A. Panel
   B. Bottom box
   C. Module
   D. RJ

5. [Multi-choice] Network tester can be used to test ().

   A. Wire Map
   B. Length
   C. Propagation Delay
   D. Insertion Lose

Chapter 3
Hardware Installation in Network Systems

A complete information network system usually consists of hardware system and software system. The software system mainly includes operating system and communication protocol; the hardware system refers to the network channel used for data processing and information transmission, including the terminals/servers, communication mediums, network devices, etc.

In the network of a general industrial park, the hardware system not only contains communication mediums, but also involves network devices such as switches, routers, access controllers (ACs), wireless access points (APs), firewalls, as well as various terminals and servers. This chapter will first introduce various network devices, lead the reader to understand the common network system, and then exemplify the common network equipment involved in the enterprise network with Huawei network devices. Finally, the reader will grasp the specific installation processes of various network devices in the network system one by one.

By the end of this chapter, you will

(1) Know the common network devices	(4) Understand the precautions for network system installation
(2) Comprehend the functions of network devices	(5) Master the installation processes of Huawei network devices
(3) Get familiar with the structure of Huawei network devices	

3.1 Hardware in Network Systems

At present, the mainstream network equipment manufacturers include Huawei, H3C, Cisco, Juniper, ZTE, Ruijie, Sangfor, etc. As a global-leading information and communications solutions provider, Huawei has developed a comprehensive product portfolio serving telecom operators, enterprises and consumers, and provides

© The Author(s) 2023
Huawei Technologies Co., Ltd., *Construction, Operation and Maintenance of Network System(Junior Level)*, https://doi.org/10.1007/978-981-19-3069-0_3

end-to-end solutions in telecom networks, terminals and cloud computing. This section will introduce Huawei's different network devices, including routers, switches, ACs, wireless APs, firewalls, etc. Through the study of this section, reader will understand the structures and functions of a range of network devices, as well as the features of Huawei network devices.

3.1.1 Routers

The router in the TCP/IP protocol stack is responsible for data exchange and transmission at the network layer. In network communication, the router also shoulders the role of identifying network address and choosing IP path, to build a flexible connection system in multiple network environments and connect subnets through different data packets and medium access mode. As the hub connecting different networks, the router system constitutes the main vein of the TCP/IP-based Internet. You could even say that routers form the backbone of the Internet. However, the processing speed of router is one of the main bottlenecks of network communication, and router reliability directly affects the quality of network interconnection. Therefore, in the field of industrial park network, regional network and even the whole Internet, router technology is always in the core of research and development, and the course and direction of router development can be summarized as an epitome of the whole Internet research.

There are a wide variety of routers on the market. By location in the network and function, routers can be roughly divided into access routers, convergence routers, core routers, etc.; and by style and profile, they can be further divided into case-shaped routers (see Fig. 3.1) and chassis-shaped routers (see Fig. 3.2).

At present, Cisco, H3C, Huawei, etc. constitute the mainstream router manufacturers. Cisco RV260 VPN Router, as an access router, is designed for small- and medium-sized enterprises. H3C MSR 5600 Series Routers adopt the non-blocking switching architecture, which are a type of convergence router helpful for improving the concurrent processing capacity of multiple services. H3C SR8800 Series Routers allow flexible scalability by virtue of multi-slot performance to meet the needs from different locations in the network.

The following will be a detailed introduction of the types and functions of Huawei routers.

(1) Cisco RV260 VPN Router   (2) H3C MSR 5600 Router

Fig. 3.1 Case-shaped routers

(1) Cisco NCS 5500 Router

(2) H3C SR8800 Router

Fig. 3.2 Chassis-shaped routers

Fig. 3.3 Huawei AR1200 Series Routers

1. Case-shaped routers

Taking AR series routers as an example, the case-shaped routers are developed by Huawei for large- and medium-sized enterprises and small office home offices (SOHO). The AR1200 Series Routers are deployed at the connection between the internal network and external network of the enterprise, as the only passageway for the data flow between the internal and external network, as shown in Fig. 3.3. This series enables multiple service networks to be deployed on the same equipment, which greatly saves the initial investment and long-term operation and maintenance costs of network construction.

The AR Series, as case-shaped routers, adopts the non-blocking switching architecture with multi-core CPU, and integrates Wi-Fi, voice security and other functions, which can be applied to the multiservice routers for small- and medium-sized offices or enterprise branches. With its flexible scalability, the

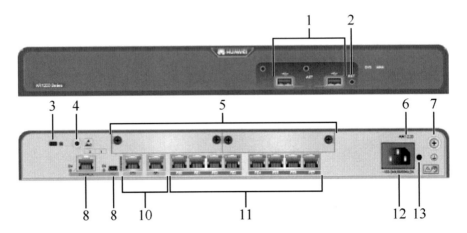

Fig. 3.4 Appearance of Huawei AR1200 Series Routers

AR1200 Series Routers can provide customers with flexible networking capabilities with full functions. The appearance of AR1200 routers is shown in Fig. 3.4, and the explanation is detailed in Table 3.1.

2. Chassis-shaped routers

Huawei NetEngine 8000 Routers is a chassis-shaped router series introduced by Huawei, as shown in Fig. 3.5. It is a high-end Ethernet oriented network product profile that focuses on the access, convergence and transmission of metropolitan Ethernet services. Based on hardware forwarding mechanism and non-blocking switching technology, it adopts the Versatile Routing Platform (VRP) independently developed by Huawei to achieve carrier-level reliability, full-line speed forwarding capacity, perfect QoS management mechanism, powerful service processing capacity and good scalability. In addition, thanks to strong network access, Layer 2 switching and EOMPLS transmission capabilities, and the convergence of a wide range of interface types, it has the ability to access broadband, provide fixed-line triple-play services that integrate voice, video, and data, as well as IP dedicated line and VPN services. Together with the NE, CX and ME series developed by Huawei, NetEngine 8000 builds a well-structured metropolitan Ethernet network with richer business capabilities.

Huawei NetEngine 8000 M8 chassis-shaped routers have the following features.

(a) Large capacity. The NetEngine 8000 M8 has a maximum switching capacity of 1.2 Tbit/s and can be smoothly evolved to 2 Tbit/s to accommodate future traffic growth. Its multiple types of business interfaces can meet the different needs (100GE/50GE/40GE/25GE/10GE/GE/CPOS/E1/POS).

(b) Small profile. The deep 220 mm chassis can be flexibly deployed, with low power consumption. The compact design allows it to take up less space in the equipment room, easy to fit the 300 mm cabinet.

Table 3.1 Appearance explanation of Huawei AR1200 Series Routers

No.	Component	Explanation
1	2 USB interfaces (host)	If you use the USB interface for a 3G USB modem, a plastic cover for USB interface (optional) is recommended to protect the interface, which can be mounted through the two screw holes above the USB interface. The plastic cover looks like
2	RST button	Used for resetting the device manually. This button should be used with caution, as resetting the device means a business interruption
3	Anti-theft lockhole	–
4	ESD jack	Used for connecting one end of an anti-static wrist strap that must be worn for maintenance or operation of equipment
5	2 SIC slots	Used for grounding equipment reliably with grounding cable to protect against lightning and interference
6	Silkscreen of product model	–
7	grounding point	–
8	CON/AUX interface	The AR1220-AC does not support AUX functionality
9	MiniUSB interface	Cannot be enabled at the same time with the Console port
10	WAN-side interface: 2 GE electrical interfaces	The GE0 interface is used as the management interface for upgrading the device
11	LAN-side interface: 8 FE electrical interfaces	In V200R007C00 and later firmware, all FE LAN interfaces can be switched to WAN interfaces
12	AC power cable interface	Used for connecting the device to external power supply with AC power cable
13	Mounting hole for power cable buckle	Used for fix power cable buckle that binds the power cable to prevent it from loosening

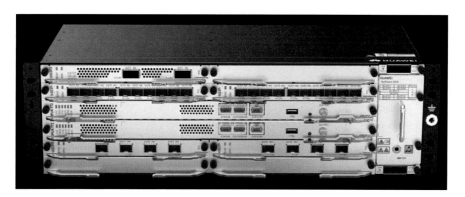

Fig. 3.5 Huawei NetEngine 8000 chassis-shaped routers

(c) High reliability. Key component control, forwarding, power redundancy backup and other functions ensure the high reliability of multi-service access. SRV6 support simplifies network configuration, making it possible to more simple VPN implementation. Based on full compatibility with existing IPv6 networks, normal IPv6 forwarding can be achieved even if MPLS forwarding is not supported on the node. Efficient protection of fast reroute (FRR) facilitates traffic tuning of the IPv6 forwarding path.

(d) Better scalability. The EVPN extended to BGP moves the MAC address learning and publishing process between the two layer networks from the data plane to the control plane. The load-sharing function optimizes the rational utilization of network resources and reduces network congestion. The series supports the deployment of route reflectors on the public network to avoid the deployment of full connections between PE devices on the public network and reduce the number of logical connections. It also helps reduce network resource consumption caused by ARP broadcast traffic.

3.1.2 Switches

Switch is an important equipment in computer network. The switches mentioned in this section are Ethernet switches. In their early days, Ethernets were half duplex networks with shared bus lines. The birth of switch realized full duplex communication, and the automatic learning of MAC address brought by it greatly improved the efficiency of data forwarding. Early switches operated at the data link layer of the TCP/IP model and were therefore called layer 2 switches. Later, the layer 3 switches realized the data forwarding across network segments. The development of technology is constantly strengthening the functions of switches, including supporting wireless, supporting IPv6, programmability and other functions.

Switch types from various manufacturers emerge in an endless stream. Generally speaking, by network structure, switches can be divided into access layer switches, convergence layer switches and core layer switches; by layer of TCP/IP model on which they based, they can be divided into layer 2 switches and layer 3switches; and by appearance, case-shaped switches and chassis-shaped switches. At present, the mainstream switch manufacturers include Cisco, H3C, Huawei, etc. The switches provided by Cisco and H3C are shown in Figs. 3.6 and 3.7, respectively. Cisco Catalyst 3650 Series supports both standalone and stacked deployments, while

(1) Catalyst 3650 Switch   (2) Catalyst 9300 Switch

Fig. 3.6 Cisco switches

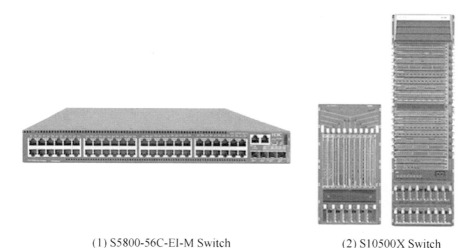

(1) S5800-56C-EI-M Switch   (2) S10500X Switch

Fig. 3.7 H3C switches

Fig. 3.8 Huawei
CloudEngine S5731-S
Ethernet Switch

Catalyst 9300 is a stacked series. H3C S5800-56C-EI-M is a case-shaped switch series, while the S10500X is for chassis-shaped switches. Huawei has launched a complete range of switches, covering all types of switches for all layer. Now we will go into more detail below.

1. Case-shaped switches

Huawei case-shaped switch switches are represented by S-Series Ethernet switches. Huawei CloudEngine S5731-S Ethernet Switches shown in Fig. 3.8 are case-shaped switches. As a new generation of Gigabit access switches launched by Huawei, the series is based on Huawei's unified VRP software platform. Thanks to the enhanced layer-3 feature, simple operation and maintenance, intelligent iStack, flexible Ethernet networking, mature IPv6 features and other characteristics, they are widely used for access and convergence in industrial parks, access to data centers and other application scenarios.

The S-Series is equipped with a centralized hardware platform, whose hardware system consists of case, power supply, fan, plug-in card and switch control unit (SCU). An example of this is the S5731-S24T4X Switch, as shown in Fig. 3.9, whose components are listed in Table 3.2.

The interfaces are described below.

(a) 10/100/1000BASE-T Ethernet electrical interface: adopts the RJ-45 connector; mainly used for receiving and sending of 10 Mb/100 Mb/Gigabit services; used with network cables.

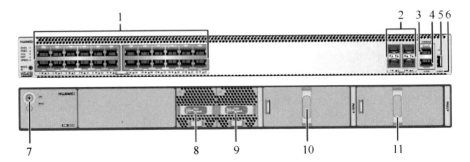

Fig. 3.9 S5731-S24T4X Switch

(b) 10GE SFP+ Ethernet optical interface: adopts the LC/PC connector; supports 1000 Mbit/s self-adaption; mainly used for receiving and sending of Gigabit/10-Gigabit services.

(c) Console port: adopts the RJ-45 connector; used for connecting the console; conforms to RS-233 standard; supports field configuration; used with the console communication cable. When first powered on, the device needs to be configured through the Console port.

(d) ETH management interface: adopts the RJ-45 connector; used for configuring the interface connection of terminals or network management workstations, and building on-site and remote configuration environment; used with network cables. Under the Bootload menu, you can select the ETH management interface to load the software version package. Its transmission rate is faster than that of the Console port.

(e) USB interface: used with USB flash disk; used for site deployment, configuration file transfer, file upgrading, etc. The USB flash disk should support USB 2.0 standard.

2. Chassis-shaped switches

Huawei CloudEngine S12700E Switches shown in Fig. 3.10 are chassis-shaped switches. They are the flagship core switches launched by Huawei for the Intent-Driven Network (IDN), featuring high-quality massive switching capacity, deep integration of wired and wireless networks, full-stack opening and smooth upgrade. They can help customers transform from the traditional park network to the business experience-oriented IDN Park, and provide three versions, with 4, 8 and 12 different business slots respectively, to satisfy customers of different scales with the park network deployment. The CloudEngine S12700E Series Switches have the following features.

(a) Super performance. They are equipped with an exchange capacity up to 57.6 Tbit/s and compatible with 288 × 100GE port, and supports 10 K AP management, nearly twice as much as standalone AC management, and 50 K multi-client concurrency access.

Table 3.2 Components of 3-2 S5731-S24T4X Switch

No.	Explanation
1	24 10/100/1000BASE-T Ethernet electrical interfaces
2	4 10GE SFP+ Ethernet optical interfaces Compatible with following modules and cables: (a) GE optical module; (b) GE-CWDM colored optical module; (c) GE-DWDM colored optical module; (d) GE photoelectric module (supporting 100 Mbit/s/1000 Mbit/s self-adaption); (e) 10GE SFP+ optical module (OSXD22N00 is not supported); (f) 10GE-CWDM optical module; (g) 10GE-DWDM optical module; (h) 1 m, 3 m, 5 m and 10 m SFP+ high-speed cables; (i) 3 m and 10 m AOC optical cables; (j) 0.5 m and 1.5 m SFP+ stacked cables (only for stacking without configuration)
3	1 Console port
4	1 ETH management interface
5	1 USB interface
6	1 PNP button (a) Long press (for 6 s): restoring factory settings and resetting the device. (b) Short press: resetting the device. This button should be used with caution, as resetting the device means a business interruption.
7	Grounding screw Used with the grounding cable
8	Fan Module Slot 1 Fan module supported: FAN-023A-B Fan Module
9	Fan Module Slot 2 Fan module supported: FAN-023A-B Fan Module
10	Power Module Slot 1 Power module supported: (a) 600 W AC power module (PAC600S12-CB); (b) 1000 W DC power module (PDC1000S12-DB); (c) 150 W AC power module (PAC150S12-R)
11	Power Module Slot 2 Power module supported: (a) 600 W AC power module (PAC600S12-CB); (b) 1000 W DC power module (PDC1000S12-DB); (c) 150 W AC power module (PAC150S12-R)

(b) Super high reliability. The distributed switching architecture separates the main control network board and the switching network board, achieving the carrier-grade service reliability above 99.999%. The switching network board can be configured on demand to support flexible capacity expansion. Thanks to the independent fan module design, redundant backup and intelligent speed regulation, any single fan module failure will not affect the normal operation of the equipment. The innovative cell switching technology based on

Fig. 3.10 Huawei CloudEngine S12700E Switches

dynamic load balancing algorithm enables non-blocking switching in high concurrency and full load working environment.

(c) Agility and opening. Based on fully programmable chips, new services and new features can be realized through software programming without hardware upgrading, which accelerates business monetization. According to statistics, by 2020, this switch series has completed docking and verification with 10 proprietary protocols, more than 400 network devices and more than 30 authentication/network management systems launched by mainstream manufacturers, helping smooth network upgrade.

3.1.3 WLAN devices

Wireless Local Area Network (WLAN) refers to the network system that interconnects computer devices through wireless communication technology, which can communicate with each other and realize resource sharing. WLAN has abandoned the use of communication cables to connect the computer with the network, but takes wireless connection to make the network construction and terminal movement more flexible. It uses the radio frequency (RF) technology to replace the traditional wired cables with the wireless electromagnetic waves in the short-distance communication, so as to build the wireless local area network. Huawei WLAN equipment adopts simple storage architecture, so that users can experience the ideal realm of "portable information". In general, the common networking architecture of WLAN system consists of ACs and wireless APs.

Fig. 3.11 H3C WX2500H
AC

Fig. 3.12 Ruijie
RG-WS7208-A
Multiservice Wireless AC

1. ACs

The access control device of WLAN is responsible for gathering data from different APs and accessing the Internet, plus the control functions such as AP configuration management, wireless user authentication and management, broadband access and security. Meanwhile, they also manage the APs in the wireless network in a certain area. H3C WX2500H Series ACs are gateway wireless controllers, as shown in Fig. 3.11. It provides a variety of services, integrating fine user control and management, perfect RF resource management, 24/7 wireless security management and control, fast Layer 2 and Layer 3 roaming, flexible QoS control, IPv4/IPv6 dual stack and other functions into one, and presents a powerful wired and wireless integrated access capability.

Figure 3.12 shows Ruijie RG-WS7208-A Multiservice Wireless AC, which can implement intensive centralized visual management and control for wireless network, and significantly alleviate the implementation difficulties and complex deployment issues of wireless network. By coordinating with RG-SNC, an unified management platform for wired and wireless devices, and wireless APs, it can flexibly control the configuration of wireless APs, optimize the RF coverage effect and performance, and reduce deployment of devices in the network.

AC6600 Series Wireless ACs from Huawei, provide wireless data control featuring large capacity, high performance, high reliability, ease to install, and ease to maintain, with flexible networking, energy saving and other advantages. Its appearance is shown in Fig. 3.13, whose interfaces are introduced in Table 3.3.

Huawei AC6600 Series Wireless AC has the following features and functions:

(a) Integrates access and convergence functions;
(b) Provides power supply capability of POE (15.4 W) or POE + (30 W) through 24 interfaces, which can directly access wireless APs;
(c) Provides rich and flexible user policy management and authority control capabilities;
(d) No matter in AC or DC, supports double power backup and hot plug, to ensure long time trouble-free operation of equipment;

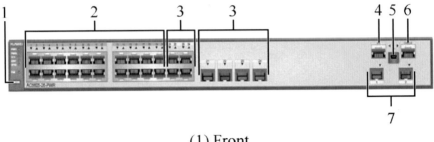

(1) Front

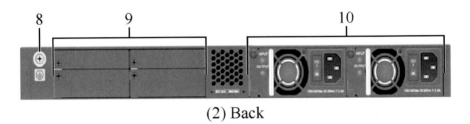

(2) Back

Fig. 3.13 Huawei AC6600 Series Wireless AC

Table 3.3 Introduction to interfaces of Huawei AC6600 Series Wireless AC

No.	Explanation
1	MODE button, used to switch the indicator light mode of the service port
2	20 10/100/1000BASE-T Ethernet electrical interfaces: (a) Support 10 Mbit/s/100 Mbit/s/1000 Mbit/s self-adaption (b) Support Power over Ethernet (POE) through 20 interfaces
3	4 pairs of Combo interfaces, as the electrical interfaces: (a) Support 10 Mbit/s/100 Mbit/s/1000 Mbit/s self-adaption (b) Support Power over Ethernet (POE) through 4 interfaces
4	ETH management interface
5	MiniUSB interface
6	Console port
7	2 10GE SFP+ Ethernet optical interfaces
8	grounding point
9	Filler panel
10	2 power module slots, supporting 3 power modules: (a) 150 W DC power module; (b) 150 W AC power module; (c) 500 W AC PoE power module

(e) Support equipment maintenance through the network management system eSight, Web network management system, and command line interface (CLI).

Fig. 3.14 Ruijie
RG-AP320-I Wireless AP

Fig. 3.15 TP-Link
TL-AP301C 300 M
Wireless AP

2. APs

As the bridge of communication between wireless network and wired network, wireless AP is the core equipment for building WLAN. It provides the mutual access between wireless workstations (i.e. wireless mobile terminal devices) and WLAN. In WLAN, it plays the role as the transmitting base station in mobile communication network, so that wireless workstations within the AP signal coverage can communicate with each other through it.

Ruijie RG-AP320-I Wireless AP is shown in Fig. 3.14. It adopts dual-channel dual-frequency design and supports simultaneous operation in the IEEE 802.11a/n and IEEE 802.11b/g/n modes. The product is designed for wall-mounted installation, which can be safely and conveniently mounted on walls, on ceilings or at other positions. The RG-AP320-I enables users to choose between local power supply and remote PoE according to the field power supply environment, especially suitable for large-scale campus, corporate office, hospital, commercial hot spot and other scenarios.

TP-Link TL-AP301C 300 M Wireless AP, as shown in Fig. 3.15, supports 11 N wireless technology and 300Mbit/s wireless transmission. With its miniaturized design and flexible deployment, it can be easily mounted on the ceilings or walls or placed on the desktop. Thanks to the passive POE and integrated advantages of fat AP and fit AP, it can choose different working modes in different environments. Its wireless transmission power is linearly adjustable, and users can adjust the signal coverage as needed. Independent hardware

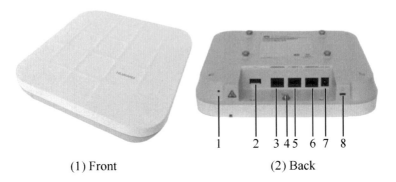

(1) Front   (2) Back

Fig. 3.16 Huawei AP7050DE Wireless AP

Table 3.4 Introduction to interfaces of Huawei AP7050DE Wireless AP

No.	Explanation
1	Default button: used to restore factory settings by holding for more than 3 s
2	USB interface: used to connect USB flash disk to expand storage, with external output power up to 2.5 W
3	Console port: used to implement device configuration and management by connecting maintenance terminals
4	Grounding screw: used to connect the equipment to the grounding cable
5	GE1: 10/100/1000 Mbit/s for wired Ethernet connections
6	GE0/POE: 10/100/1000 Mbit/s for wired Ethernet connections; for PoE devices to power wireless APs
7	Power input interface: 12 V DC
8	Lock interface: used to protect the device against theft

protection circuit can automatically restore the AP working abnormally, supporting remote view/management on TP-Link commercial cloud application.

The AP7050DE is a new-generation technology-leading wireless AP released by Huawei, which supports IEEE 802.11ac Wave 2 standard. It enables wireless network bandwidth beyond Gigabit and supports 4 × 4 MU-MIMO and 4 spatial streams at a maximum rate of 2.53 Gbit/s. The built-in smart antenna realizes the smooth transition between IEEE 802.11n and IEEE 802.11ac standards, ideal for satisfying the quality requirements of high-definition video streaming, multimedia, desktop cloud applications and other large bandwidth services in colleges and universities, large-scale campus and other scenarios. Its appearance is shown in Fig. 3.16, whose interfaces are introduced in Table 3.4.

Huawei AP7050DE Wireless AP has the following features:

(a) Supports IEEE 802.11ac Wave 2 standard and MU-MIMO; provides 2.4GHz and 5GHz RFs, with the former reaching 800 Mbit/s, the latter reaching 1.73 Gbit/s, and the maximum access rate of the whole device reaching 2.53 Gbit/s;

(b) Adopts the smart antenna array for the precise directional coverage of the mobile terminal, which reduces the interference while improving the signal quality, and supports millisecond-level switching with the movement of the user terminal;

(c) Provides built-in Bluetooth to achieve the precise positioning of Bluetooth terminals in cooperation with eSight;

(d) Supports link aggregation with dual Ethernet interface, ensuring link reliability while enhancing service load balancing capability;

(e) Provides USB interface for external power supply or storage;

(f) Supports fat AP, fit AP and cloud AP;

(g) Supports cloud management for managing, operating and maintaining wireless AP devices and services through Huawei SDN controller, so as to save network operation and maintenance costs.

3.1.4 Firewalls

With the development of network, an endless stream of new applications bring more convenience to people's network life, and more security risks at the same time.

1. IP address is not equal to user identity. In the new network, it has become the simplest means of attack to use the legitimate IP address to launch the network attack by manipulating the botnet host, or to cheat and obtain the rights by forging and imitating the source IP address. Today, it is no longer possible to identify the network user who sent a message from its source IP address. At the same time, due to the emerging office forms such as telecommuting and mobile office, the IP address of the host used by the same user may change at any time, so the traffic control through IP address has been unable to meet the needs of modern network.

2. Ports and protocols are not equal to applications. Traditional network services always run on fixed ports, such as HTTP on Port 80 and FTP on Port 20 or 21. However, in the new network, more and more network applications are beginning to use unknown ports that are not explicitly assigned by the Internet Assigned Numbers Authority (IANA), or use randomly assigned ports (such as P2P). These applications tend to be difficult to control and abuse bandwidth, resulting in network congestion. Meanwhile, some well-known ports may be used to run very different services. The most typical situation is that, with the development of web technology, more and more services of different risk levels run on ports 80 and 443 under the banner of HTTP and HTTPS, such as web mail, web game, video website, web chat, etc.

3. Message is not equal to content. Single-packet detection mechanism can only analyze the security of a single message, and can not prevent the virus, Trojan horse and other network threats produced in a normal network access. Intranet hosts are now easy to inadvertently introduce worms, Trojans and other viruses from the Internet in the process of accessing the Internet, resulting in the

Fig. 3.17 Cisco Firepower
4100 Firewalls

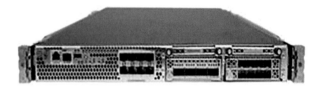

Fig. 3.18 H3C SecPath
F1000-AI Series Firewalls

Front View

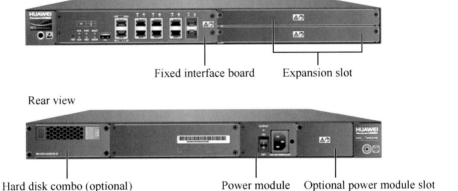

Fixed interface board   Expansion slot

Rear view

Hard disk combo (optional)   Power module   Optional power module slot

Fig. 3.19 Huawei USG6300 Series Firewall

disclosure of confidential enterprise data and huge losses to the property of
enterprises. Therefore, in order to guarantee network security management, it is
necessary for enterprises to deeply identify and monitor the real content of traffic
transmission on the basis of controlling the source and purpose of traffic.

In response to new threats to new networks, the next generation of firewall products
is emerging from various manufacturers. Cisco Firepower 4100 Firewalls, shown in
Fig. 3.17, displays network dynamics in real time, enabling users to detect attacks
earlier and take promptly action to reduce security risks.

H3C SecPath F1000-AI Series Firewalls (see Fig. 3.18), as a high-performance
multi-10-Gigabit firewall VPN integrated gateway product, is a 1 U standalone box
firewall series based on multi-core processor architecture. This series provides rich
interface expansion capabilities.

Huawei USG6300 Firewall is shown in Fig. 3.19, whose interfaces are introduced
in Table 3.5. As a security gateway product designed and developed for small
enterprises, market segments and chain businesses, it sets a variety of security

Table 3.5 Introduction to interfaces of Huawei USG6300 Series Firewall

Name	Explanation
Fixed interface board	The fixed interface board serves as the core of system control and management, which provides the management plane, forwarding plane, and control plane for the whole system, and provides the intelligent perception engine for service processing (a) Management plane: provides configuration, testing, maintenance and other interfaces for system status monitoring, environmental monitoring, log and alarm processing, system loading, system upgrade and other functions (b) Forward plane: carries out the basic analysis and processing of the message, and carries out the forwarding, discarding or conversion of the message in cooperation with other planes (c) Control plane: obtains the network user authentication information and feedback the results to the forwarding plane, so that the forwarding plane can conduct user-based processing of the message (d) Intelligent perception engine: conducts service awareness and content parsing of the message, and identifies the application to which the message corresponds, as well as information such as files, viruses, URL addresses, mail fields, intrusions, attacks, etc. that are hosted in a message or stream, and delivers the detection results to the forwarding plane for further processing
Expansion slot	Supports for plug-in expansion cards for more interfaces or other specific functions. The supported expansion cards are shown in Table 3.6
Power module	Provides built-in standard 150 W single power supply, and supports optional 170 W redundant power supply, constituting 1 + 1 mode redundancy backup. The PWR6 power module supports hot swapping under the premise that the PWR5 power supply works normally
Hard disk combo (optional)	Used to store log and report data, and supports the optional hard disk combo SM-HDD-SAS300G-B

capabilities in one to fully support multiple IPv4/IPv6 routing protocols, suitable for a range of network access scenarios. It features the following advantages.

1. Security functions: provides complete and comprehensive application identification and protection against threats to and attacks on the application layer by inheriting and developing traditional security functions.
2. Product performance: integrates the message content based on the same intelligent perception engine, with high detection performance that content that meets the processing requirements for all content security features can be extracted in a single inspection.
3. Control dimension: user + application + content + quintuple (source/destination IP address, source/destination port, and service).
4. Detection granularity: realizes stream-based cache-free integrated detection and real-time monitoring which, with only a small amount of system resources, can detect the applications, intrusion behavior and virus files in the fragmented/packet messages in real time, effectively improving the security of the whole network access process.

Table 3.6 Expansion cards expansion card Huawei USG6300 Series Firewall

Name	Explanation
8GE WSIC Interface Card	Provides 8 Gigabit RJ-45 Ethernet interfaces
2XG8GE WSIC Interface Card	Provides 8-Gigabit RJ-45 interfaces and 2 10-Gigabit SFP+ interfaces
8GEF WSIC Interface Card	Provides 8-Gigabit SFP interfaces
4GE-Bypass WSIC Card	Provides 2 bypasses for electrical links

5. Support for cloud computing and data center: conduct comprehensive virtualization from three aspects of routing and forwarding, configuration management and security to provide perfect security protection for cloud computing and data center.

Huawei USG6300 Series Firewall provides the following interfaces.

1. The fixed interface board provides:

   (a) 1 out-of-band management interface (RJ-45 interface)
   (b) 1 Console port (RJ-45 interface)
   (c) 1 USB 2.0 interface
   (d) 2 GE photoelectric mutex interfaces
   (e) 4 10 Mbit/s/100 Mbit/s/1000 Mbit/s self-adaptive Ethernet interface

2. The expansion slot is compatible with the expansion card as shown in Table 3.6. Huawei USG6300 Series Firewall provides the following interfaces.

   (a) Powerful content security and protection functions. Perfect application-layer security capabilities based on in-depth application and content resolution constitute the biggest advantage of the next generation firewall products.
   (b) Flexible user management. With the development of application protocols, IP address has lost the significance of representing the real identity of network users, which leads to many security risks. However, the user-based management can effectively solve these problems.
   (c) Perfect traditional firewall security functions. Huawei USG6000 completely inherits the network layer protection function of the traditional firewall. These security mechanisms are simple but efficient, thus effectively dealing with the network layer threats.
   (d) Fine traffic management. Despite the rapid development of network services, network bandwidth cannot expand indefinitely. Therefore, if necessary, administrators need to manage the bandwidth occupancy of traffic, limit the bandwidth occupancy of low-priority network services, and provide guarantee for high-priority network services.
   (e) Comprehensive support to routing and switching protocols. Huawei USG6000 provides comprehensive routing and switching protocol support, which can well adapt to a variety of network environments and deployment requirements.

(f) Intelligent route selection strategy. When multiple export links exist, Huawei USG6000 can dynamically select the outbound interface through intelligent routing strategy to ensure that traffic is forwarded according to the preset strategy, so as to improve the utilization rate of link resources and improve the user's Internet experience.

(g) Leading IPv6 support. Huawei USG6000 provides comprehensive support for the next generation IP network technology—IPv6, which meets various IPv6 networking modes and effectively protect the security of IPv6 network.

(h) Multiple VPN access methods. VPN technology makes it possible to build cheap and secure private networks, and plays an important role in modern enterprise networks. The varied VPN access methods enabled by Huawei USG6000 expand the network boundary for enterprises and meet various private network requirements.

(i) Stable high-reliable mechanism. The influence of network on enterprises has reached the degree that its normal operation directly affects the profits of enterprises, especially for the network information, network communication and e-commerce enterprises that rely on the network to carry out services. Therefore, it is critical to ensure the stability and high reliability of network equipment.

(j) An easy-to-use virtual system. A virtual system logically divides a physical device into multiple independent virtual devices, and equip each of them with its own administrator, routing table, and security policy.

(k) Visual equipment management and maintenance. Based on the new design and improved web interface provided by Huawei USG6000, administrators can easily carry out an array of operations such as initial deployment, configuration, maintenance, fault diagnosis, status monitoring, update and upgrade of equipment on the web interface.

(l) Abundant logs and reports. Logging and reporting are one of the key links in device management, which provide the conditions for network administrators to record and track the events that occur in the long run of the equipment.

Enterprises can gain the following benefits from Huawei USG6300 Series Firewalls.

(a) The original employee management system of the enterprise (such as active directory users) can be well inherited to realize user-based traffic detection and control.

(b) The latest network threats can be dealt with through a single equipment of high integration and high performance, which greatly saves the purchase, maintenance and management costs of network security equipment.

(c) Efficient "single detection" mechanism can upgrade the enterprise network security while avoiding obvious delay or other effects on the normal transmission of network traffic, so as to ensure the normal network experience.

(d) Visual management of applications and content can significantly improve the management efficiency of enterprises, and help the enterprises to increase profits by carrying out more network services in a safe environment.

3.1.5 Network Management Equipment

The management of network devices such as routers and switches introduced above is accomplished by network management devices. Typical network management devices include Huawei's eSight and iMaster NCE, and their corresponding hardware devices are servers.

1. eSight

   eSight is an integrated operation and maintenance management solution launched by Huawei for enterprise data centers, campus/branch networks, unified communications, video conferencing, and video surveillance. Through the unified management of the whole network equipment, it provides automatic deployment, visual fault diagnosis, intelligent capacity analysis and other functions for enterprises' ICT equipment, which can effectively help enterprises improve the efficiency of operation and maintenance, improve the utilization rate of resources, reduce the cost of operation and maintenance, and ensure the stable operation of the ICT system. It features the following characteristics.

   (a) Unified management of the whole network equipment.

      (i) Supports the unified management of servers, storage, virtualization, switches, routers, WLAN, firewalls, ELTE terminal equipment, base stations, business engines, equipment room facilities, unified communication, telepresence, video monitoring, application systems, etc.
      (ii) Pre-integrates the capability to manage other non-Huawei equipment such as those from HP, Cisco and H3C.
      (iii) Customizes quick access based on visual wizards for devices not pre-integrated.

   (b) Componentized architecture.

      eSight adopts a componentized architecture, that is, on the unified eSight management platform, providing a rich variety of components for customers to choose according to their own circumstances.
   (c) Independent equipment adaptation.

      The extension point mechanism used by eSight delivers incremental development of features and network element version adapter packs, allowing new features to be added or new devices to be adapted without modifying the original distribution code. When there is a new feature that needs to be supported, you just need to develop a new feature plug-in pack and deploy it to the system; and when there is a new device, you only need to add a new adapter pack.
   (d) Lightweight and web-based design.

      eSight adopts the B/S architecture that frees the customers from the installation of any plug-in and enables access anytime and anywhere. When the system is upgraded or maintained, only the server software needs to be

updated, which simplifies the system maintenance and upgrade and reduces the overall cost for the customers.
(e) Security and protection.

Considering the network security issues and the characteristics of enterprise operation and maintenance, eSight provides comprehensive security protection solutions.

(i) Platform security: The system reinforcement, security patches and antivirus means, by improving the security level of the operating system and database, ensures the security and reliability of the platform.
(ii) Application security: It delivers solutions including transmission security, user management, session management, log management, etc.

2. iMaster NCE

The iMaster NCE Autonomous Network Management and Control System provides an efficient connection between the physical network and the commercial intent. It, downstream, realizes centralized management, control and analysis of the global network, cloud-based resources and full-lifecycle automation for businesses and business intent, and intelligent closed loop driven by data analysis; and for the upstream, it empowers fast integration between open API and IT. iMaster NCE is mainly used in 5G bearer, IP metropolitan area network (MAN)/backbone network, quality optical dedicated line, quality broadband, data center, enterprise campus and other scenarios, aiming to create a simpler, smarter, open and secure network to accelerate the business transformation and innovation of enterprises and operators. As the industry's first network automation and intelligence platform integrating management, control, analysis and AI, iMaster NCE has the following features.

(a) Full-lifecycle automation

On the basis of unified resource modeling and data sharing services, it provides full-lifecycle automation across multiple network technology domains to realize device plug-and-play, network swap-and-pass, business self-service, fault self-healing and risk pre-warning.
(b) Intelligent closed loop based on big data and AI

It builds a complete intelligent closed-loop system based on four sub-engines: intention, automation, analysis and intelligence. With Telemetry-based acquisition and aggregation of massive network data, iMaster NCE achieves real-time cyberspace situation awareness and builds big data-based global network analysis and insight through unified data modeling. It built into the architecture Huawei's AI algorithms based on 30 years of telecoms experience, which realizes the automated, closed-loop analysis, prediction and decision making for user intent, so as to solve problems before customer complaints, reduce business interruption and customer impact, improve customer satisfaction, and continue to improve the intelligent level of the network.

(c) Scenarialized APP ecology enabled by open programmability

iMaster NCE provides a programmable integrated development environment, namely Design Studio, and developer community for docking with
third-party network controllers or network devices in the south, and fast
integration with cloud-based AI training platform and IT applications in the
north. In addition, it also endows users with the freedom to choose Huawei
Apps, or develop Apps independently or with the support of third-party
system integrators.

(d) A full-cloud platform with large capacity

Based on the cloud-based architecture derived from the Cloud Native,
iMaster NCE supports operating in both private and public clouds, as well as
on-premise deployment. Thanks to its large capacity and scalability, it also
provides the world's largest system capacity and user access capacity, which
enables the network to transform from the offline mode of data decentraliza-
tion and multi-level operation and maintenance to the online mode where data
sharing and process connection are enabled.

As a product built on a unified cloud-based platform, iMaster NCE provides a series of solutions for different application scenarios such as 5G
bearer, optical network, IP MAN/backbone network, IP+ optical cross-layer
collaboration, quality broadband, home network, data center, campus network, etc. IMaster NCE provides multiple feature module packages
according to application scenarios, forming a product portfolio for customers
to choose as needed. Among them, NCE-Super is suitable for 2B dedicated
line, IP+ optical collaboration, cloud-network collaboration and other scenarios; NCE-IP is suitable for IP MAN/backbone network scenarios; NCE-T, for
transmission networking scenarios such as backbone network, MAN and
enterprise access; NCE-FAN, for home broadband access, home network
and other scenarios; NCE-Fabric, for cloud data center scenarios; and
NCE-Campus, for campus networking scenarios. The management, control
and analysis modules of iMaster NCE can be deployed independently. It is
not mandatory for customers to deploy all of them. Instead, different modules
can be selected for different application scenarios.

3. Servers

The following will focus on the servers with eSight as an example. Table 3.7
lists eSight's configuration requirements for servers.

At present, mainstream servers are mainly from HP, Lenovo, Inspur, Huawei,
etc., as shown in Fig. 3.20. Users can choose the server according to the
configuration requirements of eSight network management software.

Huawei provides RH2288H, Taishan 200 and other servers. For both
RH2288H and Taishan 200 servers shown in Fig. 3.21, the versions with
12 hard disks are exemplified. The RH2288H V3 is a widely used 2 U2 rack
server launched by Huawei for the needs of Internet, data center, cloud computing, enterprise market and telecom business applications. It is suitable for

Table 3.7 eSight's configuration requirements for servers

Server	Management capacity	Minimum configuration (exclusive resource)	Remarks
eSight master server	0–5000 equivalent network elements	2 × 6-core 2 GB CPU, 32 GB memory, 500 GB hard disk	1. Supports symbiotic deployment of network traffic collectors (up to 10 nodes, 2000 flow/s, up to a total of 100 APs for network traffic collection + monitoring interfaces) 2. Supports symbiotic deployment of WLAN location collectors (up to 50 APs and 500 clients) 3. Supports deployment of application managers
		4 × 8-core 2 GB CPU, 64 GB memory, 1 TB hard disk	1. Required as the infrastructure managers and asset managers are needed 2. Supports symbiotic deployment of network traffic collectors (up to 10 nodes, 2000 flow/s, up to a total of 100 APs for network traffic collection + monitoring interfaces) 3. Supports symbiotic deployment of WLAN location collectors (up to 50 APs and 500 clients) 4. Supports deployment of application managers
	5000–20,000 equivalent network elements	4 × 8-core 2 GB CPU, 64 GB memory, 1 TB hard disk	1. Supports the infrastructure managers, application managers and asset managers 2. Supports symbiotic deployment of network traffic collectors (up to 10 nodes, 2000 flow/s, up to a total of 100 APs for network traffic collection + monitoring interfaces) 3. Supports symbiotic deployment of WLAN location collectors (up to 50 APs and 500 clients)
Network traffic collector extension	0–350 collection nodes	2 × 6-core 2 GB CPU, 32 GB memory, 500 GB hard disk	1. Required when there are more than 10 network traffic collection nodes, and only one node can be deployed; up to 350 nodes, 30,000 flow/s, up to a total of 1000 APs for network traffic collection + monitoring interfaces) 2. No database is required, and the operating system should be consistent with the eSight master server

(continued)

Table 3.7 (continued)

Server	Management capacity	Minimum configuration (exclusive resource)	Remarks
Location server	0–2000 APs; 0–24,000 clients	2 × 6-core 2 GB CPU, 32 GB memory, 500 GB hard disk	1. Required when there are more than 50 APs or 500 clients as WLAN location collection nodes, and only one node can be deployed; up to 5000 APs and 64,000 clients)
	2000–5000 APs; 24,000–64,000 clients	4 × 8-core 2 GB CPU, 64 GB memory, 1 TB hard disk	2. No database is required, and the operating system should be consistent with the eSight master server

(1) HP ProLiant DL388 Gne9

(2) Lenovo ThinkSystem SR550

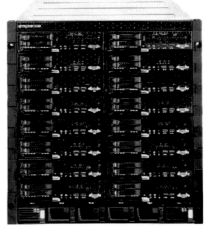

(3) Inspur NX8480M4

Fig. 3.20 Servers from different manufacturers

(1) RH2288H V3 Server

(2) Taishan 200 Server (Model 2280)

Fig. 3.21 Appearance of Huawei Servers

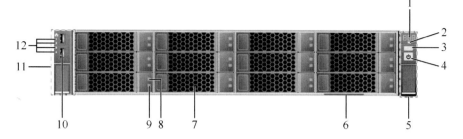

Fig. 3.22   Front panel of the RH2288H V3 (with 12 inch × 3.5 inch [approximately 30 cm × 9 cm] hard disks)

Table 3.8   Panel composition of the RH2288H V3

No.	Explanation	No.	Explanation
1	Nixie tube for fault diagnosis	7	Hard disk (slots in order from 0 to 11, from top to bottom and left to right)
2	Health LED	8	Fault LED for hard disk
3	UID button/LED	9	Active LED for hard disk
4	Power switch/LED	10	USB 2.0 interface
5	Right mounting ear	11	Left mounting ear
6	Label card (including ESN label)	12	Link LEDs at network port (in order from 1 to 4, from top to bottom)

distributed storage, data mining, electronic photo album, video and other storage services, as well as basic enterprise applications and telecom business applications. It is equipped with an E5-2600 V3/V4 processor, supporting up to 22 cores per processor, and offers 24 DDR4 memory slots and 9 PCIe expansion slots. For local storage applications, it can be expanded from 8 hard disks to 28 hard disks, and supports 12 Gbit/s SAS technology, which can meet the high bandwidth transmission requirements of big data.

Taishan 200 Server is a data center server based on Huawei Kunpeng 920 processor. The Model 2280 Server in this series is a 2U2 rack server. The server is oriented to the Internet, distributed storage, cloud computing, big data, enterprise business and other fields, presenting the advantages of high-performance computing, large-capacity storage, low energy consumption, easy management, easy deployment and so on. The system provides up to 128 cores and up to 27 SAS/SATA HDDs or SSDs, with computing power of 2.6 GHz.

Let's take the RH2288H V3 Server as an example to analyze the server's appearance and architecture. The front panel of the RH2288H V3 (with 12 inch × 3.5 inch [approximately 30 cm × 9 cm] hard disks) is shown in Fig. 3.22, and the panel composition is shown in Table 3.8.

The RH2288H V3 has a rear panel as shown in Fig. 3.23, whose components are introduced in Table 3.9.

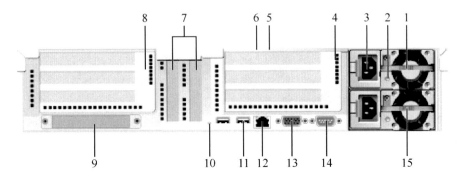

Fig. 3.23 Rear panel of the RH2288H V3

Table 3.9 Rear panel composition of the RH2288H V3

No.	Explanation	No.	Explanation
1	Power module 1	9	Flexible I/O card
2	Power supply LED	10	UID LED
3	Power supply interface	11	USB 3.0 interface
4	I/O Module 2 (Slot 6, Slot 7, Slot 8 in top to bottom order), or switch module for PCIe NVMe SSDs (paired with CPU 2; Slot 6, Slot 7 in top to bottom order)	12	MGMT (management) port
5	Connection Status LED	13	VGA interface
6	Transmission Status LED	14	Serial port
7	On-board PCIe card slots (Slot 4, Slot 5 in left to right order)	15	Power Supply Module 2
8	I/O Module 1 (Slot 1, Slot 2, Slot 3 in top to bottom order)		

3.2 Network System Installation

Before a network system is put into normal operation and provides services, it must undergo hardware installation, which includes installation preparation, equipment installation, board installation, cable connection and so on. This section describes the installation process of various network devices such as routers, switches, ACs/APs, firewalls, and servers.

3.2.1 Installation of Routers

Following the brief introduction of the classification of Huawei routers in Sect. 3.1.1, this section will introduce the installation specifications, methods and steps of AR Series case-shaped routers and NE Series chassis-shaped routers in detail. For the case-shaped routers, the AR1200 Series will be taken as an example, while the chassis-shaped routers will be introduced with the NE40E-X16 Series as an example.

1. Installation of case-shaped routers

    (a) Installation preparation

        (i) Read through safety precautions carefully.

            To protect personal safety and the safety of your router, please follow the signs on your router and any safety precautions in the manual when installing, operating and maintaining the router. Precautions and hazards shown in the manual do not cover all safety precautions to be followed, only as supplementary precautions. Staff responsible for installation, operation and maintenance of Huawei routers must receive strict training, understand various security precautions and master correct operation methods before they can implement the installation, operation and maintenance of routers.

        (ii) Check the installation environment.

            Before installing a router, please check whether the installation environment meets the requirements to ensure the normal operation of the router. The checklist for installation environment inspection is shown in Table 3.10.

        (iii) Check the cabinet.

            Before installing the router, please check whether the cabinet meets the requirements. The checklist for cabinet inspection is shown in Table 3.11.

        (iv) Check the power condition.

            The requirements of the router for power conditions are shown in Table 3.12.

        (v) Prepare installation tools.

            Installation tools to be prepared include ESD gloves, protective gloves, ESD wrist strap, snap-off knife, tape measure, marker pen, flat-head screwdriver, Phillips screwdriver, diagonal pliers, network tester, multimeter, percussion drill and adjustable wrench.

    (b) Installation of the main body of the case-shaped router

        The AR1200 Series case-shaped routers are suitable for three installation scenarios: mounting to workbench, mounting to vertical plane, and installing into cabinet. The installation process for each scenario is described below.

        (i) Scenario 1: mounting to workbench. The AR1200 Series routers are generally placed on a clean flat workbench. This method is relatively simple, just requires the installer to ensure the stability and good grounding of the workbench, and ensure a space of more than 50 mm around the router for heat dissipation. Never pile up sundries on the router. Prepare four adhesive pads.

Table 3.10 Checklist for installation environment inspection

Item	Requirements
Ventilation and heat dissipation	A space of more than 50 mm is provided around the router to facilitate its heat dissipation
Cleanliness	1. The router is installed in a clean, dry and well-ventilated place with stable temperature 2. Water seepage, leakage and condensation are strictly prohibited in the installation site
Temperature and humidity	1. Operating ambient temperature: 0–45 °C 2. Working condition relative humidity: 5–95%, non-condensation Note: If the relative humidity is greater than 70%, dehumidification equipment (such as air conditioning with dehumidification function, special dehumidifier, etc.) should be equipped
Electrostatic protection	1. The router is properly grounded as per the grounding requirements 2. The ESD wrist strap is used to avoid damage of the router by electrostatic discharge 3. One end of the ESD wrist strap is grounded, and the other end is in good contact with the wearer's skin
Corrosive gas resistance	Acid, alkaline and other corrosive gases are avoided in the installation site
Lightning protection	1. Signal cables are routed along indoor walls, especially avoiding outdoor aerial cabling 2. The signal cables are routed in a manner of avoiding high risk cables such as power line and down-conductor system of lightning rod
Electromagnetic environment	The electromagnetic environment requirements are met

Table 3.11 Checklist for cabinet inspection

Item	Requirements
Width	The standard 19-inch (about 48 cm) cabinet is used
Installation space	Sufficient installation height ($\geq$3 U) is reserved for the cabinet, and the cabinet depth is not less than 600 mm
Grounding	The cabinet provides a reliable grounding point for the router
Heat dissipation	1. A certain gap is reserved around the cabinet 2. The closed cabinet is provided with good ventilation conditions
Slide rail	1. An L-style slide rail is mounted for AR2220/AR2240/AR2240C/AR3260/AR3670 router 2. When the spacing of the mounting bars of the cabinet does not meet the requirements, an L-shaped slide rail is installed to bear the load

The steps are as follows.

- Paste the four adhesive pads onto the circular embossing areas at the bottom of the router, as shown in Fig. 3.24.
- Place the router on the workbench stably, as shown in Fig. 3.25.

Table 3.12 Requirements of the router for power conditions

Item	Requirements
Preparation	The power supply is ready before the installation of the router
Voltage	The router conforms to the normal operating voltage range. Please refer to the hardware manual of the corresponding product for the voltage range that supports the normal operation of AR series routers
Socket and cable	1. If the external power supply is provided via the AC socket, the local standard AC power cable is adopted. 2. If the external power supply is provided via the DC distribution box, the DC power cable is adopted 3. Any power cable supplied with the product as an accessory is only used for the product in the package, not for other devices

Fig. 3.24 Paste the adhesive pads

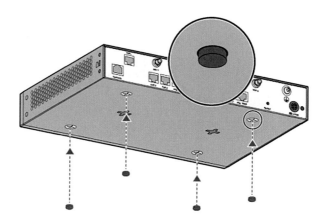

Fig. 3.25 Place the router stably

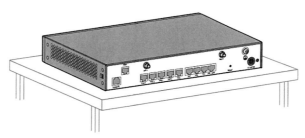

(ii) Scenario 2: mounting to vertical plane. The router should be mounted with the interface facing down to prevent the router from water infiltration through the interface. The mounting screws should be tightened firmly and reliably, otherwise the router may fall down due to the tension when the cable is connected. Flammable and explosive items are prohibited under the router, and foreign objects are prohibited within 100 mm around the router. The router should be mounted at a height that facilitates the check of the indicator LEDs. Before drilling a hole into the wall, make sure there is no electrical circuit in the drilling area to avoid

Fig. 3.26 Mark the
mounting holes

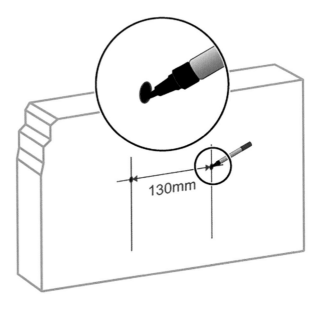

Fig. 3.26 Mark the mounting holes

personal injury. Tools and accessories to be prepared include percussion
drill, claw hammer, plastic expansion tubes and screws.

The steps are as follows.

- Position the two mounting holes on the wall with a steel tape measure
  and mark them with a marker pen. The two holes should be in a
  horizontal line, as shown in Fig. 3.26. The spacing of the mounting
  holes varies with the router models, which should be determined
  according to the actual situation.
- Drill and mount the screws as shown in Fig. 3.27.

  - Choose the drill bit according to the outer diameter of the screw,
    and the outer diameter should not exceed 4 mm.
  - Knock the plastic expansion tubes into the mounting holes respec-
    tively with a claw hammer.
  - Align the screws to the plastic expansion tubes, and then screw
    them into the tubes using a Phillips screwdriver with 2 mm body
    of the screws left outside the wall.

- Align the mounting holes on the back of the router with the screws to
  hang the router on the wall, as shown in Fig. 3.28.

(iii) Scenario 3: installing into cabinet. Before installation, the following
      points need to be confirmed: the cabinet is fixed; the place of the router
      is arranged in the cabinet; the router to be installed is prepared and

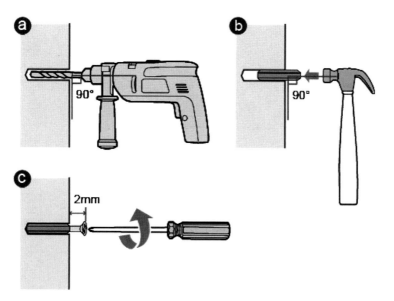

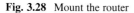

Fig. 3.27 Drill holes and mount the screws

Fig. 3.28 Mount the router

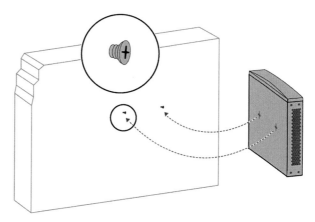

placed close to the cabinet for easy handling. Tools and accessories to be prepared include floating nuts, mounting ears, M4 screws and M6 screws.

The steps are as follows.

- Fix the mounting ears to both sides of the router with a Phillips screwdriver and M4 screws, adjacent to the front or rear panel of the router, as shown in Fig. 3.29.

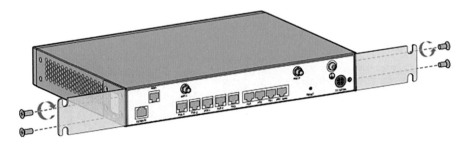

Fig. 3.29 Attach the mounting ears

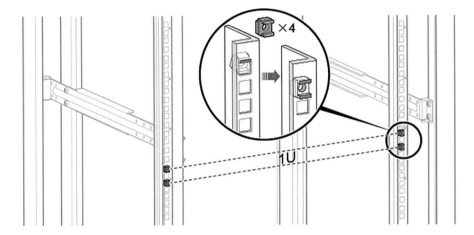

Fig. 3.30 Install the floating nuts

- Install four floating nuts on the front mounting bars of the cabinet, with two for each of the left and right side, and the upper and lower nuts are spaced by one mounting hole. The holes on the mounting bars are not all spaced 1 U apart. So attention should be paid to identifying and referring to the scale on the bars. The floating nut can be installed with a flat-head screwdriver, as shown in Fig. 3.30.
- Install the router into the cabinet.

  - Set the M6 screws into the two lower floating nuts with the Phillips screwdriver. Do not tighten them first, but keep the screws exposed about 2 mm.
  - Move the router into the cabinet and hold the router with one hand, so that the mounting ears on both sides hooks the exposed part of the M6 screws.
  - Tighten the M6 screws below the mounting ears and then the upper M6 screws with the Phillips screwdriver, as shown in Fig. 3.31.

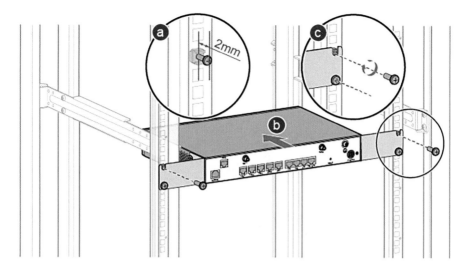

Fig. 3.31 Install the router into the cabinet

After installing the main body of the router in the above three scenarios, you can also install optional accessories such as PoE power supply, RPS150 power supply, DSP chip, VoIP card, module bar and security unit as required. The installation of optional accessories will not be described here. Readers who have demands can consult relevant information as required.

(c) Router connection

　(i) Connect the grounding cable.
　　　Wear the ESD wrist strap, ensuring that one end of the ESD wrist strap is grounded, and the other end is in good contact with the wearer's skin. Connect the grounding cable as shown in Fig. 3.32.

- Unscrew the M4 screw from the grounding terminal on the rear panel of the router with a Phillips screwdriver and place the it properly.
- Align the M4 end of the grounding cable to the screw hole on the grounding terminal, and then fix it with the M4 screw with a torque of 1.4 N • m.
- Connect the M6 end of the grounding cable to the grounding terminal of the workbench, wall or cabinet, and then tighten the M6 screw with a torque of 4.8 N • m.

After the grounding cable is connected, the following checks should be completed: confirm that the grounding cable and the grounding terminal are

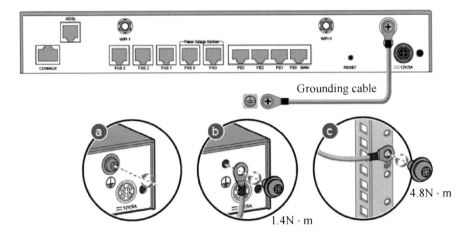

Fig. 3.32 Connect the grounding cable

firmly and reliably connected; check that the resistance between the router grounding point and the grounding terminal is less than 5 Ω with a multimeter in Ohm mode.

(ii) Connect the Ethernet cable.

Select the corresponding number of network cables with corresponding length according to the number of ports and surveyed distance. Attach a temporary label to both ends of each cable for writing the cable No. with a marker. Connect one end of the cable to the Ethernet port of the router and the other end to the Ethernet port of the corresponding device, as shown in Fig. 3.33. Straighten the connected network cables to prevent them from intersecting, and then bind them with the binding strap, and cut off the redundant part of the strap with the diagonal pliers. Remove the temporary labels on the cables, and attach the formal label at both ends of each cable, with the labels keeping 2 cm away from the connectors.

After connecting the Ethernet cables, check the following: the labels on both ends of the Ethernet cables are correct, clear, neat, and oriented in the same way; the network cables and plugs are free of damage and break, and the connections are correct and reliable.

(iii) Connect the power adapter.

Check that the router is well grounded at the grounding point. Wear the ESD wrist strap, ensuring that one end of the ESD wrist strap is grounded, and the other end is in good contact with the wearer's skin. And then connect the grounding cable as shown in Fig. 3.34.

- Connect one end of the power adapter to the router's power port.
- Connect the other end of the power adapter to the AC socket.

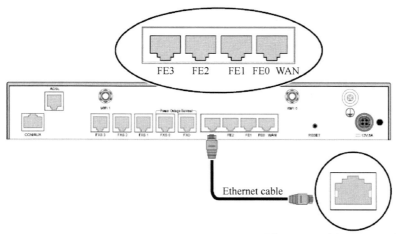

Fig. 3.33   Connect the Ethernet cable

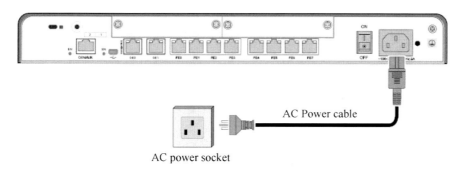

Fig. 3.34   Connect the power adapter

And then connect the power cable buckle as shown in Fig. 3.35.

- Plug the power cable buckle in the mounting hole for power cable buckle on the rear panel of the router.
- Adjust the power cable buckle to its proper position.
- Fasten the AC power cable with the power cable buckle.

After the power adapter is connected, the following checks should be completed: check that the connection between the power cable and the power interface is firm and reliable; if more than one device is installed, attach a label with code to both ends of each power cable for identification.

(d) Power on and off

Before the router is powered on, the following checks should be completed: check that the power adapter is properly connected; check that the input voltage is 90–264 V AC.

Fig. 3.35 Connect the
power cable buckle

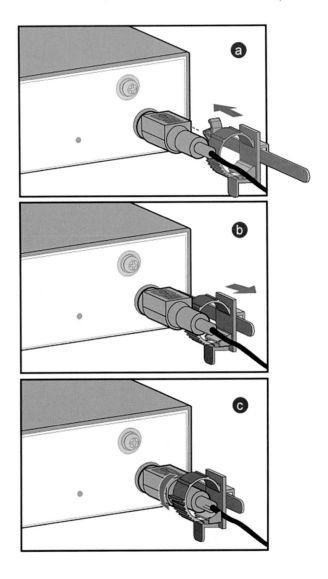

The steps are as follows.

(i) Power on the router. Turn on the power switch of the router, and check
that the router is running normally according to the state of the indicator
LEDs on the front of the router. When the router is running normally, the
indicator LEDs are displayed as shown in Fig. 3.36. The meanings of the
indicator states are shown in Table 3.13.

(ii) Power off the router. Turn off the power switch of the router. The power
switch should be turned off with caution, as that will cause a business
interruption.

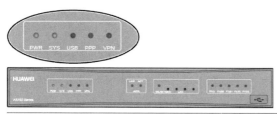

Indicator	State and Meaning
PWR	Green constant light: The system power supply is normal.
SYS	Green slow flashing light: The system is running properly.

Fig. 3.36 Indicator state when the router is running normally

Table 3.13 Indicator states and meanings

Indicator	State and meaning
PWR	The indicator remains at steady green: the system is powered normally
SYS	The indicator flashes slowly: the system is running normally

2. Installation of chassis-shaped routers

 (a) Installation preparation

  (i) Tools to be prepared: diagonal pliers, Phillips screwdriver, flat-head screwdriver, level ruler, adjustable wrench, marker, ladder, network tester, heat gun, ESD gloves, ESD gloves, torque drive, multimeter, snap-off knife, stripping pliers, vacuum cleaner, cable cutters, RJ clamping pliers, power cable clamping pliers, posting plumb, hydraulic pliers, protective gloves, socket wrench, clamping pliers, percussion drill, tape measure, torque wrench, and hammer.
  (ii) Installation accessories: screw, insulating tape, cable buckle, binding strap for optical fiber, heat-shrinkable sleeve, corrugated pipe, and cable label.

 (b) Installation of the main body of the chassis-shaped router

  (i) The chassis is so heavy that it takes four people to handle it. To handle the chassis, the load-bearing handle of the chassis should be used. It is strictly prohibited to pull the handle of any other module, so as to avoid damaging the chassis. Never step on the dust screen at the bottom of the cabinet when installing the chassis. The handling method is shown in Fig. 3.37.

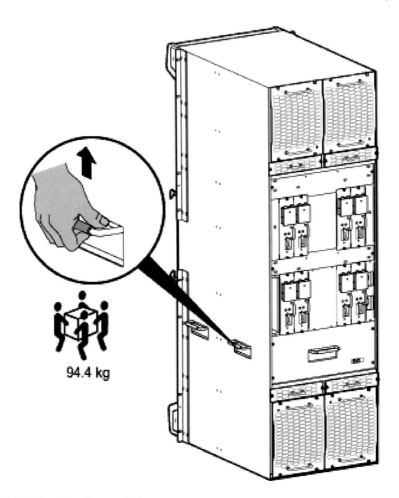

Fig. 3.37 Chassis handling method

(ii) Remove the package according to the unpacking instructions on the packaging box and take out the main body of the router. Install the cabinet slide rails, as shown in Fig. 3.38.

(iii) When the third-party cabinet is adopted, the retractable slide rails can be installed, as shown in Fig. 3.39. Pre-fix the slide rails on the mounting bars through the locating pin at both ends of the retractable slide rails, and then fasten them at both front and rear ends with M6 screws. When installing the retractable slide rails, do not confuse the left and right slide rails and the front and rear ends of them to avoid reverse installation. Make sure the front and rear ends of the retractable slide rails are on the same horizontal level. The third-party cabinet used should meet the following conditions.

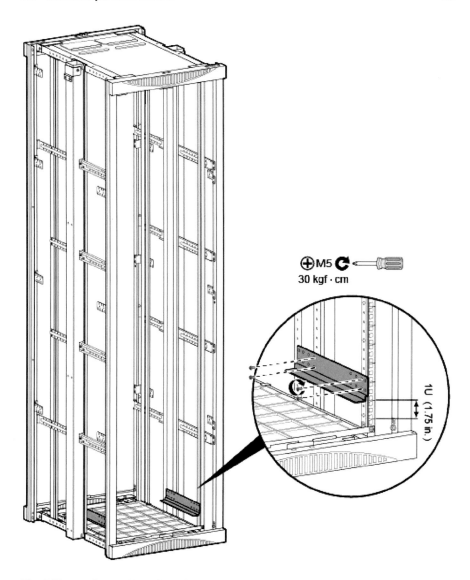

Fig. 3.38 Install the cabinet slide rails

- A 19-inch (about 48 cm) cabinet that meets IEC standards is selected.
- The mounting area of the cabinet provides mounting bars with square holes not less than 9.0 mm × 9.0 mm.
- The front and rear mounting bars of the cabinet are 500–850 mm apart (the Huawei code is 21242246).
- The chassis suitable for the slide rails weighs no more than 425 kg.

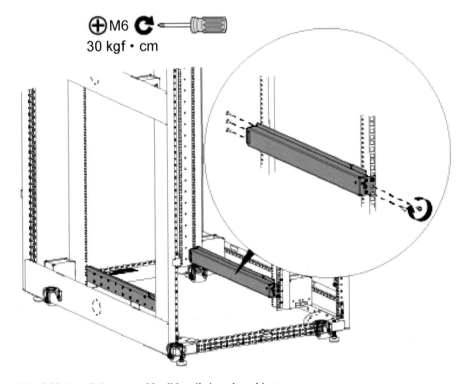

Fig. 3.39 Install the retractable slide rails into the cabinet

(iv) Position the screw holes for the mounting ear panels with a tape measure to determine the mounting positions of the floating nuts, and install the floating nuts on the mounting bars, as shown in Fig. 3.40.

(v) Lift the chassis onto the slide rails of the cabinet and push it into the cabinet, and then fix it in the cabinet with M6 screws, as shown in Fig. 3.41.

(c) Installation of power supply

(i) Install the grounding cable and PGND cable.

There are two ways to install the grounding cable of the chassis: if the chassis is close to the grounding bar of the equipment room of the equipment room, connect the grounding cable directly to the grounding bar of the equipment room; if not, connect the grounding cable to the grounding point of the cabinet.

Next, we will take the scenario of connecting the grounding cable to the grounding bar of the equipment room as an example. The following

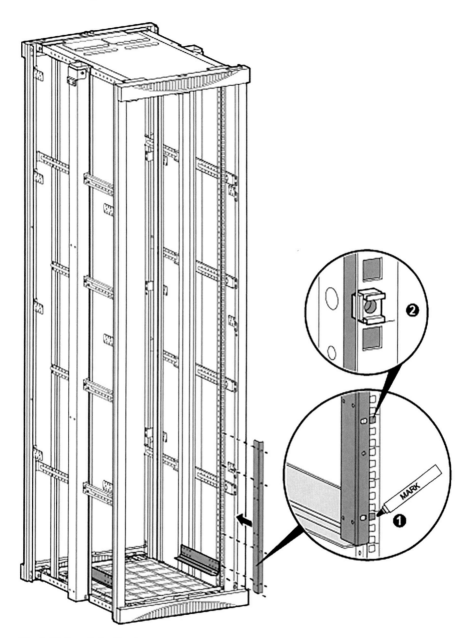

Fig. 3.40 Install the floating nuts

case grounding wire is connected to the computer room grounding row as an example. The grounding cable must be connected to the grounding network. The steps are as follows.

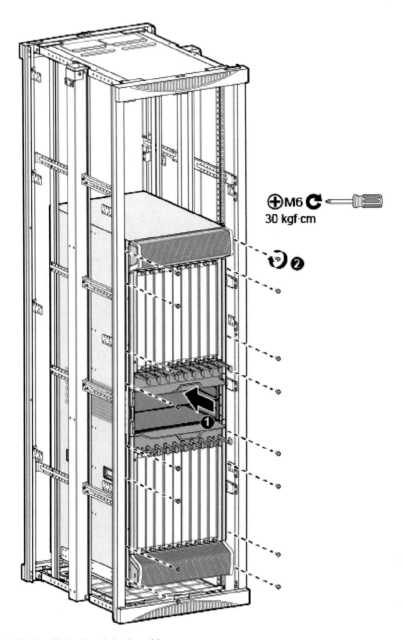

Fig. 3.41 Install the chassis in the cabinet

- Attach temporary labels at both ends of the grounding cable. Lay the grounding cable along the cable ladder and connect it to the grounding terminal at the top of the cabinet, as ❶ in Fig. 3.42. Connect the

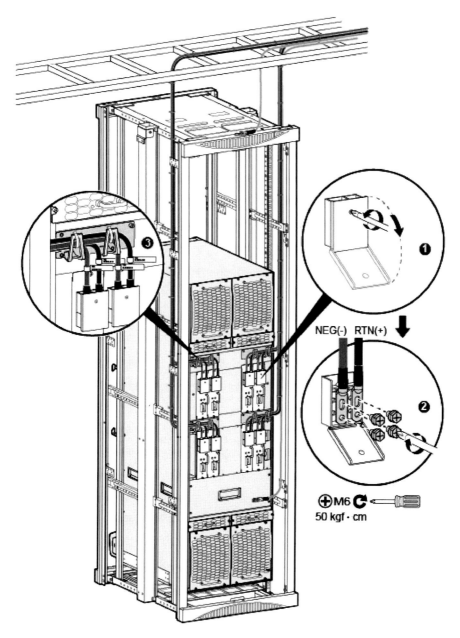

NEG(-) RTN(+)

M6
50 kgf · cm

Fig. 3.42 Connect the grounding cable and PGND cable

other end of the grounding cable to the grounding bar of the
equipment room.
- Connect the PGND cable of the cabinet, with the other end of the
  PGND cable connecting to the grounding bar of the equipment room,
  as ❷ in Fig. 3.42.
- Remove the temporary labels and attach the formal labels 20 mm
  away from both cable ends, as ❸ and ❹ in Fig. 3.42.

(ii) DC distribution guidance and cable specification requirements are illus-
      trated with the NE40E-X16 as an example. The cable specifications are
      listed in Table 3.14.
(iii) Install the power cable.

- Attach temporary labels at both ends of the power cable.
- Lay the power cable towards the device along the cable ladder.
- Open the plastic protection plate for the junction box of the power
  module and connect the DC power cable to the corresponding port, as
  ❶ and ❷ in Fig. 3.43. Then connect the other end of the power cable
  to the distribution panel.
- After the power cable is connected, restore the plastic protection plate
  to the junction box.
- Fix the cable to the cable rack and tie it with cable buckles every
  150 mm from bottom to top.
- Attach formal labels 20 mm away from both ends of the power cable.
  In order to obtain a power cable of the right length, the following
  should be noted when installing the power cable.

  – Cut the power cable according to the measured distance from the
    power module of the device to the distribution panel and allow
    some redundancy.
  – First assemble the power cable terminal at the device side, and
    then install the power cable onto the device end.
  – After completing the cabling and tying of the power cable, cut the
    redundant cable part according to the actual situation of the
    distribution panel; after the terminal is assembled, connected the
    power cable to the distribution panel.

(iv) AC distribution guidance
      When AC power distribution is adopted, one NE40E-X16 router
      needs to be equipped with two EPS200-4850A/4850B AC distribution
      boxes, as shown in Fig. 3.44. The EPS200-4850A/4850B AC distribu-
      tion box should be installed in the same cabinet with the NE40E-X16
      router. If Huawei cables are not used, you need to choose cables

Table 3.14 Cable specification requirements (for NE40E-X16)

Distance between distribution panel and router	Item	Specifications	Huawei code	Remarks
≤15 m	AC power cable	16 mm^2 (6 AWG)	25030430	Blue power cable
			25030428	Black power cable
			25030722	Red power cable
	JG2/OT terminal	16 mm^2 (6 AWG)—M6 JG2 double-hole bare crimping terminal	14170116	Connects to the device
		16 mm^2 (6 AWG)—M8 OT single-hole bare crimping terminal	14170024	Connects to the distribution panel
>15 m, <25 m	AC power cable	25 mm^2 (4 AWG)	25030101	Blue power cable
			25030432	Black power cable
			25030433	Red power cable
	JG2/OT terminal	25 mm^2 (4 AWG)—M6 JG2 double-hole bare crimping terminal	14170119	Connects to the device
		25 mm^2 (4 AWG)—M8 OT single-hole bare crimping terminal	14170060	Connects to the distribution panel
>25 m, <35 m	AC power cable	35 mm^2 (2 AWG)	25030199	Blue power cable
			25030420	Black power cable
			25030418	Red power cable
	JG2/OT terminal	35 mm^2 (2 AWG)—M6 JG2 double-hole bare crimping terminal	14170159	Connects to the device
		35 mm^2 (2 AWG)—M8 OT single-hole bare crimping terminal	14170063	Connects to the distribution panel
>35 m	–	Requires the user to set up the distribution panel or the array cabinet nearby	–	–

according to local regulations. Cable specification requirements for the EPS200-4850A/4850B AC distribution boxes are shown in Table 3.15.

For the cabling of AC cabinet and AC distribution panel, when the distance between local points measured by field survey is greater than

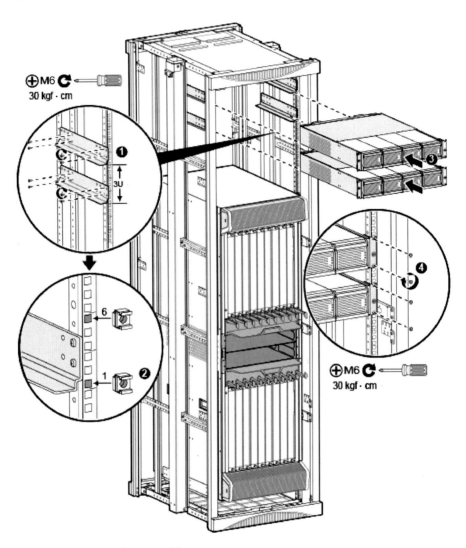

Fig. 3.43 Install the DC power cable

20 m, AC power distribution panel or array cabinet should be set up nearby.

(v) Install the AC distribution boxes.

It is recommended to reserve 2 U of space between an AC distribution box and the top of the cabinet, and 1 U of space between AC distribution boxes. The steps are as follows.

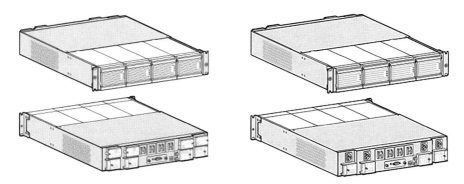

Fig. 3.44 EPS200-4850A AC distribution box (left) and EPS200-4850B AC distribution box (right)

Table 3.15 Cable specification requirements

Item	Specifications	Huawei code	Remarks
AC input cable	6 mm^2—black sheath (core wire: blue, brown)—43A, two core wires with equal sectional area	25030461	–
OT/JG terminal	Bare pressed terminal—OT—6 mm^2—M6—tin-plated—pre-insulated round terminal—12–10 AWG—yellow	14170023	Connects to the EPS200-4850A AC distribution box
	Bare pressed terminal—OT—6 mm^2—M8—tin-plated—pre-insulated round terminal—12-10 AWG—yellow	14170013	Connects to the distribution panel
	25 mm^2—M6 JG2 double-hole bare crimping terminal	14170119	Grounding cable terminal for the EPS200-4850A AC distribution box
	25 mm^2—M6 OT single-hole bare crimping terminal	14170147	
Grounding cable	25 mm^2	25030431	Grounding cable for the EPS200-4850A AC distribution box
DC cable	16 mm^2	25030430	Blue power cable
		25030428	Black power cable
		25030722	Red power cable
JG terminal	16 mm^2—M6 JG2 double-hole bare crimping terminal	14170116	–
Monitoring and alarm cable	Monitoring and alarm cable -3 m—(D9 male)—(CC4P0.48 black (S))—(D9 male)	04080076	–

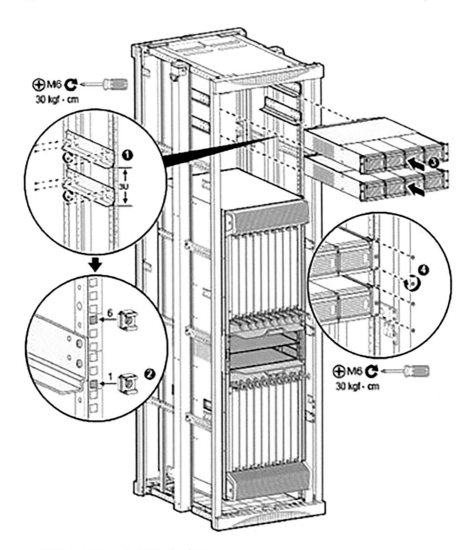

Fig. 3.45 Install the AC distribution box

- Install the slide rails, as ❶ in Fig. 3.45.
- Install floating nuts respectively at the first and sixth holes of the mounting bar starting from the bottom of the slide rail, as ❷ in Fig. 3.45.
- Install the AC distribution box and fix it in the cabinet with M6 screws, as ❸ and ❹ in Fig. 3.45.
- Install the PGND cable for the AC distribution box, and ensure the power system is safely grounded, as shown in Fig. 3.46. The ground cable of each AC distribution box should be connected to the nearest grounding bar of the equipment room.

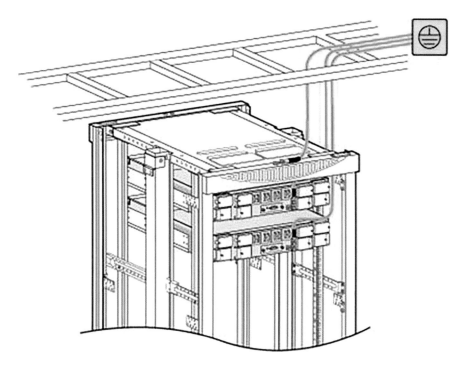

Fig. 3.46 Install the PGND cable for the AC distribution box

- Install the monitoring cable for the AC distribution box, as shown in Fig. 3.47.
- Connect the AC distribution box with the device power cable. To ensure the correct main-standby relationship between the power modules and the distribution boxes, the cable should be connected in strict accordance with the relationship shown in Fig. 3.48.

(vi) Install the AC power cable

- Attach temporary labels at both ends of the power cable.
- Lay the AC power cable along the cable ladder and connect one end of the power cable to the input terminal of the AC distribution box, as ❶ in Fig. 3.49.
- Connect the input end of the power module with the output end of the AC distribution box, as ❷ in Fig. 3.49.
- Restore the plastic protection plate to the junction box.
- Fix the power cable to the cable rack and tie it with cable buckles every 150 mm from bottom to top.
- After the power cable is installed, attach the formal labels 20 mm away from both cable ends, as ❸ in Fig. 3.49.

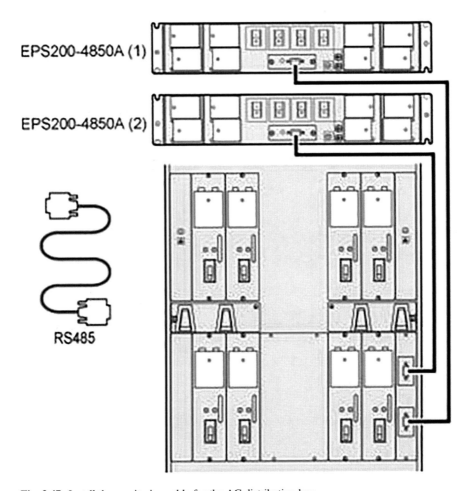

EPS200-4850A (1)

EPS200-4850A (2)

RS485

Fig. 3.47 Install the monitoring cable for the AC distribution box

(d) Installation of board and sub-board

Install the board and sub-board. The board slot layout is shown in Fig. 3.50.

(i) The interface should be coded in the format of "PCB slot No./service interface card No./port No."

- PCB slot No.: The slot numbers of the NE40E-X16 router should be marked 1 through 16, starting from 1.
- Service interface card No.: Starts from 0. If there is no service interface card on the board, this card number should be marked as "0".
- Port No.: Starts from 0.

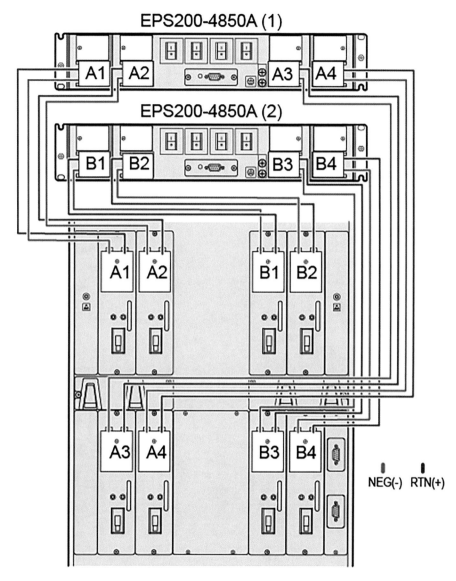

Fig. 3.48 Connection relationship between the AC distribution boxes and the device power cables

(ii) Install the board and sub-board. Before installing the board, make sure there is no condensation on the device and board. To prevent ESD-sensitive components from damage by static electricity, The ESD wrist strap or ESD gloves must be wore before the installation. The unoccupied slot should be installed with a filler panel. The board at the

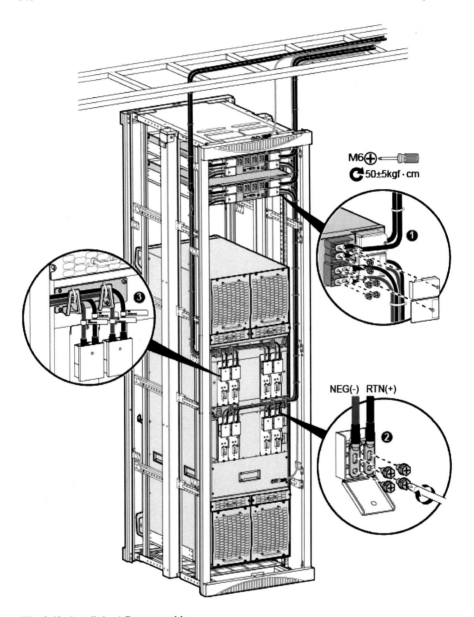

Fig. 3.49 Install the AC power cable

lower ledge of the NE40E-X16 router should installed upside down in the same way as that at the upper ledge. During the installation, if the board cannot be inserted, confirm the selected slot by verifying that the colors of both ends of the panel is the consistent with those of the chassis plate name bar.

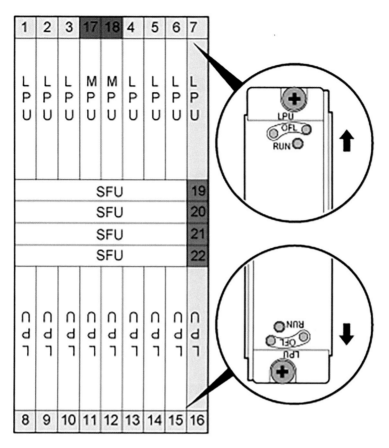

Fig. 3.50 Board slot layout

- To install a sub-board of 1/2 width or full width, you need to remove the redundant slide rails for sub-cards. Remove the fixing screws with a Phillips screwdriver, and then remove the slide modules from the motherboard, as shown in Fig. 3.51.
- Install the board, as ❶ and ❷ in Fig. 3.52. First remove the filler panel on the slot, and then insert the board along the rail for the slot smoothly and fasten it, and finally tighten the two loose screws with the Phillips screwdriver.
- Install the sub-board, as (3) in Fig. 3.52. Insert the sub-board along the rail for the slot smoothly, and then tighten the two loose screws with the Phillips screwdriver.

Fig. 3.51 Remove the redundant slide rails for sub-cards

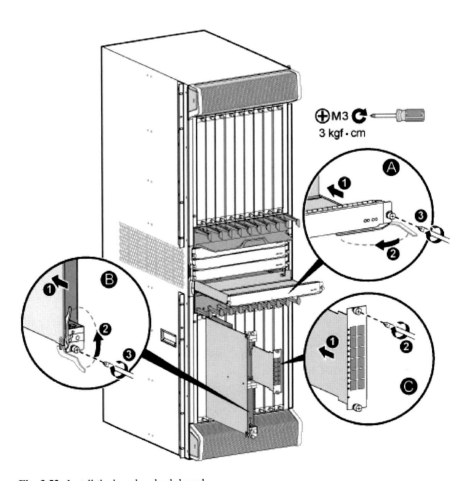

Fig. 3.52 Install the board and sub-board

(e) Router connection

(i) Connect the network cable, and then test the connectivity with the network cable tester before tying the network cable.

> **注意**
> - Keep the distances between the power cable, grounding cable and signal cable greater than 30 mm.
> - Tie the cable into a rectangle, and keep the cable buckles neat and oriented in the same way.

The steps are as follows.

- Attach temporary labels at both ends of the network cable.
- Lay the network cable along the cable trough and connect it to the corresponding interface, as ❶ in Fig. 3.53.
- Test the connectivity with the network cable tester.
- Fix the cable to the rack and tie it with cable buckles every 150 mm, as ❷ in Fig. 3.53.
- Attach the formal labels 20 mm away from both cable ends, as ❸ in Fig. 3.53.

(ii) The connection of optical fiber includes the respective installation of the side fiber management tray and optical module, optical fiber and corrugated pipe.

- The ESD wrist strap or ESD gloves must be wore to install the side fiber management tray and optical module. In the installation scenario of combining cabinets, it is necessary to install the side fiber management tray before combining cabinets, otherwise the side fiber management tray cannot be installed after cabinet combination. The side fiber management tray should be installed in the barrier-free space above the device, the number of which depends on the requirements of the scenario. In order to facilitate the fiber management and cabling, the second side fiber management tray, if any, should be installed on the other side of the cabinet. The installation of the side fiber management tray is shown as ❶ in Fig. 3.54; the installation of the optical module is as ❷ in Fig. 3.54; the optical port with no optical module installed should be provided with a dust cap, as ❸ in Fig. 3.54.
- Optical fiber installation should meet the following requirements.

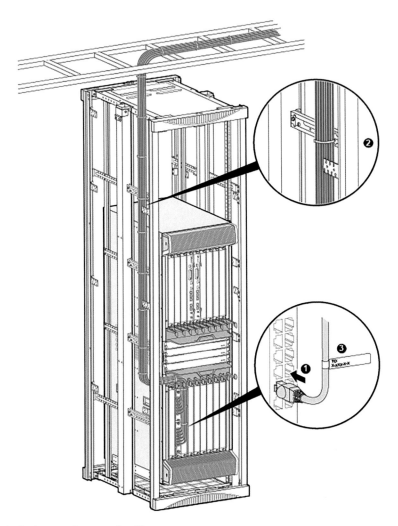

Fig. 3.53 Connect the network cable

– Keep the distances between the power cable, grounding cable and
  signal cable greater than 30 mm. Keep the minimum bending
  radius at the optical fiber turning point greater than 40 mm.
– The optical module with no optical fiber connected should be
  provided with a dust cap.
– The optical fiber should not be bond too tightly. After binding, the
  optical fiber should be able to be twitched freely.

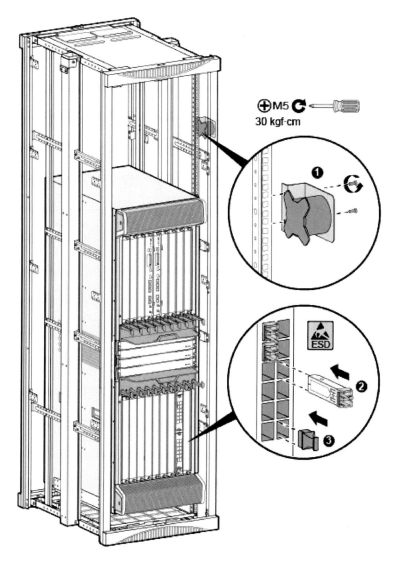

Fig. 3.54   Install the side fiber management tray and optical module

The steps are as follows.

– Lay the optical fibers along the cabling area, and then remove the dust caps from the optical modules and optical fibers and connect each optical fiber to the corresponding optical module, as ❶ in Fig. 3.55.
– Connect the other end of the optical fiber to the ODF.
– Coil the redundant optical fiber part around the side fiber management tray, as ❷ in Fig. 3.55.
– Bind the optical fibers with binding straps every 150 mm. Fix the fiber bundle to the cable rack with cable buckle at the place of each binding strap.

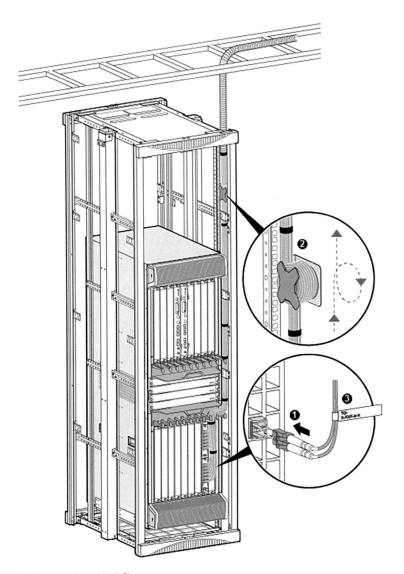

Fig. 3.55 Connect the optical fibers

- Attach the formal labels 20 mm away from both fiber ends, as ❸ in Fig. 3.55.

- The steps for installation of the corrugated pipe are as follows.

  - Attach temporary labels at both ends of each optical fiber.
  - Straighten the optical fibers and bind them into a fiber bundle, and then run the fiber bundle through the corrugated pipe.
  - Use adhesive tape at both ends of the corrugated pipe to prevent cuts, as ❶ in Fig. 3.56.

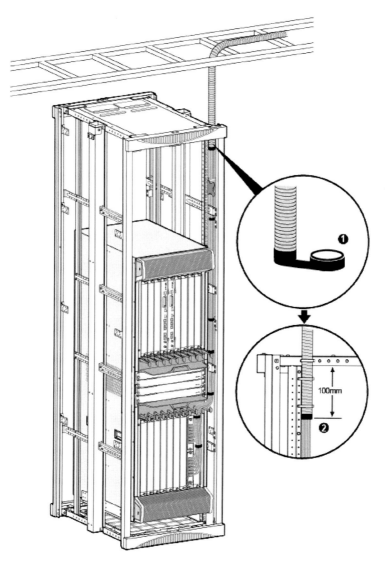

Fig. 3.56 Install the corrugated pipe

    – Lay the corrugated pipe along the cable ladder.
    – Push the corrugated pipe through the leading-out hole at the top of the
      cabinet and extend it into the cabinet for about 100 mm, and then fix it
      onto the cabinet with a cable buckle, as ❷ in Fig. 3.56.

(f) Checks for power on and off What you are checking here is the power on of
    the device. Take the power-on check process in the AC scene as an example,
    which is similar to the check process in the DC scene. The power-on check
    process is shown in Fig. 3.57.

Fig. 3.57 Power-on check process

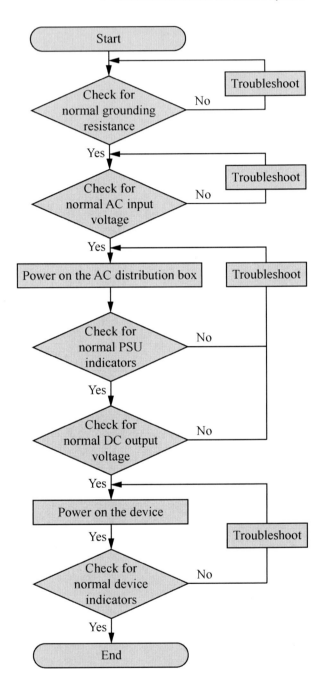

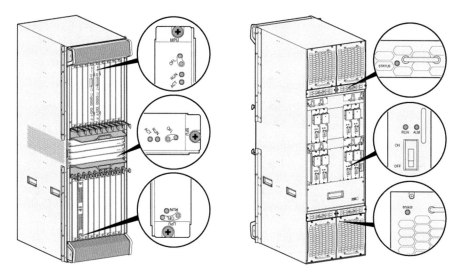

Fig. 3.58 Front view (left) and rear view (right) of the device

All air switches on the back of the AC distribution box must be placed in OFF state before power-on check, as shown in Fig. 3.58.

3.2.2 Installation of Switches

This section will take case-shaped switches, especially the Huawei S5700 Series, as examples to explain the installation process of switches.

1. Installation preparation

   (a) Read through safety precautions carefully.

   To protect personal safety and the safety of your switch, please comprehend the general safety norms and general safety practices provided in Chap. 1, and follow the signs on your switch and any safety precautions in the manual when installing, operating and maintaining the switch. Staff responsible for installation, operation and maintenance of switches must receive strict training, understand various security precautions and master correct operation methods before they can implement the installation, operation and maintenance of switches.

   (b) Check the installation environment.

   Installation staff should carefully review the installation instructions to make sure that the switch can be installed indoors or outdoors. The checklist for installation environment of switches is shown in Table 3.16. The S5700

Table 3.16 Checklist for installation environment of switches

Item	Requirements
Cleanliness	The switch is installed in a clean, dry and well-ventilated place where temperature is controlled. Water seepage, leakage and condensation are strictly prohibited in the installation site
Dust prevention	Dust prevention measures in the installation site are in place. Dust falling on the indoor device may cause poor contact with metal connectors or metal contacts due to electrostatic adsorption, which not only damages the service life of the switch, but also is prone to device failure
Temperature and humidity	The installation site maintains the temperature and relative humidity that support the normal operation of the switch. If the relative humidity is greater than 70%, dehumidification equipment (such as air conditioning with dehumidification function, special dehumidifier, etc.) should be equipped
Corrosive gas resistance	Acid, alkaline and other corrosive gases are avoided in the installation site
Space for heat dissipation	A space of more than 50 mm is provided around the switch to facilitate its heat dissipation
Lightning protection requirements for service ports	1. The buried cabling or steel pipe for cable threading should be adopted, instead of the outdoor aerial cabling, in order to avoid damage to the device by lightning strike 2. The network port of the S5720I-SI Series Switches supports the interconnection with the devices on the nearby utility poles on the street, so there is no need to install a lightning protector; but for interconnection with a device on a tower or in other harsh environments, the lightning protector is necessary 3. The 8-core lightning protector should be selected preferably as a network port lightning protector 4. When installing a lightning protector, it is necessary to connect the IN end of the lightning protector to the terminal side and the OUT end to the network port side of the switch 5. If the optical fiber reinforcing rib is used, it must be well grounded outside the device, in order to avoid lightning damage to the device via the reinforcing rib
Lightning protection for power interfaces	When the S5720I-SI Series Switch is installed in the outdoor cabinet, lightning protection requirements are as follows. 1. For AC switch: If it is directly powered by 220 V mains, it is recommended to install a 20 kA lightning protector between the power port of the switch and the mains; if it is powered by an isolated inverter near the outdoor cabinet, the lightning protector is not required between the power port of the switch and the inverter 2. For DC switch: The switch should be powered by the isolated power supply, and the isolated power supply and the switch should be placed in the same outdoor cabinet. The power supply of outdoor cabinet must be processed with lightning protection. An equipotent reference should be established for the lightning protector, power supply and switch, and the outdoor cabinet should be well grounded, with

(continued)

Table 3.16 (continued)

Item	Requirements
	grounding resistance not greater than 10 Ω. If the DC switch is powered by the PAC-260WA-E or PAC240S56-CN power module that is powered by the 220 V mains, it is recommended to install a 20 kA lightning protector between the power input port of PAC-260WA-E or PAC240S56-CN power module and the mains. A power cable of a specific length (5–10 m) is required to connect the 20 kA lightning protector and the S5720I-SI switch, or a decoupling inductor is required for decoupling. In all installation scenarios, each of the switch, cabinet, isolated power supply and lightning protector need to be grounded separately

Table 3.17 Requirements for the cabinet/rack

Item	Requirements
Width	The standard 19-inch (about 48 cm) cabinet/rack is used
Installation space	The cabinet/rack purchased by the user is provided with sufficient space for installation. The device using a 1150 W POE power module is not installed in a cabinet 600 mm deep
Grounding	The cabinet provides a reliable grounding point for the switch
Spacing of the front and rear mounting bars of the cabinet	1. In view of the fact that the switch needs to be installed on the cabinet through the front and rear mounting ears, the spacing of the front and rear mounting bars in the cabinet/rack should meet the requirements detailed later 2. When the above spacing requirements are not met, the slide rails or trays should be used, which should be prepared by the user

Series Switches can only be used indoors (except for the S5720I-SI, which can be installed in an outdoor cabinet).

(c) Check the cabinet/rack.

Check that the dimensions, grounding and other items of the cabinet or rack meet the requirements as shown in Table 3.17.

a, b and c in Fig. 3.59 indicate the cabinet width, depth and spacing of the mounting bars, respectively.

(d) Check the power condition.

Check to meet the requirements of the router for power conditions as shown in Table 3.18.

(e) Prepare installation tools and accessories.

Installation tools to be prepared include ESD gloves or ESD wrist strap, protective gloves, snap-off knife, tape measure, marker pen, flat-head screwdriver, Phillips screwdriver, diagonal pliers, network tester, multimeter, percussion drill and adjustable wrench.

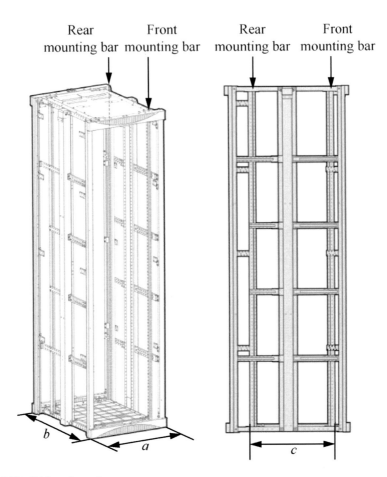

Fig. 3.59 Cabinet dimensions

The installation accessories to be prepared include insulating tape, cable buckle, binding strap for optical fiber, and corrugated pipe.

2. Installation of switches (main body)

The installation scenario varies with the switch profile and size, including installing into cabinet/rack, mounting to workbench, mounting to wall, and mounting to ceiling. Installation personnel may consult the product manual about the installation scenario corresponding to the model and size. It should be noted that some models have high housing temperature during operation, so it is recommended to install such a device in the area of restricted contact, for example, in the network box or cabinet, or on the workbench in the equipment room, so as to hinder the contact of unskilled technical personnel and ensure safety.

Table 3.18 Requirements of the switch for power conditions

Item	Requirements
Preparation	The power supply is ready before the installation of the switch
Voltage	The equipment room provides the switch with operation voltage conforming to the voltage range for normal operation. Please refer to the manual of the corresponding switch for the voltage range that supports the normal operation
Socket and cable	1. If the external power supply is provided via the AC socket, the switch is equipped with built-in AC power or provided with AC power module, and the local standard AC power cable is adopted 2. If the external power supply is provided via the power distribution unit (PDU), the switch is equipped with built-in AC power or provided with AC power module, and the C13 female—C14 male power cable is adopted 3. If the external power supply is provided via the DC distribution box, the switch is equipped with built-in DC power or provided with DC power module, and the DC power cable is adopted 4. Any power cable or plug supplied with the product as an accessory is only used for the product in the package, not for other devices

(a) Scenario 1: installing into cabinet/rack.

First consult the product manual to check that the switch model is suitable for the installation scenario. This scenario includes three installation methods, namely, by front mounting ears, by front mounting ears + rear mounting ears, and by front mounting ears/cabling teeth + rear mounting ears. The following is an example of the first method to explain the installation steps. The other two methods are similar. You can refer to the corresponding installation instructions.

The following items should to be confirmed before installation.

(i)   The cabinet is fixed and meets the requirements of cabinet/rack.

(ii)   The place of the switch is arranged in the cabinet.

(iii)   The switch to be installed is prepared and placed close to the cabinet for easy handling.

(iv)   The ESD protection measures is in place, such as wearing the ESD wrist strap or ESD gloves.

(v)   In general, the heat dissipation modes of the switch include forced heat dissipation through the fan, quasi-natural heat dissipation and natural heat dissipation. When more than one switch is installed in the cabinet/rack, the natural heat dissipation mode requires that the spacing between the upper and lower switcher must be no less than 1 U, while the modes of forced heat dissipation through the fan and quasi-natural heat dissipation recommend the spacing of 1 U.

(vi)   When installing, the mounting ears on the left and right sides of the switch should be aligned horizontally in the cabinet/rack. Forced installation is prohibited, otherwise it may cause the switch to bend and deform.

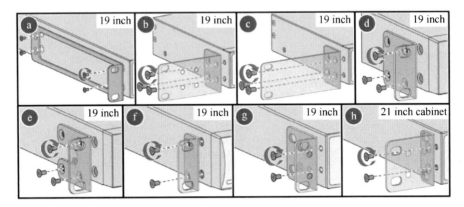

Fig. 3.60 Installation methods for different mounting ears

Tools and accessories to be prepared include floating nuts (4 for each device, purchased by the user), M4 screws, M6 screws (4 for each device, purchased by the user), front mounting ears (2 for each device), grounding cable, slide rail (optional).

The steps are as follows.

(i) Wear the ESD wrist strap or ESD gloves. If the ESD wrist strap is selected, ensure that one end of the ESD wrist strap is grounded, and the other end is in good contact with your skin.

(ii) Install the front mounting ears onto the switch with the M4 screws. The standard model and installation method of the mounting ears depends on the switch model, as shown in Fig. 3.60 (19 inches ≈ 48 cm; 21 inches ≈ 53 cm). The mounting ears must match the switch. Figure 3.60 shows the installation method for the left ear, the same for the right ear. To install the ears shown in (f), (g) and (h) in Fig. 3.60, two screws are needed for each side.

(iii) Connect the grounding cable to the switch (optional). Grounding is an important step in switch installation. Correct grounding is an significant guarantee for lightning protection, interference resistance and ESD protection of the switch, as well as an important premise to ensure that the PoE switch can normally power the PD. Depending on the environment in which the switch is installed, the grounding cable of the switch may be connected to the grounding point or grounding bar of the cabinet/rack. The following scenario is illustrated with the connection of grounding cable from the switch to the grounding point of the cabinet.

- Remove the M4 screw anticlockwise with a Phillips screwdriver at the switch grounding point, as shown in Fig. 3.61. The removed M4 screw should be placed properly.
- Connect the grounding cable to the switch grounding point. Fix the M4 end of the grounding cable (the end with the smaller connector

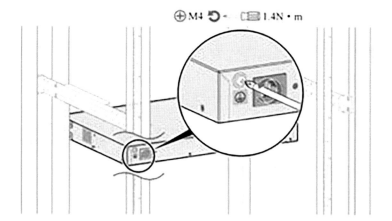

Fig. 3.61 Remove the M4 screw from switch grounding point

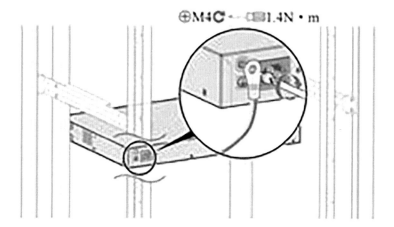

Fig. 3.62 Connect the grounding cable to the switch grounding point

aperture) to the switch grounding point with the removed M4 screw, and then tighten the M4 screw with a torque of 1.4 N • m, as shown in Fig. 3.62.

• Connect the grounding cable to the cabinet grounding point. Fix the M6 end of the grounding cable (the end with the larger connector aperture) to the cabinet grounding point with a M6 screw, and then tighten the M6 screw with a torque of 4.8 N • m, as shown in Fig. 3.63.

After the grounding cable is connected, check that the resistance between the switch grounding point and the grounding terminal is less than 0.1 Ω with a multimeter in Ohm mode.

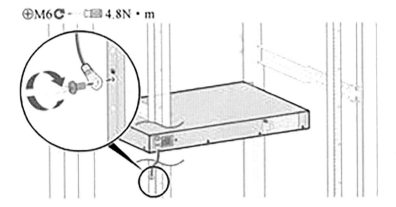

Fig. 3.63 Connect the grounding cable to the cabinet grounding point

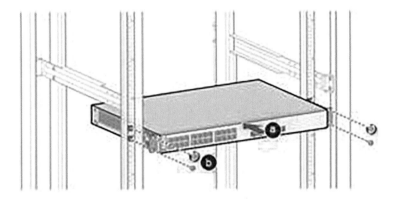

Fig. 3.64 Install the switch into the cabinet

(iv) Fix floating nuts to the mounting bars of the cabinet According to the nut positions determined, install four floating nuts on the front mounting bars of the cabinet using a flat-head screwdriver, with two for each of the left and right side, and the upper and lower nuts are spaced by one mounting hole on the mounting bar. Make sure the left and right corresponding floating nuts are on the same horizontal level. The holes on the mounting bars are not all spaced 1 U apart. So attention should be paid to identifying and referring to the scale on the bars.

(v) Install the switch into the cabinet. Although the switches uses different front mounting ears, the method of installing the switch into the cabinet is the same. So the following installation instructions take a switch using one type of the front mounting ears as an example, as shown in Fig. 3.64.

- Move the switch into the cabinet and hold the switch with both hands so that the mounting holes of the ears on both sides are aligned with the floating nuts on the mounting bars of the cabinet.

Fig. 3.65 Mount the switch
to the workbench

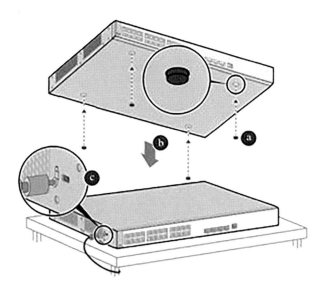

- Hold the switch with one hand, and with the other hand, fix the
  mounting ears to the mounting bars of the cabinet using the Phillips
  screwdriver and the M6 screws (two for each side of the switch).

(b) Scenario 2: mounting to workbench.

First consult the product manual to check that the switch model is suitable
for the installation scenario. Ensure that the ESD protection measures is in
place, such as wearing the ESD wrist strap or ESD gloves. Ensure the stability
and good grounding of the workbench. Ensure a space of more than 50 mm
around the switch for heat dissipation. Never pile up sundries on the switch.

Tools and accessories to be prepared include adhesive pads (4 for each
device) screws and anti-theft lock (optional, purchased by the user).

The steps are as follows.

(i) Wear the ESD wrist strap or ESD gloves. If the ESD wrist strap is
selected, ensure that one end of the ESD wrist strap is grounded, and the
other end is in good contact with your skin.

(ii) Paste the adhesive pads to the switch. Carefully invert the switch, and
paste the four adhesive pads onto the circular embossing areas at the
bottom of the switch, as shown in Fig. 3.24(a).

(iii) Place the switch onto the workbench. Place the switch normally and
stably on the workbench, as shown in Fig. 3.65(b).

(iv) Install the anti-theft lock (optional). After mounting the switch on the
workbench, you can fix the switch to the workbench through the anti-
theft lock, as shown in Fig. 3.65(c).

Fig. 3.66 A sign of anti-
theft lockhole on the switch.

Check whether a sign of anti-theft lockhole is provided on the switch to confirm whether it supports the installation of the anti-theft lock, as shown in Fig. 3.66. Switches without an anti-theft lockhole do not support the anti-theft lock.

(c) Scenario 3: mounting to wall.

First consult the product manual to check that the switch model is suitable for the installation scenario. Before drilling a hole into the wall, make sure there is no electrical circuit in the drilling area to avoid personal injury. Ensure that the ESD protection measures is in place, such as wearing the ESD wrist strap or ESD gloves. It is recommended to take waterproof and dustproof measures for the switches to be mounted on the wall to avoid the switch from damages due to water or dust infiltration at the interfaces. Flammable and explosive items are prohibited under the switch, and foreign objects are prohibited within 100 mm around the switch.

The tools and accessories to be prepared include percussion drill (Φ8 drill bit), M6 explosive expansion bolts (4 for each device), M4 screws (4 or 6 for each device, depending on the switch model), and front mounting ears (2 for each device).

The steps are as follows.

(i) Wear the ESD wrist strap or ESD gloves. If the ESD wrist strap is selected, ensure that one end of the ESD wrist strap is grounded, and the other end is in good contact with your skin.

(ii) Install the front mounting ears onto the switch with the M4 screws. The standard model and installation method of the mounting ears depends on the switch model, so the mounting ears must match the switch. The installation methods for different mounting ears are shown in Fig. 3.67. The mounting ears should be installed on both sides of the switch, and the installation method is the same on both sides. The following is an example of the installation on one side.

(iii) Mark the drilling holes on the wall with a marker according to the size of the switch and the positions of the mounting ears.

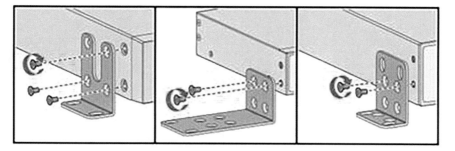

Fig. 3.67 Installation methods for different mounting ears

Fig. 3.68 Mount the switch
to the wall

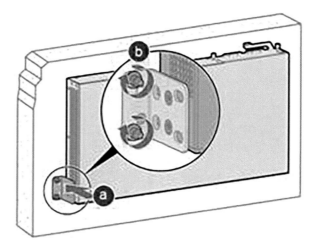

(iv) Install M6 explosive expansion bolts.

- Use a percussion drill (Φ8 drill bit) to drill holes perpendicular to the wall at the marked positions, about 35–40 mm deep.
- Insert the M6 explosive expansion bolts into the holes drilled and then rotate the nuts clockwise to secure the bolts into the wall.
- Remove the nuts from the M6 explosive expansion bolts by counter-clockwise rotation.

(v) Mount the switch to the wall, as shown in Fig. 3.68.

- Align the mounting ear holes on both sides of the switch with the M6 explosive expansion bolts on the wall and hang the ears on the bolts.
- Fasten the removed nuts on the M6 explosive expansion bolts.

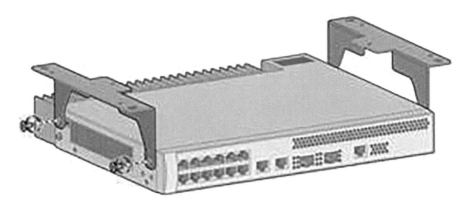

Fig. 3.69 Installation method of the ceiling-mounting ears

(d) Scenario 4: mounting to ceiling.

First consult the product manual to check that the switch model is suitable for the installation scenario. Before drilling a hole into the ceiling, make sure there is no electrical circuit in the drilling area to avoid personal injury.

The tools and accessories to be prepared include percussion drill (Φ8 drill bit), M6 explosive expansion bolts (4 for each device), M4 screws (4 for each device), and ceiling-mounting ears (2 for each device).

The steps are as follows.

(i) Wear the ESD wrist strap or ESD gloves. If the ESD wrist strap is selected, ensure that one end of the ESD wrist strap is grounded, and the other end is in good contact with your skin.

(ii) Install the ceiling-mounting ears onto the switch. Align the ceiling-mounting ears with the ear holes on the device and fix the ceiling-mounting ears to the switch using the M4 screws, as shown in Fig. 3.69. The installation method of the ears is the same on both sides. The following is an example of the installation on one side.

(iii) Mark the drilling holes on the ceiling with a marker according to the size of the switch and the positions of the mounting ears. The marking method is similar to that in Scenario 3.

(iv) Install M6 explosive expansion bolts.

- Use a percussion drill (Φ8 drill bit) to drill holes perpendicular to the wall at the marked positions, about 35–40 mm deep.
- Insert the M6 explosive expansion bolts into the holes drilled and then rotate the nuts clockwise to secure the bolts into the wall.
- Remove the nuts from the M6 explosive expansion bolts by counter-clockwise rotation.

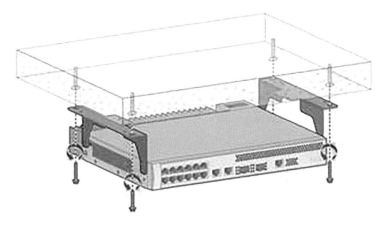

Fig. 3.70   Mount the switch to the ceiling

(v) Mount the switch to the ceiling, as shown in Fig. 3.70.

- Align the mounting ear holes on both sides of the switch with the M6 explosive expansion bolts on the ceiling and hang the ears on the bolts.
- Fasten the removed nuts on the M6 explosive expansion bolts.

3. Installation of boards

The installation of the main body of the switch should be followed by the installation of boards, including such modules as power module, fan module and optical module.

(a) Installation of pluggable power module and fan module.

For switches that have a power module and fan module pre-installed, this step can be omitted. The installation method of the fan module is the same as that of the power module, including the fixations with loose screw and with latch. Here, the power module is taken as an example for installation instructions.

Tools and accessories to be prepared include the ESD wrist strap or ESD gloves, and Phillips screwdriver.

The steps are as follows.

(i) Wear the ESD wrist strap or ESD gloves. If the ESD wrist strap is selected, ensure that one end of the ESD wrist strap is grounded, and the other end is in good contact with your skin.

(ii) Remove the filler panel on the power slot of the switch, and properly save it for subsequent use.

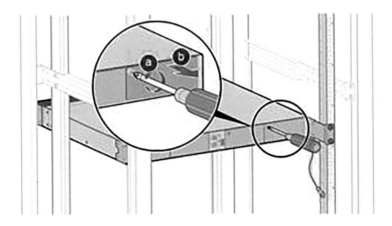

Fig. 3.71 Remove the filler panel fixed with the loose screw

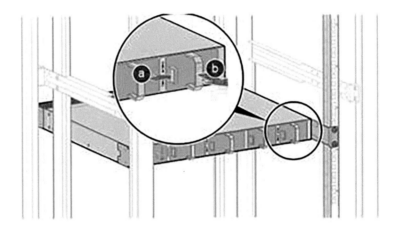

Fig. 3.72 Remove the filler panel fixed with the latch

There are two ways to fix the power module of the switch (with loose screw and with latch), and accordingly, the filler panel also adopts these two ways.

If the loose screw is used, the filler panel should be removed as shown in Fig. 3.71.

- Loosen the loose screw fixing the filler panel using the Phillips screwdriver anticlockwise.
- Pull the loose screw to pull out the filler panel.

If the latch is used, the filler panel should be removed as shown in Fig. 3.72.

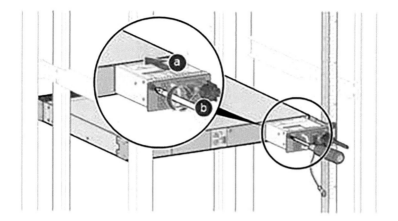

Fig. 3.73 Install the filler panel fixed with the loose screw

- Snap the latch fixing the filler panel to right with your thumb and hold it down.
- Pull the handle on the filler panel to pull out the filler panel.

(iii) Install the power module

Again, the above two installation methods can be used. The power module fixed with loose screw should be installed as shown in Fig. 3.73.

- Hold the handle on the power module with one hand and the bottom of the power module with the other hand, and insert the power module horizontally and completely into the power slot.
- Tighten the loose screw on the power module clockwise with the Phillips screwdriver.

The power module fixed with latch should be installed as shown in Fig. 3.74. Hold the handle on the power module with one hand and the bottom of the power module with the other hand, and insert the power module horizontally into the power slot until the latch locks automatically.

(b) Installation of plug-in card

Some switch models support the installation of a pluggable plug-in card. Different types of plug-in cards have the same installation method, so the following 4-port front plug-in card is taken as an example for installation instructions.

Tools and accessories to be prepared include the ESD wrist strap or ESD gloves, and Phillips screwdriver.

The steps are as follows.

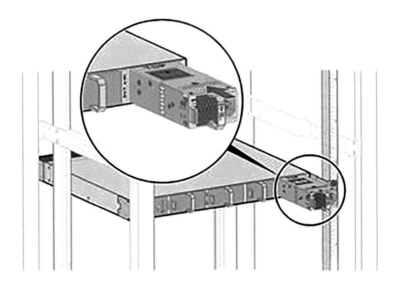

Fig. 3.74 Install the filler panel fixed with the latch

    (i) Wear the ESD wrist strap or ESD gloves. If the ESD wrist strap is selected, ensure that one end of the ESD wrist strap is grounded, and the other end is in good contact with your skin.

   (ii) Remove the filler panel on the plug-in card slot of the switch, and properly save it for subsequent use.

- Loosen the loose screw fixing the filler panel using the Phillips screwdriver anticlockwise.
- Pull the loose screw to pull out the filler panel.

  (iii) Install the plug-in card to the switch.

- Open the lever of the plug-in card about 45°, and then push the card into the device by pushing its left and right sides with both thumbs (below the loose screw) until the whole screw above the card enters the device case.
- When the screw fully enters into the device case, turn the level so that the card is fully inserted into the case.
- Tighten the loose screw with the Phillips screwdriver.

(c) Installation of optical module.

    The optical module is used to receive and transmit optical signals. To install it, tools and accessories to be prepared include the ESD wrist strap or ESD gloves, and dustproof plug.

    The steps are as follows.

(i) Wear the ESD wrist strap or ESD gloves. If the ESD wrist strap is selected, ensure that one end of the ESD wrist strap is grounded, and the other end is in good contact with your skin.

(ii) Pull out the dustproof plug in the optical interface, and properly save it for subsequent use.

(iii) Install the optical module to the optical module. Slide the optical module into the optical interface smoothly until it is fully inserted. After proper installation, the spring plate of the optical module will make a "snap" sound. During the installation, if the optical module cannot be fully inserted, stop pushing it in, but turn it over 180° and try to insert it again.

(iv) Check that the optical module is installed in place. Without opening the pull ring, press both sides of the optical module with your thumb and forefinger and gently pull the module to check if it can be pulled out. If cannot, the optical module is properly installed; otherwise, it is not installed correctly and should be re-installed.

4. Connection of switches

(a) Connection of power cable

The case-shaped switches can be powered by a built-in power supply, a pluggable power module, or a stand-alone power module, with different power cables and connection methods required for each scenario. For switches other than the S5720I-SI series, if the external power supply is provided via the AC standard socket, the switch should be equipped with built-in AC power or provided with AC power module, and the local AC standard power cable should be adopted; if via the AC PDU, the switch should be equipped with built-in AC power or provided with AC power module also, and the C13 female—C14 male power cable should be adopted; and if via the DC distribution box, the switch should be equipped with built-in DC power or provided with DC power module, and the DC power cable should be adopted. For the S5720I-SI Series Switches and PAC-260WA-E or PAC240S56-CN power modules, Phoenix terminals and supporting power cables are required. Here we will take the use of a built-in AC power supply or AC power module as an example to explain the connection method. For other types of power supply, please consult the corresponding product manuals.

Tools and accessories to be prepared include the ESD wrist strap or ESD gloves, and captive buckle for AC terminal (optional).

The steps are as follows.

(i) Wear the ESD wrist strap or ESD gloves. If the ESD wrist strap is selected, ensure that one end of the ESD wrist strap is grounded, and the other end is in good contact with your skin.

(ii) Turn off the power switch of the external power supply for the switch.

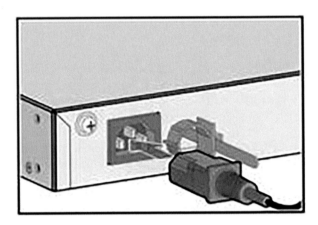

Fig. 3.76 Usage of the
captive buckle

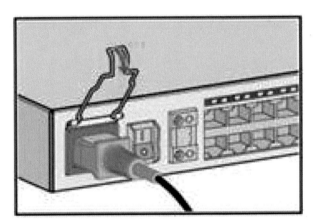

(iii) Turn off the power switch of the switch or power module. If there is no
power switch, skip this step.

(iv) Connect the power cable to the switch or power module. Here the built-
in AC power supply is taken as an example to illustrate the connection
method of the AC power cable.

- Install the captive buckle for AC terminal (optional).
- Plug the AC power cable into the power interface of the switch or AC
power module, as shown in Fig. 3.75.
- If the captive buckle for AC terminal is installed, adjust its position
according to the size of the AC cable connector to grip the AC power
cable (optional).

  Some switch models provide a captive buckle for the AC power
interface, whose usage is shown in Fig. 3.76.

Table 3.19 Requirements for the use of different types of network cables (the vertical distance excludes the length of the photoelectric module)

Cable type	Vertical Distance from Switch's Front Panel to Cabinet's Front Door (X)
Cat 5 unshielded cable	$X \geq 80$ mm, for 48-electrical-port switch, double-sided cabling is required
Cat 5 shielded cable	$X \geq 110$ mm, for 48-electrical-port switch, double-sided cabling is required
Cat 6 cable	$X \geq 120$ mm, for 48-electrical-port switch, double-sided cabling is required

(b) Connection of network cables

The connection of networks cable follows the power cable connection. The following points need to be noted in the connection.

(i)   Test their connectivity before laying the network cables.

(ii)   The outdoor aerial cabling is prohibited, in order to avoid damage to the device by lightning strike.

(iii)   The buried cabling or steel pipe for cable threading should be adopted.

(iv)   Keep the distances between the power cable and signal cable greater than 10 cm.

(v)   When the 48-optical-port switch is used with the photoelectric module for the 600 mm deep cabinet, only Cat 5 unshielded cables can be used.

(vi)   When the 48-electrical-port switch is used for the 600 mm deep cabinet, only Cat 5 unshielded cables can be used.

If the switch does not support or use a rear plug-in card, the type of network cable used for the electrical port and the vertical distance from the front panel of the switch to the front door of the cabinet should meet the following requirements listed in Table 3.19.

If the switch using the rear plug-in card is to be installed in a cabinet with a depth greater than 600 mm, the type of network cable used by the electrical port and the vertical distance from the switch's front panel to the cabinet's front door should meet the requirements shown in Table 3.18, and there is no special requirement for the vertical distance between the switch's rear panel and the cabinet's rear door; if such a switch is to be installed in a 600 mm deep cabinet, the type of network cable used in the electrical port, the type of network cable used by the electrical port, the type of optical fiber used for the rear plug-in card and the vertical distance between the switch panel and the cabinet door should meet the requirements shown in Table 3.20.

Double-sided cabling refers to that the network cables connected to the first 24 ports of the switch are routed from the left side of the switch and those connected to the last 24 ports are routed from the right side. In case of double-sided cabling, it is recommended to reserve 1 U for the cabling rack below the switch. After the cabling is completed, the cables should be bond and fixed on the side of the cabinet to ensure that the cabinet bears the weight of the cables. For 10GBASE-T Ethernet electrical interfaces, if any, it is recommended to

Table 3.20 Requirements for the use of different types of network cables and optical fibers (the vertical distance excludes the length of the photoelectric module)

Cable type	Vertical distance from Switch's Front Panel to Cabinet's Front Door (X)	Vertical distance from Switch's Rear Panel to Cabinet's Rear Door (Y)		
		Ultra-short tail fiber	Short tail fiber	Conventional fiber or QSFP +
Cat 5 unshielded cable	80 mm < X < 100 mm	Y ≥ 60 mm	Y ≥ 72 mm	Y ≥ 80 mm
Cat 5 shielded cable	X = 110 mm	Y ≥ 60 mm, double-sided cabling is required	Y ≥ 72 mm, double-sided cabling is required	No use in combination
Cat 6 cable	X = 120 mm	Y ≥ 60 mm, double-sided cabling is required	No use in combination	No use in combination

use Cat 6e shielded cables or those of higher standard, because Cat 6e shielded cables and Cat 7 cables are able to avoid external crossover. But these cables are heavier that require proper binding and fixing. They can be installed in combination with other types of cables. The MultiGE interface (10GBase-T and IEEE 802.3bz) may produce bit error rate no greater than 10^{-7} in the case of strong interference, so it is suggested to keep it away from the interference source or take necessary shielding measures. When the Fast Retrain function is triggered, there will be a large number of bit errors around 30 ms.

Tools and accessories to be prepared include the ESD wrist strap or ESD gloves, diagonal pliers, binding strap, marker and cable labels.

The steps are as follows.

(i) Confirm the number of interfaces to be connected and the connection relationship, and determine the easy cabling path.

(ii) Select the corresponding number of network cables with corresponding length according to the number of ports and surveyed distance.

(iii) Attach a temporary label to both ends of each cable and write the cable No.

(iv) Lay the cables. If there are many cables to be routed, in order to facilitate cabling, you can lay the cables in the cabinet first, and then make the cable connectors for connections with the device. The connectors made on site must be standardized, firm, reliable and aesthetically pleasing.

(v) Wear the ESD wrist strap or ESD gloves. If the ESD wrist strap is selected, ensure that one end of the ESD wrist strap is grounded, and the other end is in good contact with your skin.

Cable bundle diameter (mm)	Binding interval (mm)
<10	150
10–30	200
>30	300

Table 3.21 Intervals of the cable binding straps

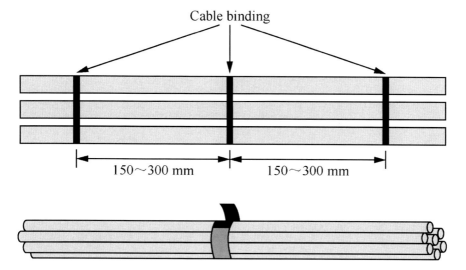

Fig. 3.77 Cable binding method

(vi) Connect the network cables to the switch interfaces. Insert each network cable connector into the corresponding switch interface according to the network cable No. Ensure that all network cables are properly connected to the switch before Step G.

(vii) Bind the cables. Straighten the connected network cables to prevent them from intersecting, and then bind them with the binding straps at the intervals shown in Table 3.21, and cut off the redundant part of the straps with the diagonal pliers, as shown in Fig. 3.77. The cable binding should be as loose as possible, preferably lined with a protective pad. Note that a cable bundle is recommended to have no more than 12 cables, and must not have more than 24 cables.

(viii) Replace all temporary labels with formal cable labels.

(c) Connect the optical fibers

The following points need to be noted in the connection.

(i) Test their connectivity before laying the optical fibers.

(ii) Keep the distances between the power cable and signal cable greater than 10 cm.

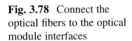
Fig. 3.78 Connect the optical fibers to the optical module interfaces

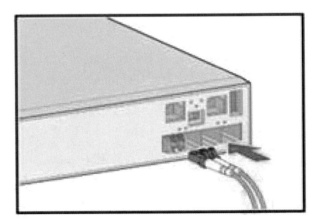

(iii) The optical fibers must enter the cabinet/rack with being cased by the corrugated pipe. The radius of curvature of an optical fiber should be at least 20 times of its diameter, and no smaller than 40 mm in general.

(iv) Ensure that the section at the optical fiber interface is clean and tidy, so as to avoid pollution affecting the communication effect. If this section is polluted, use a dedicated fiber cleaning cloth to clean it.

Tools and accessories to be prepared include the ESD wrist strap or ESD gloves, corrugated pipe, optical fiber binding strap, marker, optical fiber labels and fiber extraction tool (optional).

The steps are as follows.

(i) Confirm the number of interfaces to be connected and the connection relationship, and determine the easy cabling path.

(ii) Select the corresponding number of optical fibers with corresponding length and mode according to the optical module type, number of ports and surveyed distance.

(iii) Wear the ESD wrist strap or ESD gloves. If the ESD wrist strap is selected, ensure that one end of the ESD wrist strap is grounded, and the other end is in good contact with your skin.

(iv) Attach a temporary label to both ends of each optical fiber and write the fiber No.

(v) Pull out the dustproof plug of each optical module and the dustproof cap of each optical fiber connector,

(vi) Connect the optical fibers to the optical module interfaces. Align and insert the optical fiber connector into the optical module interface. After that, if a "snap" sound is heard, the connector is in place, as shown in Fig. 3.78. Never confuse the transmitting end and receiving end of the optical fiber connector, and you can refer to the signs at the interface of the optical module.

Fig. 3.79 Pull out the
optical fibers

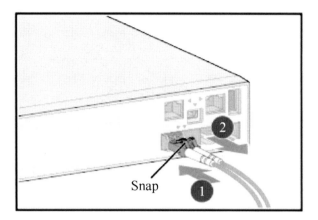

Snap

If the optical fiber needs to be removed, gently push the optical fiber
connector inward, and then pinch the snap to pull it out, as shown in
Fig. 3.79. It is prohibited to pull out the optical fiber connector directly.
In the case that the interfaces are densely deployed and inconvenient to
be operated by hand, the fiber extraction tool can be used to assist the
operation.
(vii) Bind the optical fibers. Straighten the connected optical fibers to
       prevent them from intersecting, and then bind them with the binding
       straps in intervals of 150–300 mm.
(viii) Replace all temporary labels with formal optical fiber labels.

(d) Connection of high-speed cables
    The following points need to be noted in the connection.

   (i) High-speed cables that are not in use require an ESD protective cap at
        both plugs.
  (ii) Ensure that the section of the high-speed cable interface is clean and
        tidy, so as to avoid pollution affecting the communication effect. If this
        section is polluted, use a dedicated fiber cleaning cloth to clean it.
 (iii) Ensure that the cable and optical fiber keep the bending radius greater
        than the minimum bending radius to avoid damage to the core wires. For
        bending radius of the cable, please refer to the corresponding product
        instructions.

    Tools and accessories to be prepared include the ESD wrist strap or ESD
    gloves, diagonal pliers, binding strap, marker and high-speed cable labels.
       The steps are as follows.

   (i) Confirm the number of interfaces to be connected and the connection
        relationship, and determine the easy cabling path.

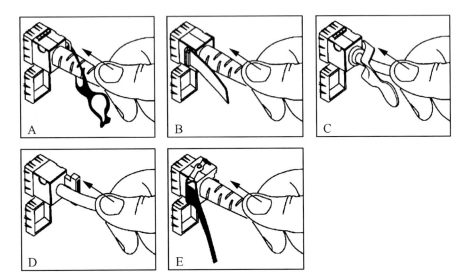

Fig. 3.80 Connect the high-speed cable to the switch interface

(ii) Select the corresponding number of high-speed cables with corresponding length according to the number of ports and surveyed distance.

(iii) Wear the ESD wrist strap or ESD gloves. If the ESD wrist strap is selected, ensure that one end of the ESD wrist strap is grounded, and the other end is in good contact with your skin.

(iv) Attach a temporary label to both ends of each high-speed cable and write the fiber No.

(v) Connect the high-speed cables to the switch interfaces. Insert each high-speed cable connector into the corresponding switch interface according to the high-speed cable No. Insert the cable connector into the optical module interface in the correct direction. After that, if a "snap" sound is heard, the connector is in place, as shown in Fig. 3.80. Ensure that all high-speed cables are properly connected to the switch before Step F.

If the optical fiber needs to be removed, gently push the cable connector inward, and then hold the handle to pull it out, as shown in Fig. 3.81. It is prohibited to pull out the cable connector directly.

(vi) Bind the high-speed cables Straighten the high-speed cables to prevent them from intersecting, bind them with the binding straps in intervals of 150–300 mm, and then cut off the redundant part of the straps with the diagonal pliers.

(vii) Replace all temporary labels with formal high-speed cable labels.

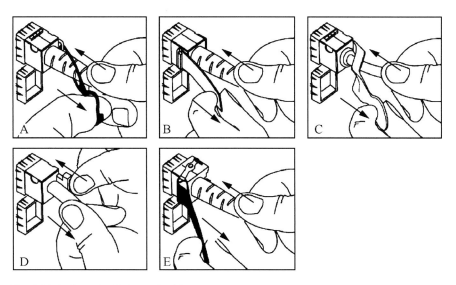

Fig. 3.81 Pull out the high-speed cable

(e) Connection of stacking cables

Some switch models support stacking through stack-in card or service port.

(i) Stacking through stack-in card: Devices are connected through special stack-in cards and stacking cables.

(ii) Stacking through service port: Devices are connected through physical member ports bound to logical stacking ports, without the need for a dedicated stack-in cards.

To confirm whether the specific switch model supports stacking, or to confirm the stacking mode supported, the software and hardware requirements of stacking, and the connection method of stacking cable, please refer to the corresponding product manual.

3.2.3   Installation of WLAN Devices

As described in Sect. 3.1.3, the thin AP+AC networking architecture of WLAN network is divided into AP and AC. This section will introduce the installation processes for each of these parts. For AC, Huawei AC6605 will be taken as an example; and for AP, Huawei AP7050 Series products.

1. Installation of AC

   Pre-installation preparation: Read through safety precautions carefully; check the installation site, cabinet/rack, and power supply condition; prepare installation tools and accessories, as shown in Table 3.22.

   (a) AC6605 supports two installation scenarios, namely installing into cabinet/rack and mounting to workbench, and generally does not support mounting to wall.

      (i) Scenario 1: installing into cabinet/rack.

         There are two cases. One is the installation of the device through the front and rear mounting ears without the need for slide rail or a tray for support. Examples of such installation are described below. The other is the use of a slide rail or tray for support, without the installation of the rear mounting ear, but the slide or tray needs to be purchased separately.

         The steps are as follows.

         • Install front and rear mounting ears (two for each of the front and rear side). It is recommended to install the front mounting ears on both sides of the side of the device outbound interface and the rear mounting ears on both sides of the side of the device outlet power module, as shown in Fig. 3.82.
         • Install the floating nuts Install four floating nuts on the front mounting bracket, two for each of the left and right sides. Because the AC6605 is 1 U high, the mounting holes on the mounting ears correspond to the two mounting holes separated by one hole on the front mounting bracket; install four floating nuts on the corresponding rear mounting bracket, two for each of the left and right sides, as shown in Fig. 3.83. Note that the floating nut on the rear mounting bracket should be in line with the floating nut on the front mounting bracket.
         • Install the slide rail for the rear mounting ears on the rear mounting bracket, as shown in Fig. 3.84.

            When installing the device into the cabinet/rack, the difference in spacing between two mounting bars in the cabinet determines the difference in installation mode of the slide rail for the rear mounting ears, as shown in Table 3.23.
         • Hold the device case to move it into the cabinet/rack, align the mounting ears with the rear slide rail and slowly push the case, as shown in Fig. 3.85.
         • Hold the device case with one hand, and fix the front mounting ears to the front mounting bracket with a screw driver with the other hand, and then fix the rear mounting ears to the rear slide rail on the rear side of the cabinet/rack, as shown in Fig. 3.86.

Table 3.22 Pre-installation preparation for AC6605

Item	Explanation
Read through safety precautions carefully	1. To protect personal safety and the safety of the device, please follow the signs on it and any safety precautions in the manual when installing, operating and maintaining the device 2. Precautions, warnings and hazards shown in the manual do not cover all safety precautions to be followed, only as supplementary precautions 3. Staff responsible for installation, operation and maintenance of the device must receive strict training, understand various security precautions and master correct operation methods before they can implement the installation, operation and maintenance of the device
Check the installation site	The device may only be used indoors, and the installation site must meet the following conditions 1. The device is installed in a clean, dry and well-ventilated place where temperature is controlled. Water seepage, leakage and condensation are strictly prohibited in the installation site 2. Dust prevention measures in the installation site are in place. Dust falling on the indoor device may cause poor contact with metal connectors or metal contacts due to electrostatic adsorption, which not only damages the service life of the device, but also is prone to device failure 3. The installation site maintains the temperature (at altitude from -60 to $+1800$ m: -5 °C to $+50$ °C; at altitude from 1800 to 5000 m: the maximum operating temperature decreases by 1 °C for every 300 m altitude increase) and relative humidity (5–95% RH, non-condensation) that support the normal operation of the device. If the relative humidity is greater than 70%, dehumidification equipment (such as air conditioning with dehumidification function, special dehumidifier, etc.) should be equipped 4. Acid, alkaline and other corrosive gases are avoided in the installation site 5. A space of more than 50 mm is provided around the device to facilitate its heat dissipation
Check the cabinet/rack	When installing the device, the requirements for the cabinet are as follows 1. The device has the height and width in line with the industry standards, and can be installed in the 19-inch (about 48 cm) standard cabinet/rack 2. The cabinet/rack provides a reliable grounding point for the device 3. The cabinet/rack purchased by the user is provided with sufficient space for installation and cabling
Check the power condition	When installing the device, the requirements for the power supply are as follows 1. The power supply is ready in the equipment room before the installation of the device 2. The equipment room provides the device with operation voltage conforming to the voltage range for normal operation 3. The AC power socket meets the specification of 10 A. If the power supply is provided via the standard socket, the local

(continued)

Table 3.22 (continued)

Item	Explanation
	standard AC power cable should be adopted; if via the C13 female socket, the C13 female—C14 male power cable should be adopted
Prepare installation tools and accessories	Tools: ESD gloves or ESD wrist strap, snap-off knife, tape measure, marker pen, flat-head screwdriver (M4/M6), Phillips screwdriver (M4/M6), diagonal pliers, network tester, multimeter, percussion drill and adjustable wrench (Φ8 drill bit)
	Accessories: insulating tape, cable buckle, binding strap for optical fiber, and corrugated pipe

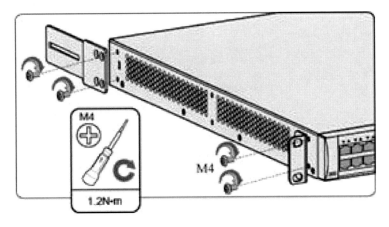

Fig. 3.82 Fix the front and rear mounting ears

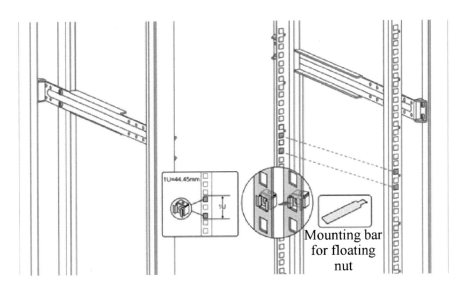

Fig. 3.83 Install the floating nuts

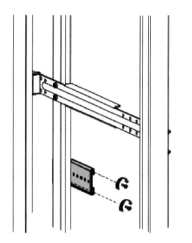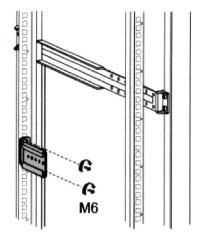

Fig. 3.84 Fix the slide rail for the rear mounting ears

Table 3.23 How to install the slide rail for the rear mounting ears

Spacing between the two mounting bars in the cabinet	How to install the slide rail for the rear mounting ears
375–454 mm	
507–566 mm	

(b) Scenario 2: mounting to workbench.

   Ensure the stability and good grounding of the workbench. Ensure a space of more than 50 mm around the switch for heat dissipation. Never pile up sundries on the device.

   The steps are as follows.

   (i) Wear the ESD wrist strap or ESD gloves, ensuring that one end of the ESD wrist strap is grounded, and the other end is in good contact with the wearer's skin.

  (ii) Paste the adhesive pads to the device. Carefully invert the device, and paste the four adhesive pads onto the circular embossing areas at the bottom of the device, as shown in Fig. 3.87(a).

 (iii) Place the device onto the workbench. Place the device normally and stably on the workbench, as shown in Fig. 3.87(b).

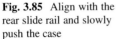

Fig. 3.85 Align with the rear slide rail and slowly push the case

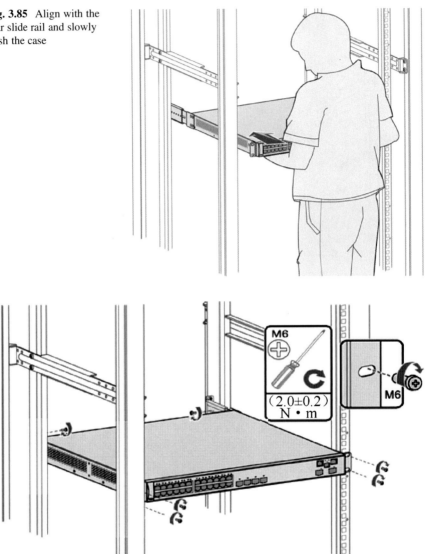

Fig. 3.86 Fix the rear mounting ears to the rear slide rail

(iv) Install the anti-theft lock (optional). After mounting the device on the workbench, you can fix the device to the workbench through the anti-theft lock provided at the left side of the device, as shown in Fig. 3.87(c).

Fig. 3.87 Mount the device
to the workbench

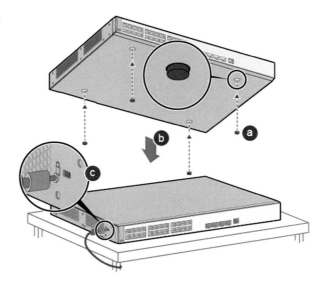

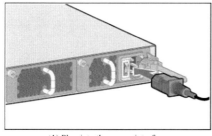
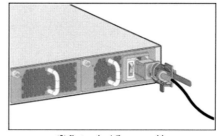

(1) Plug into the power interface   (2) Fasten the AC power cable

Fig. 3.88 How to connect the AC power cable

(c) Connect the power cable. The steps are as follows.

  (i) Wear the ESD wrist strap or ESD gloves, ensuring that one end of the
      ESD wrist strap is grounded, and the other end is in good contact with
      the wearer's skin.
 (ii) Turn off the power switch of the external power supply for the device.
(iii) Connect the power cable to the power module.

  • If AC power module is used, the connection method of AC power
    cable is shown in Fig. 3.88.

    – Plug the AC power cable into the power interface of the AC power
      module, as shown in Fig. 3.88 (1).
    – Fasten the AC power cable with the captive buckle for AC
      terminal, as shown in Fig. 3.88 (2).

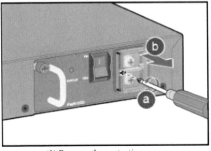

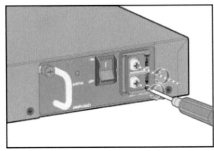

(1) Remove the protective cover   (2) Remove the OT terminals

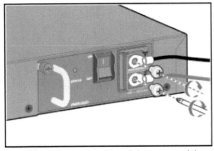

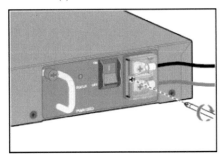

(3) Fix the DC power cable and the power module   (4) Install the protective cover

Fig. 3.89 How to connect the DC power cable

- Connect the other end of the AC power cable to the external AC power supply system.

• If DC power module is used, the connection method of DC power cable is shown in Fig. 3.89.

- Remove the protective cover of the DC terminal on the power module with a Phillips screwdriver, as shown in Fig. 3.89 (1).
- Remove the two OT terminals at the DC terminal with a Phillips screwdriver, as shown in Fig. 3.89 (2).
- Fix the DC power cable and the power module with the removed OT terminals to prevent the power cable from loosening. Connect the NEG(−) terminal of the DC power board, as shown in Fig. 3.89 (3).
- Assemble the protective cover of the DC terminal on the power module with a Phillips screwdriver, as shown in Fig. 3.89 (4).

(d) Pay attention to the following points when connecting and binding signal cables.

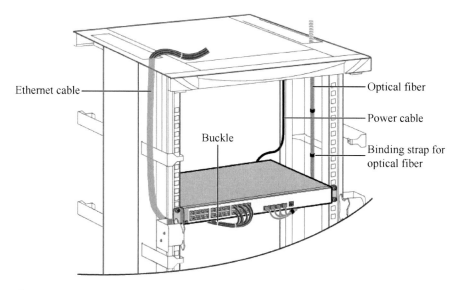

Fig. 3.90 When the cable connection is completed

   (i) The cable buckles should be even spaced. Within the cabinet, the interval of the cable buckles should not exceed 250 mm.

  (ii) The cable buckles should be moderate tightened, especially the optical fibers should not be bound too tight.

 (iii) Dust caps should be installed for temporarily unused optical fiber connectors, and dust plugs should be installed for temporarily unused optical ports on the devices.

 (iv) Excess optical fibers, cables and network cables should be wound neatly for easy search.

  (v) The connectors made on site must be standardized, firm, reliable and aesthetically pleasing.

 (vi) If there are many cables to be routed, in order to facilitate cabling, you can lay the cables in the cabinet first, and then make the cable connectors for connections with the device. Then, the cable connection is completed as shown in Fig. 3.90.

Note

Figure 3.90 is only for reference, and the specific cabling method should be adjusted according to the actual installation scenario and interface usage.

2. Installation of wireless AP

    Huawei AP7050DE provides high-performance wireless services for large and medium-sized enterprise-level scenarios with high device density (such as mobile office, general education, higher education, etc.), which can be flexibly

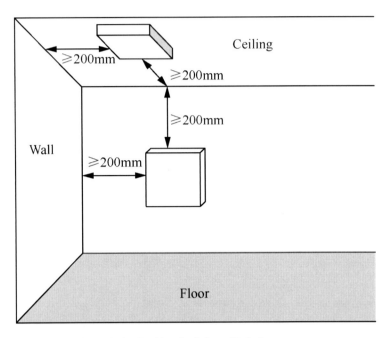

Fig. 3.91 Reference of Installation Position for Indoor AP devices

distributed according to different environments. The following describes the
installation process of wireless AP with Huawei AP7050DE as an example.

(a) Installation preparation

    (i) Read through safety precautions carefully.

        In order to ensure personal and equipment safety, appropriate safety
measures should be taken to avoid personal injury and equipment damage. Place the device in a dry and flat place; avoid the device from contact
with liquid; take dust prevention measures to keep the device clean; do
not place the device and installation tools in the walking area.

    (ii) Determine the installation position.

        Generally, indoor AP device will be directly attached to the wall or
ceiling through a sheet-metal mounting piece, so the specific installation
position of the device will be determined by engineering survey, and at
least 200 mm space will be reserved from the outlet end of the device to
the wall. Please refer to Fig. 3.91 for its installation position.

        The principles for determining the installation position are as follows.

- Minimize the number of obstacles (such as walls) between the AP and
  user terminal.
- Keep the AP away from electronic device that may produce radio
  frequency interference, such as microwave oven or other wireless
  communication device like the AP and antenna.

- The installation position should be concealed as far as possible, so as not to interfere with the daily work and life of residents.
- It is strictly prohibited to install the device under the environment of accumulated water, water seepage, dripping and condensation, and it is necessary to avoid the device from entering water due to cable condensation and water seepage.
- It is strictly prohibited to install the device in an environment with high temperature, dust, harmful gas, flammability, explosion, susceptibility to electromagnetic interference (large radar stations, transmitting stations, substations), unstable voltage, large vibration or strong noise.

(b) Installation of AP7050DE

When installing, if there is a protective film on the surface of the device, it should be torn off before installation to prevent static electricity. There are three installation methods for AP7050DE device: wall-mounted installation, indoor ceiling-mounted installation and indoor T-shaped keel installation. They will be introduced separately below.

(i) The wall-mounted installation requires the use of mounting parts and supporting expansion tubes.

The steps are as follows.

- When fixing the sheet-metal mounting piece, make sure that the arrow in the sign ⬆ is upward.
- Attach the sheet-metal mounting piece to the wall, adjust the installation positions, and mark the positions with a marker, as shown in Fig. 3.92.
- Drill holes at the installation positions with a 6 mm electric drill, with the drilling depth of 35–40 mm, and install expansion tubes to make them flush with the wall surface, as shown in Fig. 3.93.
- Attach the sheet-metal mounting piece to the wall surface, and screw three self-tapping screws into the expansion tubes in turn with a Phillips screwdriver to fasten the sheet-metal mounting piece to the wall surface, as shown in Fig. 3.94.
- Connect the AP device with cables. For details, refer to the cable connection section later. Align the screws on the back of the AP device with the mounting holes on the sheet-metal mounting piece, and push the AP vertically into the mounting piece, as shown in Fig. 3.95. After the shrapnel of the mounting piece is jacked up, press the device down hard. When the "click" sound is heard, the AP is fixed on the sheet-metal mounting piece.

  It should be noted that when the AP is installed in discos, bars and other scenes with severe vibration, M4 × 30 screws should be used to fix the AP tight to the sheet-metal mounting piece to prevent the AP

Fig. 3.92 Mark the installation positions

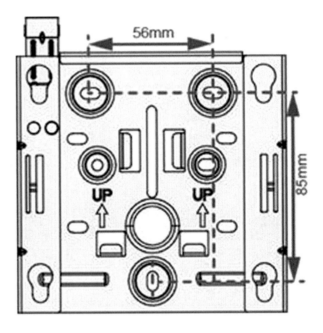

from falling off due to vibration, as shown in Fig. 3.96. Under normal circumstances, this screw need not be installed.

(ii) Indoor ceiling-mounted installation

In ceiling-mounted installation, the ceiling should be able to bear four times of the total weight of the device and sheet-metal mounting piece without being damaged. If the total weight of the device and sheet-metal mounting piece is less than 1.25 kg, the ceiling bearing capacity should be no less than 5 kg.

- Remove the ceiling, determine the positioning point according to the distance between the two mounting holes on the sheet-metal mounting piece, punch holes in the ceiling, and fix the sheet-metal mounting piece to the ceiling (the fastening torque is 1.4 N • m), as shown in Fig. 3.97. The length of screws for the ceiling-mounted installation is 30 mm, which is suitable for ceiling mounting up to 15 mm hole depth. If you need to install it on a thicker ceiling, you need prepare longer screws.
- Connect the cable of the AP. Then align the screws on the back of the AP device with the mounting holes on the sheet-metal mounting piece, and push the AP vertically into the mounting piece, as shown in Fig. 3.98. After the shrapnel of the mounting piece is jacked up, press the device horizontally hard. When the "click" sound is heard, the AP is fixed on the sheet-metal mounting piece.

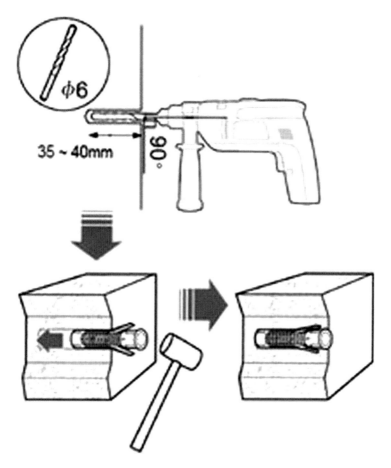

Fig. 3.93 Drill holes at the installation positions

Make sure that the AP device is correctly installed on the mounting piece to avoid falling off. It should be noted that when the AP is installed in discos, bars and other scenes with severe vibration, M4 × 30 screws should be used to fix the AP tight to the sheet-metal mounting piece to prevent the AP from falling off due to vibration, as shown in Fig. 3.99. Under normal circumstances, this screw need not be installed.

(iii) Indoor T-shaped keel installation

In T-shaped keel installation, the keel should be able to bear four times of the total weight of the device and sheet-metal mounting piece without being damaged. If the total weight of the device and sheet-metal mounting piece is less than 1.25 kg, the ceiling bearing capacity should

Fig. 3.94 Wall-mounted
installation

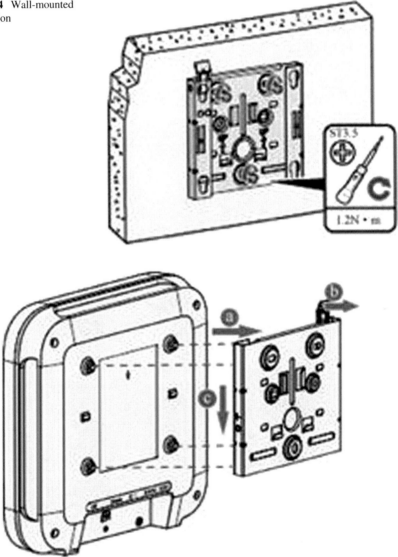

Fig. 3.95 Fix the AP to the wall

be no less than 5 kg. T-shaped keel specifications: thickness
t (0.6 mm $\leq t \leq$ 1.0 mm) and width w (24 mm $\leq w \leq$ 29 mm).

- Disassemble the two ceilings near the T-shaped keel, first tighten the
  clamping piece to the sheet-metal mounting piece with screws, then
  adjust the clamping piece so that the T-shaped keel is fastened

Fig. 3.96 Reinforced
Installation to the wall in
special scenes

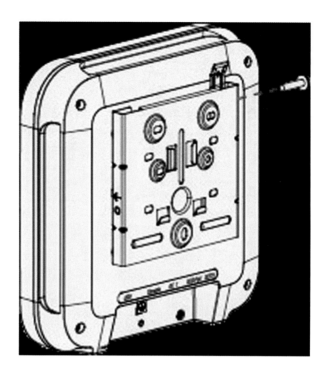

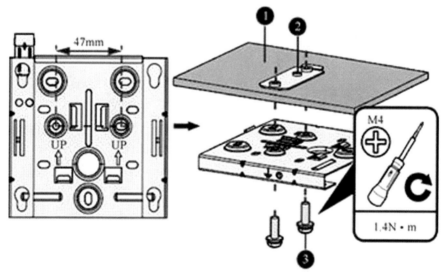

Fig. 3.97 Mark positioning points and drill holes. (1) Ceiling; (2) Clamping piece; (3) M4 × 30
screw

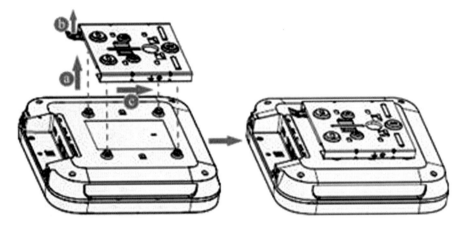

Fig. 3.98 Fix the AP

Fig. 3.99 Reinforce the installation

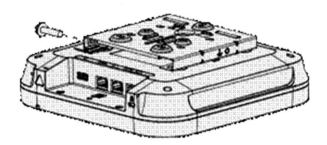

between the clamping piece and the sheet mounting lock, and finally lock the screws on the clamping piece, as shown in Fig. 3.100.

• Connect the cable of the AP. Then align the screws on the back of the AP device with the mounting holes on the sheet-metal mounting piece, and push the AP vertically into the mounting piece. After the shrapnel of the mounting piece is jacked up, press the device horizontally hard. When the "click" sound is heard, the AP is fixed on the sheet-metal mounting piece, as shown in Fig. 3.98.

It is important to note that this step can only lock the screw in the middle of the clamping piece. You can select the appropriate position to lock the screw according to the keel width. Make sure that the AP device is correctly installed on the mounting piece to avoid falling off.

When the AP is installed in discos, bars and other scenes with severe vibration, M4 × 30 screws should be used to fix the AP tight to the sheet-metal mounting piece to prevent the AP from falling off due to vibration, as shown in Fig. 3.99. Under normal circumstances, this screw need not be installed.

Fig. 3.100 Reinforce the
T-shaped keel installation.
(1) T-shaped keel;
(2) M4 × 30 screws;
(3) Clamping piece;
(4) Sheet-metal mounting
piece

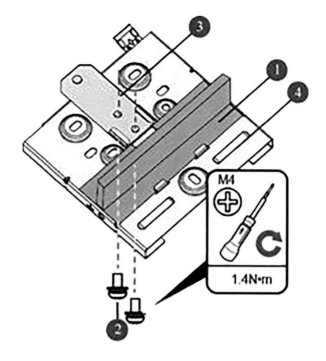

Fig. 3.101 External
connection interface of the
AP device

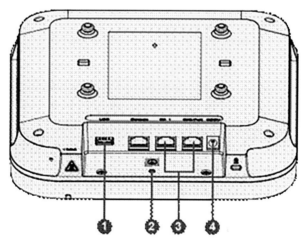

(c) Cable connection

(i) The external connection interface of the AP device is shown in Fig. 3.101, and the cable connected to the interface is described in Table 3.24.

(ii) When connecting cables, waterproof bends must be made to prevent condensation from flowing into device ports along cables, causing device damage. The specific method is as follows.

Table 3.24 Description of cable connected to the interface

Cable or device	Requirements
USB flash drive	Used to connect USB flash disk to expand storage, with external output power up to 2.5 W
Grounding cable	Used for grounding device with grounding cable
Network cable	1. Must use Cat 5e cables or higher grades. 2. The network cable for service cannot be inserted into the Console port, otherwise the device may be damaged during PoE power supply. The length of network cable cannot exceed 100 m. 3. When the AP is connected to Ethernet, it is necessary to ensure that the Ethernet cable is normal. If the network cable is abnormal (e.g., RJ short circuit), the AP may fail to power on, and the AP state is abnormal. Therefore, before connecting the network cable, you can use the network tester to check whether the network cable is normal. If it is abnormal, it should be replaced in time
DC power adapter	When using DC power supply, please use the matching power adapter, otherwise the device may be damaged

- The device service port faces down and the network cable goes up, as shown in Fig. 3.102 (1).
- The device service port faces up and the network cable goes up, as shown in Fig. 3.102 (2).
- The device service port keeps horizontal and the network cable goes up, as shown in Fig. 3.102 (3).

(iii) Pay attention to the following points when binding cables.

- Different types of cables should be laid separately, at least 30 mm apart, and it is forbidden to cross or intertwine with each other. Different types of cables should be routed in parallel or separated by special spacers.
- After binding, the cable after binding should be close to each other, keep straight and tidy, without skin damage.
- When installing the cable buckles, the cable buckles should face the same direction. The buckles in the same position should be kept on the same level, and all buckles should be trimmed flat.
- After the installation of cables is completed, labels or signs must be attached.

(iv) Connect the grounding cable (optional).

Use grounding screws and grounding cables to ground the device. Grounding cables should be made on site, with M4 OT terminals on the device side and M6 OT terminals on the grounding bar side, which can also be determined according to the site conditions. The cable length should be determined according to the site conditions to avoid waste.

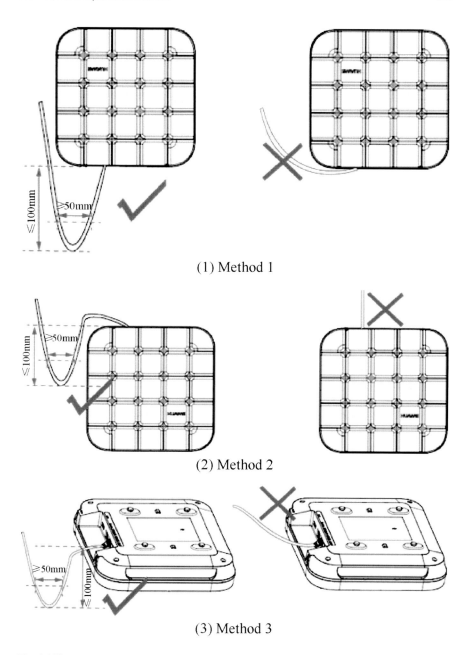

(1) Method 1

(2) Method 2

(3) Method 3

Fig. 3.102 How to make the waterproof bend

3.2.4 Installation of Firewalls

Huawei USG6000 Series Firewalls adopt a newly designed 10 Gigabit multi-core hardware platform with excellent performance. This series of firewalls provides high-density slots for expansion card, and supports rich types of interface card, realize massive service processing. Its key components are redundantly configured. With the mature link conversion mechanism and the built-in electric Bypass card design, it provides users with long-time trouble-free hardware guarantee, creating a sustained office environment. This section will provide an introduction with Huawei USG6310 as an example.

1. Installation preparation

    Before installing the USG device, please fully understand the the necessary precautions and requirements to follow, and prepare the tools needed in the installation process.

    (a) Improper operation may cause personal injury or device damage when installing the USG device. To protect personal and device safety, please follow the signs on it and any safety precautions in the manual when installing, operating and maintaining the device. Precautions, cautions, warnings and hazards shown in the manual do not cover all safety precautions to be followed, only as supplementary precautions.

    (b) Before installing a USG device, please check whether the installation environment meets the requirements to ensure the normal operation and extended service life of the device.

    (c) The following tools are needed in the installation of the USG device: Phillips screwdriver (M3–M6), socket wrench (M6, M8, M12, M14, M17, and M19), needle-nose pliers, diagonal pliers, etc.

2. Installation of the main body

    USG6310/6320/6510-SJJ supports three installation scenarios, namely, installation in a 19-inch (about 48 cm) standard cabinet, installation on a workbench and installation on a wall.

    (a) Scenario 1: Installation in a 19-inch (about 48 cm) standard cabinet.
        The steps are as follows.

        (i) Fix the mounting ears to the device case. Fix the mounting ears to both sides of the device case with a Phillips screwdriver and M4 screws, as shown in Fig. 3.103.

        (ii) Install the floating nuts The installation position of the floating nut is shown in Fig. 3.104.

        (iii) Install the floating nut matched with the M6 screw, as shown in Fig. 3.105.

Fig. 3.103 Fix the mounting ears to the device case

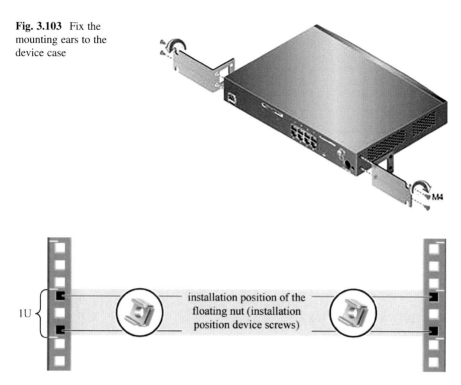

Fig. 3.104 The installation position of the floating nut

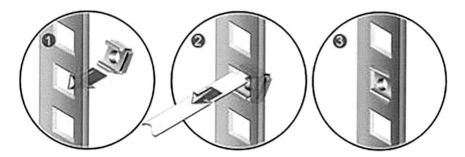

Fig. 3.105 Install the floating nut matched with the M6 screw

(iv) Install the device into the cabinet. Set the M6 screws into the two lower floating nuts with the Phillips screwdriver. Do not tighten them first, but keep the screws exposed about 2 mm, as shown in Fig. 3.106.

(v) Hold the device and move it into the cabinet slowly, so that the mounting ears on both sides hooks the exposed part of the M6 screws. Tighten

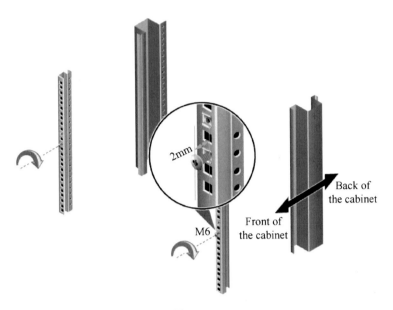

Fig. 3.106 Install the M6 screw into the cabinet

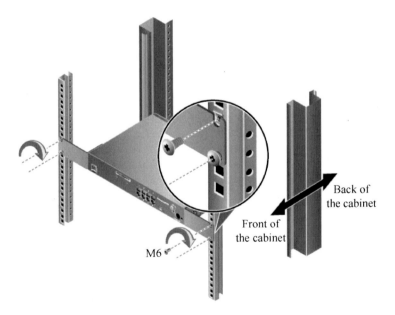

Fig. 3.107 Install the device into the cabinet

the exposed M6 screws with the Phillips screwdriver, and then install the upper M6 screws to fix the device to the cabinet with the mounting ears, as shown in Fig. 3.107.

Fig. 3.108 Place the USG
device on the clean
workbench

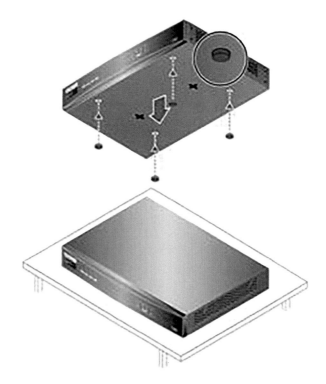

After the installation is completed, the following checks should be made: the USG device is firmly placed in the cabinet; there are no objects around the USG that hinder the heat dissipation.

(b) Scenario 2: mounting to workbench.

If there is no cabinet, the USG 6310/6320/6510-SJJ can be installed on the workbench. The USG device comes with four adhesive pads, which can be attached to the bottom of the USG to ensure the smooth contact between the device and the workbench, and avoid scratches caused by friction between the surface of the USG and the workbench.

The steps are as follows.

(i) Paste the four adhesive pads onto the circular embossing areas at the bottom of the USG device.

(ii) Place the USG device on the clean workbench, as shown in Fig. 3.108.

After the installation is completed, the following checks should be made: the USG device is firmly placed on the workbench; this is a space of more than 10 mm around the USG for heat dissipation and there are no objects around the USG that hinder the heat dissipation.

(c) Scenario 3: mounting to wall.

Fig. 3.109 Mark the
mounting holes

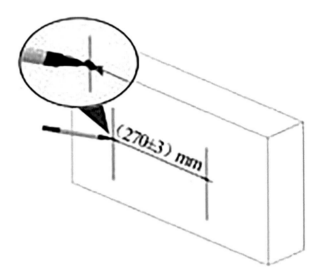

(d) When there is no cabinet, the USG6310/6320/6510-SJJ can also be installed on the wall, but the wall must be a load-bearing wall. The installation height of the device is recommended to facilitate the check of the indicator light status.

(e) The steps are as follows.

   (i) Position the two mounting holes on the wall with a ruler measure and mark them with a marker pen. The two holes should be in a horizontal line, as shown in Fig. 3.109.

   (ii) Drill holes and mount the screws The mounting screws should be tightened firmly and reliably, otherwise the router may fall down due to the tension when the cable is connected. Choose the drill bit according to the outer diameter of the screw, and the outer diameter should not exceed 4 mm. Knock the plastic expansion tubes into the mounting holes respectively. Align the screws to the plastic expansion tubes, and then screw them into the wall using a Phillips screwdriver with 2 mm body of the screws left outside the wall, as shown in Fig. 3.110.

   (iii) Mount the USG to the wall Align the mounting holes on the back of the USG device with the screws to hang the USG on the wall. USG supports two-way wall-mounted installation. To prevent device damage caused by water infiltration at the interfaces, it is recommended to install the device with the interface facing down, as shown in Fig. 3.111.

After the installation is completed, the following checks should be made: the USG device is firmly mounted on the wall; this is a space of more than 10 mm around the USG for heat dissipation and there are no objects around the USG that hinder the heat dissipation.

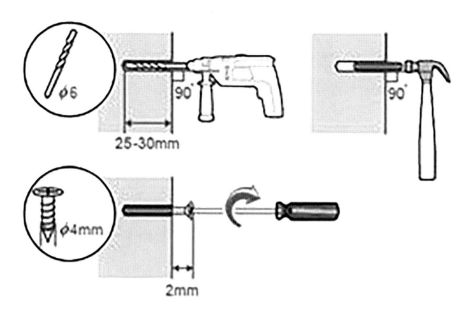

Fig. 3.110   Drill holes and mount the screws

Fig. 3.111   Mount the USG to the wall

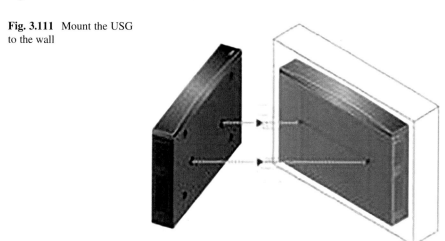

3. Connect the power adapter.

   The USG6310/6320/6510-SJJ provides a power adapter for power supply. Before connecting the power adapter, prepare an AC power cable for connecting the power adapter to the power supply of the equipment room.

   The steps are as follows.

   (a) Confirm that the protective grounding cable is well grounded.
   (b) Insert the cable buckle into the jack beside the power socket.

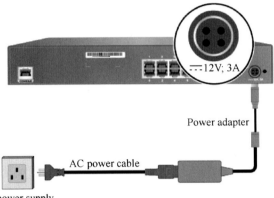

AC power supply

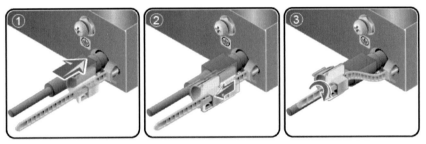

Fig. 3.112   Connect the power adapter

(c) Connect the power adapter.

(d) Insert the C13 plug of AC power cable into C14 socket end of the power adapter. Insert the 4PIN plug of the power adapter into the power socket on the back panel of the USG, and adjust the cable buckle to the appropriate position.

(e) Cover the cable of the power adapter with the cable buckle, and adjust the buckle to fasten the power adapter.

(f) Insert the other end of the AC power cable into the AC power socket or the output socket of AC power-supplied device, as shown in Fig. 3.112. The USG has no power switch. Whether USG device is powered on immediately is determined by the switch of power supply.

After the power cable is connected, the following checks should be completed: check that the connection between the power cable and the power interface is firm and reliable. If more than one USG device is installed, attach a label with code to both ends of each power cable for identification.

4. Power on and off

To ensure that the USG6310/6320/6510-SJJ can start normally and ensure personal and device safety, please operate in strict accordance with the power-on and power-off requirements. Before the device is powered on, check that the

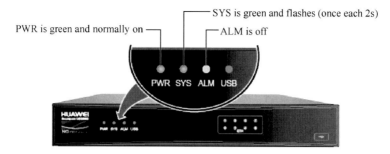

Fig. 3.113 Indicator state when the USG is running normally

power cable and the protective grounding cable are connected; and confirm the position of the power supply switch in the equipment room, so as to cut off the power supply in time in case of accident.

The steps are as follows.

(a) Power on the device. Turn on the power switch of the power supply device, and then the USG starts. After the USG is started, check whether the USG is running normally according to the indicator light status of the front panel. When the USG is running normally, the indicator LEDs are displayed as shown in Fig. 3.113.

(b) Power off the device. If the device is configured, save the data before powering off the device, otherwise the configuration will be lost. If the device is not used for a long time, it is necessary to turn off the power switch. After the device is powered off, keep it properly according to the storage requirements.

3.2.5   Installation of the Network Management Device

The following takes the RH2288H V3 Server as an example to explain the installation steps of network management device.

1. Installation preparation

   First of all, tools and accessories should be prepared, including Phillips screwdriver, flat-head screwdriver, mounting bar for floating nuts, stripping pliers, diagonal pliers, cable clamp, tape measure, multimeter, network tester, binding strap, ESD wrist strap or ESD gloves, etc.

2. Installation of the server

   (a) Install the server on the retractable slide rail (for cabinets of all manufacturers).

Fig. 3.114  Install the server

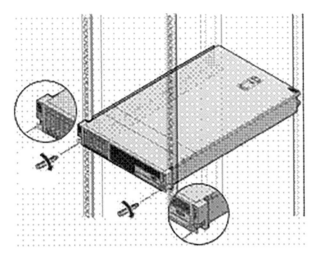

Stacking servers directly will cause damage to the servers, so the servers must be installed on the slide rails. Retractable slide rails are divided into left and right retractable slide rails. The slide rail marked with "L" is the left slide rail, and that marked with "R" is the right slide rail. Do not install them in the wrong direction. The front and rear mounting bars in the cabinet for the RH2288H V3 Server should be 543.5–848.5 mm apart. By adjusting the length of the retractable slide rails, the server can be installed in cabinets with different depths.

The steps are as follows.

(i) Install the retractable slide rails according to the installation instructions.
(ii) At least two people lift the server horizontally, place the server on the retractable slide rails and push it into the cabinet. If the disk is pulled out during transportation, the position of each disk slot should be recorded, and the disk should be inserted after the installation, otherwise the pre-installed system will fail to start. When pushing the server into the cabinet, care should be taken to avoid the server bumping into the mounting bars of the cabinet.
(iii) When the mounting ears on both ends of the server cling to the mounting bars of the cabinet, tighten the loose screws on the mounting ears to fix the server, as shown in Fig. 3.114.

(b) Install the server on the L-shaped slide rail (only for Huawei cabinets).

Stacking servers directly will cause damage to the servers, so the servers must be installed on the slide rails. The L-shaped slide rail is only suitable for Huawei cabinets.

The steps are as follows.

Fig. 3.115 Install the
floating nuts

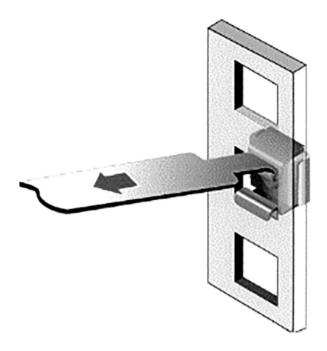

(i) Install the floating nuts, as shown in Fig. 3.115.
Floating nuts are installed inside the cabinet to provide screw holes for the M6 screws used to fix the server.

- Fasten the lower end of the floating nut in front of the cabinet and fix it on the mounting hole of the guide groove.
- Pull the upper end of the floating nut with the mounting bar and install it on the mounting hole in front of the cabinet.

(ii) Install the L-style slide rails, as shown in Fig. 3.116.

- According to the planned position, place the slide rail horizontally, close to the mounting bar of the cabinet.
- Tighten the fastening screws of the slide rail clockwise.
- Use the same method to install another slide rail.

(iii) At least two people lift the server horizontally, place the server on the retractable slide rails and push it into the cabinet. If the disk is pulled out during transportation, the position of each disk slot should be recorded, and the disk should be inserted after the installation, otherwise the pre-installed system will fail to start. When pushing the server into the cabinet, care should be taken to avoid the server bumping into the mounting bars of the cabinet.

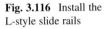

Fig. 3.116 Install the
L-style slide rails

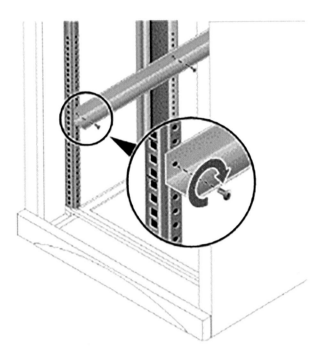

(iv) When the mounting ears on both ends of the server cling to the mounting
     bars of the cabinet, tighten the loose screws on the mounting ears to fix
     the server.

(c) Install the power cable.

   It is forbidden to install the power cable live. Before installing the power
cable, you must turn off the power switch to avoid personal injury. In order to
ensure personal and device safety, please use the matching power cables.

   The steps are as follows.

   (i) Insert one end of the AC power cable into the cable interface of the
        power module on the back panel of the server.
  (ii) Insert the other end of the AC power cable into the AC busbar of the
        cabinet. The AC busbar is located at the back the cabinet and horizon-
        tally fixed on the cabinet. You can select the jack on the nearest AC
        busbar to plug in the power cable.
 (iii) Bind the power cable to the cabinet cable groove with a binding strap, as
        shown in Fig. 3.117.

Fig. 3.117 Install the
power cable

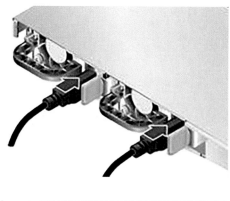

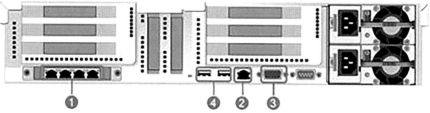

Fig. 3.118 RH2288 H V3 Server interface (rear view)

Table 3.25 Description of RH2288 H V3 Server interface (rear view)

No.	Interface	Explanation
1	Gigabit Ethernet port	Connect the service network
2	MGMT (management) port	Connection maintenance network
3	VGA interface	Connect the monitor
4	USB interface	Connect the mouse, keyboard and other devices

(d) Install the signal cable.

The RH2288 H V3 Server interface (rear view) is shown in Fig. 3.118, and
its description is listed in Table 3.25. Signal cable connection involves the
following situations.

(i) Network cable connection of stand alone system

Connect the network port of the server to the switch according to the
actual networking. For networking, the stand alone system should be
connected to at least one service network port. To remotely manage the
server, connect the MGMT port of the server to the maintenance
network.

(ii) Network cable connection of local high-availability system

The network cable connection of local high-availability system is
shown in Fig. 3.119. Connect the network port of the server to the switch
according to the actual networking. For networking, the local high-

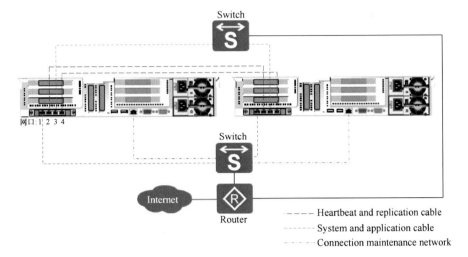

Fig. 3.119 Network cable connection of local high-availability system

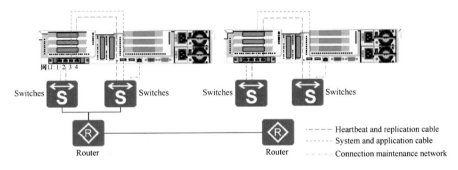

Fig. 3.120 Network cable connection of remote high-availability system

availability system needs to connect four service ports. The network ports 1 and 3 are configured with Bond as the system and application cables, and the network ports 2 and 4 are configured with Bond as the heartbeat and replication cables. The heartbeat and replication cables between the master and standby servers are directly connected, and the two directly connected network cables must be Cat 5e cables no less than 60 m. To remotely manage the server, connect the MGMT port of the server to the maintenance network.

(iii) Network cable connection of remote high-availability system

The network cable connection of remote high-availability system is shown in Fig. 3.120. Connect the network port of the server to the switch according to the actual networking. For networking, the remote high-availability system needs to connect four service ports. The network ports 1 and 3 are configured with Bond as the system and application

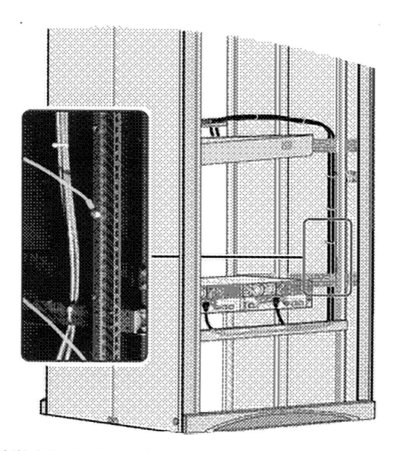

Fig. 3.121 Cabling inside the cabinet

cables, and the network ports 2 and 4 are configured with Bond as the heartbeat and replication cables. To remotely manage the server, connect the MGMT port of the server to the maintenance network.

(iv) Lay the cables.

The cabling inside the cabinet is shown in Fig. 3.121. Note that the network cable should be bound every 20 cm to ensure the cleanliness inside the cabinet. The cabling between the cabinets is shown in Fig. 3.122.

(e) Check upon installation.

Detailed inspection is required after installation, including installation inspection of power cables and signal cables. The checklists are shown in Tables 3.26 and 3.27.

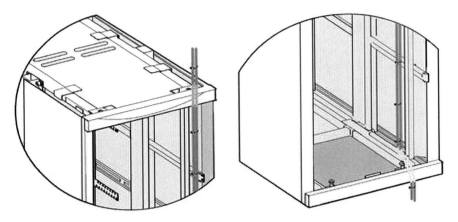

Fig. 3.122 Cabling between the cabinet (lower cabling [left] and upper cabling [right])

Table 3.26 Installation inspection of power cables

No.	Inspection items
1	All power cables and protective ground cables must be copper core cables
2	All power cables and protective ground cables must be a one-piece cable without joint
3	It is not prohibited to set disconnectable devices such as switches and fuses in the electrical connection path of the grounding system
4	GND grounding bar and PGND grounding bar should be connected to the same grounding body
5	Grounding resistance is less than 10 Ω
6	OT terminals of the power cables and protective grounding cables should be welded or crimped firmly
7	The bare wire and OT terminal handle at the connection terminal should be wrapped tightly with insulating tape or sheathed with heat shrinkable sleeve, prevented from being exposed
8	All screws should be tightened, with spring washer or plain washer (note: spring washers and plain washers are strictly forbidden to be reversed)
9	The power cable and grounding cable from the distribution box to connect each functional module, and the protective grounding cable between each module and the PGND busbar of the cabinet are installed correctly and in good contact
10	The power cables and protective grounding cables should be bound separately from other cables
11	Both ends of the power cables and protective grounding cables should be pasted with engineering labels for power cable

3.3   Summary

This chapter introduces the common routers, switches, WLAN devices, firewalls and network management devices in the network, and takes Huawei devices as examples to introduce the corresponding hardware and specific installation steps in detail. Through the study of this chapter, readers should have known the hardware

Table 3.27 Installation inspection of signal cables

No.	Inspection Items
1	All signal cables must be a one-piece cable, with no breakage and fracture
2	The signal cable plug must be intact, and installed correctly and firmly
3	The signal cables should keep an appropriate amount of redundancy at the plugs for easy plugging and unplugging
4	The signal cables should keep an appropriate amount of redundancy at turns, and the turning radius should meet the requirements for the cables
5	The cabling of the signal cables should follow the principle of "left cable goes left, and right cable goes right"
6	The signal cables should be bound separately from the power cables
7	All thread buckles shall be cut flat at the locking point.
8	The signal cable should be bound neatly with even-spaced, moderate-tightened and same-oriented buckles
9	Cables with farther plugs shall be arranged on the outer ring of the harness; otherwise, they should be arranged inside the harness. Cables shall not be laid crosswise, but shall be well-organized and routed smoothly

knowledge of common network devices, and been able to independently complete the installation of network hardware.

3.4 Exercise

1. Huawei routers can be classified into () by appearance.

    A. Case-shaped routers
    B. Chassis-shaped routers
    C. Backbone-layer routers
    D. Access layer

2. The number "48" in the model of Switch S5730S-H48T4XC-MA indicates ().

    A. Network positioning
    B. Switch sub-series
    C. Industrial symbol
    D. Number of downlink interfaces

3. The sequence of steps for installation of a case-shaped router is ().

    A. Power on and off
    B. Installation preparation
    C. Router connection
    D. Installation of the main body of the case-shaped router

    A. bdca   B. adbc   C. cadb   D. abcd

4. The sequence of steps for installation of the firewall is ().

   A. Power on and off
   B. Installation of the firewall
   C. Connection of the power adapter
   D. Installation preparation

   A. bcda   B. dbca   C. acdb   D. abcd

5. The sequence of steps for installation of a server is ().

   A. Installation preparation
   B. Installation of the server
   C. Cable laying
   D. Installation of the power cable
   E. Installation of the signal cable.

   A. deabc   B. adebc   C. abdec   D. abcde.

Chapter 4
Basic Knowledge of Network Systems

In the information network system, there are unified rules, standards or conventions that constrain all the connected devices and user terminals involved in communication. The set of these rules, standards or conventions is called protocol. For example, when a terminal user and an operator of a large server communicate in a network, they cannot understand each other's commands because of the different character sets used by their respective devices, so the communication would not be successful. In order to eliminate this communication barrier, a network device or network terminal is required to convert the characters in its private character set to those in the public standard character set before network transmission, and then further convert to the characters in the private character set of the destination terminal after arrival.

In Chap. 3, the reader is introduced to the common network connection devices in the communication network, as well as their installation, adaptation and networking processes. This chapter will mainly introduce the basic knowledge of network system, including the basic knowledge of communication network and a variety of common protocols, the basic knowledge of network address, virtual local area network (VLAN) technology and IP routing principle.

By the end of this chapter, you will

(1) Master the concept of communication network	(4) Master the planning of network address and subnet
(2) Get familiar with the OSI Reference Model	(5) Master the concept of VLAN and basic network configuration
(3) Get familiar with the TCP/IP protocol stack	(6) Master the principle of routing and static routing

© The Author(s) 2023
Huawei Technologies Co., Ltd., *Construction, Operation and Maintenance of Network System(Junior Level)*, https://doi.org/10.1007/978-981-19-3069-0_4

4.1 Basic Knowledge of Communication Network

The so-called communication is the communication and transmission of information between people through some media. A network is a data link that physically connects isolated workstations or hosts. As the physical connection of each isolated device, the communication network is to realize the information exchange and transmission between people, or between human and computers, or between computers, so as to achieve the purpose of information exchange and resource sharing.

4.1.1 Overview of Communication Network

All around us, there are networks all the time, including the telephone network, television network, computer network and so on. One of the most typical is the computer network, which combines the technology of computer and communication. These two fields cooperate closely, and complement and influence each other, promoting the development of computer network together. For the centuries before the birth of modern communication technology, interpersonal communication can only be limited to face-to-face communication, smoke signals, courier stations, flying pigeons and other restricted means. But with today's advanced technologies, the convenience brought by instant communication is like a "magic" beyond the imagination of ancient people.

Before the advent of computer networks, computers were stand-alone devices that did not cooperate or interact with each other. Later, the combination of computer and communication technologies began to exert profound impact on the way computer systems are organized, making it possible for computers to access each other. In the process that different types of computers communicate with each other through the same type of communication protocol, the computer network arises at the historic moment.

1. The development of computer networks began in the 1960s. At that time, a network was mainly a low-speed serial connection based on the host architecture, which provided application execution, remote printing and data service functions. IBM System Network Architecture (SNA) and the X.25 public data networks offered by enterprises other IBM are typical examples of this type of network. In those days, the US Department of Defense funded the establishment of a packet switching network called ARPANET, which is the prototype of today's Internet.
2. By the 1970s, a business computing model dominated by the personal computer had emerged. At first, personal computers were stand-alone devices. Later, business computing requires a large number of terminal devices to operate together, so the local area network (LAN) came into being. The LAN greatly reduced the cost of printers and disks for business users.
3. From 1980s to 1990s, the increasing demand for remote computing forced the computer industry to develop a variety of wide-area protocols (including the

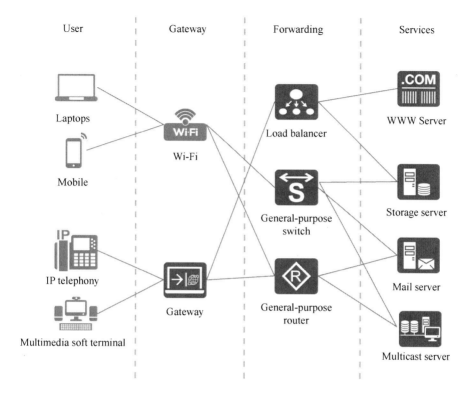

Fig. 4.1   Functions of communication network

TCP/IP and IPX/SPX protocol) for remote connections under different computing modes. The Internet technology was booming in this context, accompanied
with the widening use of the TCP/IP protocol, becoming the standard protocol of
the Internet.

The responsibility of computer network is to, with communication lines, connect
computers and special external equipment (routers, switches, etc.) distributed in
different geographical areas into a large-scale and powerful network system, so
that multitudinous computers can exchange information and share information
resources conveniently.

As shown in Fig. 4.1, in general, the communication network can provide the
following functions.

1. Resource sharing: The emergence of the network simplifies resource sharing,
   enables communication to cross spatial barriers, and makes it possible to transmit
   information anytime and anywhere.
2. Information transmission and centralized processing: Data is transmitted to the
   server through the network, and then sent back to the terminal after centralized
   processing by the server.

3. Load balancing and distributed processing: A typical example is that a large Internet content provider that places WWW servers hosting the same content in multiple locations around the world in order to support more users accessing its website. The provider adopts a specific technology to present the same Web pages to users in different geographies, that is, the pages stored on the server closest to the user. In this way, the load balancing of all servers is realized and the access time is saved for the user.
4. Integrated information service: Multiple-dimension is a major development trend of the network, that is, to provide integrated information services on a set of systems, including text and image, voice, video and so on. With the trend of multiple-dimension, new forms of network applications are emerging in an endless stream, such as instant messaging, streaming media, e-commerce, video conferencing, etc.

4.1.2 Classification and Basic Concepts of Network

1. Classification by geographical coverage
   In view of the different connection mediums, as well as the different communication protocols, the computer networks can be classified in different manners. But in general, then are divided by geographical coverage into LANs, WANs, and MANs, with the coverage between the former two.

   (a) An LAN is a network formed through the interconnection of various communication devices in a small area, whose coverage is generally limited to rooms, buildings or parks. The LAN generally refers to a network distributed within a range of several thousand meters, characterized by short distance, low latency, high data rate and reliable transmission.
   (b) The MAN reaches a medium-scale coverage between the LAN and WAN, and usually functions as a network connection within a city (the distance is about 10 km). At present, the MAN is mainly built with IP technology and ATM technology. A broadband IP MAN is a broadband multimedia communication network within a city (or a county, etc.) that is built according to the needs of business development and competition. It is an extension of the broadband backbone network (such as China Telecom's IP backbone network, China Unicom's ATM backbone network, etc.) within the city.
   (c) The WAN covers a wide area, often a country or even a continent. It provides data communication services over a wide area, primarily for Internet-based LANs. In China, the China Public Packet Switched Data Network (ChinaPAC), China Digital Data Network (ChinaDDN), China Education and Research Network (CERNET) and China Public Computer Internet (ChinaNet), as well as the China Next Generation Internet (CGNI) under building all fall into the category of WANs. The WAN is built to interconnect the LANs scattered over a large area. Its disadvantages are slow data

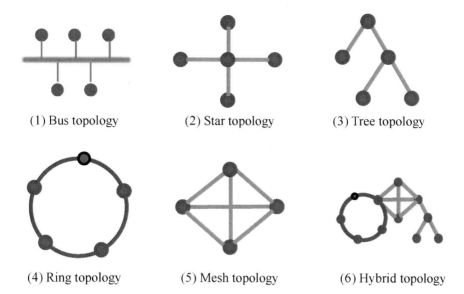

(1) Bus topology   (2) Star topology   (3) Tree topology

(4) Ring topology   (5) Mesh topology   (6) Hybrid topology

Fig. 4.2 Network topologies

transmission (typical rate from 56 Kbit s to 155 Mbit/s), relatively long delay (millisecond level), and inflexible topology structure, which makes it difficult to carry out topology classification. The WAN relies more on telecommunication data network provided by the telecom operators for network connectivity due to its mesh topology.

2. Classification of network topologies

When we talk about network topology, we are talking about the physical layout of a computer network, that is, the structure used to connect a group of devices. So it is often referred to as a topology. The basic network topology models include bus topology, ring topology, star topology and mesh topology. Most networks can be formed by one of these topologies or a mixture of several structures, as shown in Fig. 4.2. Understanding these topologies is a prerequisite for designing networks and solving difficult network problems.

(a) The bus topology adopts a bus to connect all nodes, and the bus is responsible for completing the communication between all nodes. It was widely used in the early LANs. This structure is characterized by simple structure, low cost, easy installation and use, short length of cable consumption and easy maintenance. But it has a fatal drawback—single point of failure. If the bus fails, the whole network will be paralyzed. Since the entire network shares the bandwidth of the bus, the bus network compensates for network overload, if any, with network performance. To overcome these shortcomings, the industry later invented the star topology.

(b) The star topology has a central control point. Devices connected to a LAN communicate with each other through point-to-point connections with hubs or switches. This structure is easy to design and install, allowing a network medium to be connected directly from a central hub or switch to the area where the workstation is located. It is also easy to maintain, and the layout pattern of its network medium makes it easy to modify the network, and to diagnose problems that occur. Therefore, star topology is widely used in LAN construction. However, this structure also inevitably has disadvantages: once the device located at the central control point fails, it is prone to a single point of failure; the network medium can only be connected to one device per segment of the network, so the need for a large number of network mediums drives up the installation costs correspondingly.

(c) The tree topology is a logical extension of the bus topology. In this structure, the host is connected hierarchically, not to form a closed loop structure. This structure starts with a leading terminal, and can then have multiple branching points, each of which can spawn more branches, resulting in a complex tree-like topology.

(d) The ring topology is a closed ring network, connecting each node through an end-to-end communication line. Each device can only communicate directly with one or two nodes adjacent to it. If you need to communicate with other nodes, the information must pass through each device in between in turn. The ring network supports both unidirectional and bidirectional transmission. Bidirectional transmission is the transmission of data in two directions, where the device can directly communicate with two adjacent nodes. The advantages of the ring topology include: simple structure, assigning equal status to all workstations in the system; easy networking, where only simple connection operations are required for node addition and deletion; and real-time control of data transmission, enabling prediction of network performance. The disadvantage is that in a single-ring topology, the failure of any one node will break the normal connection of all the nodes in the ring. Therefore, in practical application, multi-ring structure is generally adopted, so that in case of a single point of failure, a new ring can be formed to ensure the normal operation of the whole structure. Another disadvantage lies in that when one node sends data to another, all nodes between them are invoked to participate in the transmission, thus spending more time forwarding data than in a bus topology.

(e) Mesh topology, also known as full mesh topology, means that any two nodes conducting intercommunication are directly connected through a transmission line. So evidently, this is an extremely safe and reliable solution. The unnecessity for nodes to compete on a common line significantly simplifies communication, so that the intercommunication between any two devices does not involve any other devices. However, a full mesh topology with N nodes requires $N(N-1)/2$ connections, which makes it extremely expensive to build a full mesh topology between a large number of nodes. In addition, when the traffic between two devices is small, the line between them is underutilized, hence the underutilization of many connections. The full mesh topology is seldom used in LAN because of its high cost, complex structure, and difficult management and maintenance. In practical application, partial mesh topology is preferred. In other words, the full mesh topology is used between important nodes, while some connections are omitted for relatively unimportant nodes.

(f) Hybrid topology refers to the mixed use of two or more of the above topology structures, such as star bus + mesh + star ring topology.

3. Circuit switching and packet switching

Circuit switching and packet switching are a pair of important concepts in communication networks.

(a) Circuit switching: The concept of switching originated in the telephone system. What the telephone exchanges adopt is the circuit switching technology. Based on the principle of circuit switching in the telephone network, the circuit switching technology enable the exchange to connect a physical transmission channel between the calling user and the called user when the calling user requests to send data. The advantages of circuit switching are short delay, transparent transmission (namely, no correction or interpretation of the user's data by the transmission channel), and large throughput of information transmission. However, it also shows the disadvantages of fixed bandwidth and low utilization of network resources. In fact, circuit switching is not suitable for the direct terminal communication in the large-scale computer network, since the computer communication features high frequency, high speed, small data volume, large peak-valley traffic difference, and multi-point communication.

(b) Packet switching: Packet switching is a kind of switching for data storage and forwarding. It divides the data to be transmitted into packets of certain length or variable length, so as to store and forward them in the unit of packet. Each packet is marked with the receiving address and the sending address. In this way, a packet is transmitted on the line through the dynamic multiplexing technology, thus the bandwidth being multiplexed and the network resources being utilized more efficiently. Packet switching can prevent any user from monopolizing a transmission line for a long time, so the channel bandwidth can be fully utilized, and the parallel interactive communication can be realized. IP telephony is a new type of telephony that uses the packet switching technology, so it costs much less than traditional telephony to make calls. But packet switching introduces longer end-to-end delays because data is split into packets and consequently network devices need to forward packets one by one. This approach actually requires more bandwidth resources for a certain volume of effective data, because each packet carries additional address information. In addition, data from multiple communication nodes multiplexes the same channel, so a sudden influx of data may cause channel congestion. Due to these characteristics, packet-switched

Fig. 4.3 Standard protocol

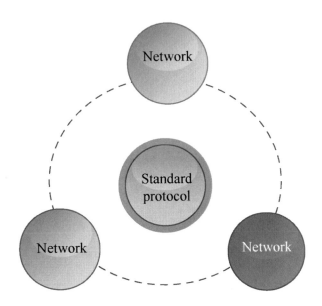

network devices and protocols need to develop the ability to handle addressing, forwarding, congestion, etc., which puts a higher demand on the processing capabilities and complexity of these devices.

4. Protocols and standards

TCP/IP, IEEE 802.1, G.952 and other such words are certainly familiar to us. What are they? Here are two concepts related to these terms in communication networks, as shown in Fig. 4.3.

(a) Protocol A network protocol is a set of formats and conventions that are made in advance for both sides of communication to understand and abide by each other, so as to enable data communication between different devices in a computer network. A network protocol is a normative description of a set of rules and conventions that define the way in which information is exchanged between network devices. Network protocol is the basis of computer network, which requires that only network devices that comply with the corresponding protocol can participate in the communication. Any device that does not support the protocol for network interconnection is ineligible to communicate with other devices.

There are many kinds of network protocols, including TCP/IP, IPX/SPX protocol of Novell, SNA protocol of IBM, etc. Today the most popular is the TCP/IP protocol cluster, having become the standard protocol of the Internet.

(b) Standard A standard is a set of rules and procedures that are widely used or officially prescribed. The standard describes the protocol requirements and sets the minimum performance set to guarantee network communication. The

IEEE 802.x standards are the dominant LAN standards. Data communication standards fall into two categories: de facto standards and legal standards.

(i) De facto standards: Standards that have not been recognized by the organizations, but are widely used and accepted in application.
(ii) Legal standards: Standards developed by an officially recognized body.

There are many international standardization organizations have made great contributions to the development of computer networks. They unify the standards of the network, so that the products from each network product manufacturer can be connected with each other. At present, there are several standardization organizations that contribute to the development of the network.

(i) International Organization for Standardization (ISO): It is responsible for the development of standards for large networks, including standards related to the Internet. ISO proposes the Open System Interconnection (OSI) reference model. This model describes the working mechanism of the network, and constructs an easy-to-understand and clearly hierarchical model for the computer network.
(ii) Institute of Electrical and Electronics Engineers (IEEE): It puts forward standards for network hardware, so that network hardware produced by different manufacturers can be connected with each other. IEEE LAN standard, as the dominant LAN standards, mainly defines the IEEE 802. x protocol cluster, among which the IEEE 802.3 is the standard protocol cluster for the Ethernet, the IEEE 802.4 is applicable for the Toking Bus networks, the IEEE 802.5 is for the Toking Ring networks, and the IEEE 802.11 is the WLAN standard.
(iii) American National Standards Institute (ANSI): It mainly defines the standards of fiber distributed data interfaces (FDDIs).
(iv) Electronic Industries Association/Telecomm Industries Association (EIA/TIA): It standardizes network connection cables, such as the RS-232, CAT 5, HSSI, V.24, etc., and defines the layout standards for these cables, such as EIA/TIA 568B.
(v) International Telecom Union (ITU): It introduces the standards of telecommunication network for wide area connection, such as X.25, Frame Relay, etc.
(vi) Internet Architecture Board (IAB): Its Internet Engineering Task Force (IETF), Internet Research Task Force (IRTF) and Internet Assigned Numbers Authority (IANA) are responsible for the definition of various Internet standards, forming the most influential international standardization organization at present.

4.1.3 OSI Reference Model and TCP/IP Protocol Cluster

1. OSI Reference Model

   Since the advent of computer networks in the 1960s, communication networks have made great strides. In order to conform to the trend of information technology and compete for the leading positions in the field of data communication network, the global major manufacturers have introduced their own network architecture systems and standards, such as IBM's SNA protocol, Novell's IPX/SPX protocol, Apple's AppleChat protocol and DEC's DECNET protocol. They have also developed different hardware and software for their respective protocols.

   These efforts have undoubtedly promoted the rapid development of network technology and the fast propagation of network equipment types. However, the coexistence of such complex protocols also makes the network society more and more jumbly—most of the network equipment from different manufacturers are not compatible with each other, which makes communication even more difficult. Therefore, the key to solve the compatibility problem between networks is to make the network equipment of each manufacturer compatible with each other. For this reason, ISO put forward the OSI Reference Model in 1984, which soon became the basic model of computer network communication. The OSI Reference Model was designed in line with the following principles.

   (a) Clear boundaries should be maintained between layers for easy understanding.
   (b) Each layer should undertake specific functions.
   (c) The division of layers should facilitate the formulation of international standards and protocols.
   (d) The sufficient layers should be provided to avoid the function overlapping among the layers.

   The OSI Reference Model consists of seven layers, with the first layer at the bottom and the seventh layer at the top. From bottom to top, there are physical layer, data link layer, network layer, transport layer, session layer, presentation layer and application layer, as shown in Fig. 4.4.

   The OSI Reference Model is endowed with the following advantages:

   (a) Simplified network operations;
   (b) Plug-and-play compatibility and standard interfaces to connect different manufacturers;
   (c) Support to all manufacturers to design interoperable network devices, promoting network standardization;
   (d) Separation of the structure to avoid the mutual interference between regional networks due to network changes, so that each regional network can be upgraded separately and quickly;
   (e) Disassembling of complex network problems into simple problems for easy learning and operation.

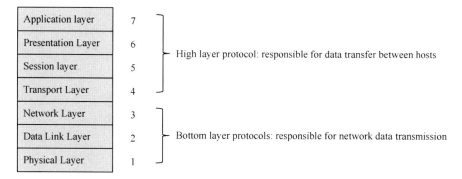

Fig. 4.4   OSI Reference Model

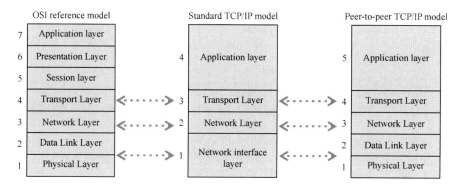

Fig. 4.5   The correspondence between the TCP/IP protocol cluster and the OSI Reference Model

2. TCP/IP protocol cluster

TCP/IP originated from the design and implementation of ARPANET, and then was continuously enriched and improved by the IETF. The name "TCP/IP" is taken from two critical protocols in this protocol cluster: TCP and IP.

Like the OSI Reference Model, the peer-to-peer TCP/IP Model consists of multiple layers responsible for different communication functions. It is a combination of the OSI Reference Model and TCP/IP standard model, including the physical layer, data link layer, network layer, transport layer and application layer from bottom to top. The TCP/IP protocol cluster maintains a clear correspondence with the OSI Reference Model, as shown in Fig. 4.5, where the application layer embraces all the high-level protocols of the OSI Reference Model. The protocols of each layer of the TCP/IP protocol cluster are shown in Table 4.1.

(a) Physical layer and data link layer

The physical layer and data link layer involve the raw bit stream transmitted over the communication channel. They play the role to realize the

Table 4.1 The layers of the TCP/IP protocol cluster

Layer number	TCP/IP layer	Common protocols	Functions
5	Application layer	HTTP, Telnet, FTP, and TFTP	Provides network interfaces for applications
4	Transport layer	TCP and UDP	Establishs end-to-end connections
3	Network layer	IP	Searches IP addresses and routing options
2	Data link layer	Ethernet and PPP	Enables point-to-point, point-to-multipoint communication and error detection in the data link
1	Physical layer	–	Transmits bit stream on the medium to realize the transmission and reception of physical signals

mechanical, electrical, functional and process means needed for data transmission, enabling error detection, error correction, synchronization and other measures, so as to show a fault-free line for the network layer, accompanied with additional flow control.

(b) Network layer

The network layer examines the network topology to determine the best route for transmitting packets, and performs data forwarding. It undertakes the key responsibility is to determine how packets are routed from source to destination. The main protocols used in the network layer include IP, Internet Control Message Protocol (ICMP), Internet Group Management Protocol (IGMP), Address Resolution Protocol (ARP), etc.

(c) Transport layer

The basic function of the transport layer is to enable end-to-end communication for applications between two hosts. It receives data from the application layer, and breaks it up into smaller units for passing them on to the network layer when necessary, ensuring that each piece of information that reaches the other side is correct. The main protocols applicable to the transport layer include Transmission Control Protocol (TCP) and User Datagram Protocol (UDP).

(d) Application layer

The application layer handles specific application details, displays received information, and transmits user data to the lower layer, providing network interfaces to the applications. Application layer contains a large number of commonly used applications, such as Hypertext Transfer Protocol (HTTP), Telnet, File Transfer Protocol (FTP), Trivial File Transfer Protocol (TFTP) and so on.

The similarities and differences between the OSI Reference Model and the TCP/IP protocol cluster are as follows.

(a) Similarities

(i) Both models adopt layered structure and the same working mode, and both require close collaboration between layers.
(ii) Both models include application layer, transport layer, network layer, data link layer and physical layer.
(iii) Both models employ the packet switching technology.

(b) Differences

(i) The TCP/IP protocol cluster classifies the presentation layer and session layer into the application layer.
(ii) The TCP/IP protocol cluster has fewer layers, so the structure is relatively simple.
(iii) The TCP/IP protocol cluster is established with the development of the Internet, based on practice, which is highly reliable; the OSI Reference Model, on the other hand, is based on theory and is born as a guide.

4.2 Basic Knowledge of Network Addresses

Communication network is a generic term for the network formed by the interconnection of network devices. When a networked device communicates on the network, the information sent must contain the location flags of the sending device address and the receiving device address, namely the source address and the destination address. This is just like sending express, to specify the addresses and telephones of the recipient and the sender and other location information. This set of location flags is the MAC address and IP address to be introduced in this section.

4.2.1 MAC Address

This section focuses on the definition and classification of media access control (MAC) addresses. As shown in Fig. 4.6, the MAC address, also known as the physical address or the hardware address, is typically recorded by the network card manufacturer into the EPROM of the network card. It corresponds to the data link layer of the TCP/IP protocol stack and is an address used to define the location of network devices. MAC addresses are used to uniquely identify a network card in the network. If a device has one or more network cards, each card needs a unique MAC address. The MAC address consists of 48 bits, usually represented as a string of 12 hexadecimal digits. Viewed from left to right, the Bits 0 to 23 represent the code applied by a manufacture to an organization such as the IETF to identify the manufacture, known as the organizationally unique identifier (OUI); the Bits 24 to

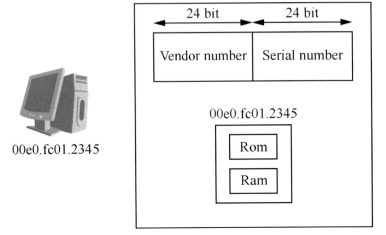

Fig. 4.6 MAC address

47 represent the unique number assigned by the manufacture to represents the network card manufactured by this manufacture, known as the extended unique identifier (EUI).

There are three types of MAC addresses.

1. Physical MAC address: uniquely identifies a terminal in the Ethernet as the globally unique hardware address, also known as unicast MAC address.
2. Broadcast MAC address: consists of all binary 1 s (FF-FF-FF-FF-FF-FF-FF), used to represent all terminal devices in the LAN.
3. Multicast MAC address: the MAC address with Bit 8 as 1 (e.g. 01-00-00-00-00-00) other than broadcast MAC address, which is used to represent a group of terminals in a LAN.

4.2.2 IP Address

This section is a detailed introduction to IP addresses. An IP address is a set of digits used to uniquely identify a device in a computer network. IP addresses can be divided into IPv4 and IPv6 addresses. Unless otherwise stated, all IP addresses mentioned in this book are IPv4 addresses. IPv4 address protocol cluster is the most core class of TCP/IP protocol cluster, which works in the network layer of TCP/IP protocol cluster, also known as logical address.

IPv4 addresses are made up of 32-bit binary digits, but they are represented in dotted decimal notation for ease of identification and memory. This notation represents an IPv4 address as four dotted decimal integers, each of which corresponds to one byte. For example, an IPv4 address represented as 00001010 00000001 00000001 00000010 in binary can be adjusted to 10.1.1.2 in dotted decimal notation.

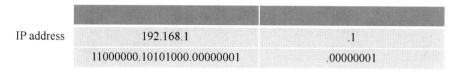

IP address	192.168.1	.1
	11000000.10101000.00000001	.00000001

Fig. 4.7 Two-level IP address structure

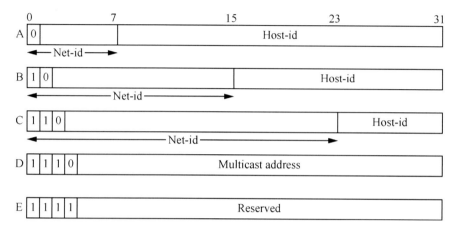

Fig. 4.8 Five IP address classes

The network mask, which is of the same length the IP address bit, 32 bits in total and, when represented in binary, consists of a series of consecutive "1 s" and a series of consecutive "0 s", is also usually represented in dotted decimal notation. The number of "1" in the network mask is regarded as the length of the network mask. For example, the length of the network mask 252.0.0.0 is 6.

A network masks are typically used in conjunction with an IP address. The bit positions with a "1" correspond with the bit positions in the IP address that are part of the NET_ID, and the bit positions with a "0" corresponds the HOST_ID in the IP address. Thus identifying the network ID and host ID in an IP address.

The IP address consists of two parts as shown in Fig. 4.7.

1. Network ID (NET-ID): Used to identify a network. Network ID is the result of converting the IP address and network mask into digits in the binary notation, and then carrying out bitwise calculation.

2. Host ID (HOST-ID): Used to distinguish different hosts within a network. Devices with the same network number are in the same network regardless of their actual physical locations. Host ID is the result of converting the IP address and network mask into digits in the binary notation, performing bitwise NOT operation on the network mask, and then carrying out bitwise calculation.

In order to facilitate IP address management and networking, IP addresses fall into five classes, as shown in Fig. 4.8.

Table 4.2 Address ranges of different IP address classes

IP address class	Address range	Explanation
A	0.0.0.0– 127.255.255.255	The IP address with all host bits as "0" is a network address, used for network routing; that with all host bits as "1" is a broadcast address for broadcasting to all hosts in the network. See Table 4.3
B	128.0.0.0– 191.255.255.255	
C	192.0.0.0– 223.255.255.255	
D	224.0.0.0– 239.255.255.255	Multicast address
E	240.0.0.0– 255.255.255.255	Reserved. 255.255.255.255 is a LAN broadcast address

Table 4.3 Common special IP addresses

Network ID	Host ID	Available as source address?	Available as destination address?	Description
All 0	All 0	Yes	No	Used for this host in this network
All 0	Host-ID	Yes	No	Used for the specific host in the network
127	Any value other than all 0 and all 1	Yes	Yes	Used for loopback addresses
All 1	All 1	No	Yes	Used for Restricted Broadcasts (never to be forwarded)
Net-ID	All 1	No	Yes	Used to broadcast to a network for Net-ID purposes

In Fig. 4.8, Classes A, B and C IP addresses are called host addresses, for identifying devices and hosts in the network; Class D addresses are multicast addresses; and Class E addresses are reserved. The address ranges of different IP address classes is shown in Table 4.2.

Some 32-bit IP addresses are reserved for special purposes and are not available to general users. The common special IP addresses are shown in Table 4.3.

Besides, to address the shortage of IP addresses, some of Class A, B, and C addresses are planned as private IP addresses, that is, the internal network addresses or host addresses that can only be used for the internal networks, rather than public networks. A private IP address can be reused in an internal network, as shown in Table 4.4.

Table 4.4 Private IP addresses	IP address class	Address range
	A	10.0.0.0–10.255.255.255
	B	172.16.0.0–172.31.255.255
	C	192.168.0.0–192.168.255.255

4.3 VLAN

The Ethernet is a CSMA/CD-based data network communication technology that enables sharing communication medium. In case of host gathering, there will be serious problems such as serious conflicts, broadcast flooding, significant performance degradation, and even network unavailability. Although the serious conflicts can be addressed by building LAN interconnection via switches, it still cannot isolate broadcast messages or improve the network quality. In this case, VLAN technology arises at the historic moment. On the basis of not changing the hardware of the switch, it defines the logical grouping in the network by software, becoming the mainstream technology used to divide the broadcast domain.

4.3.1 Ethernet Technology

1. LAN

In the 1970s, with the reduction of the size and price of computers, there emerged a business computing model dominated by personal computers. The complexity of business computing requires resource sharing and cooperative operation of a large number of terminal devices, which leads to the need for network connection of a large number of computer devices, and hence the emergence of LAN.

LAN is short for local area network. It is a computer communication network that connects all kinds of computers, peripherals, databases and so on within a local geographic scope (usually limited to a few kilometers).

The Ethernet is the most common communication protocol for the existing LANs, which defines the cable types and signal processing methods adopted in the LANs. It was first developed by Xerox, and later promoted by Xerox, DEC and Intel to form the DIX (Digital/Intel/Xerox) standard. In 1985, the IEEE 802 Committee incorporated the Ethernet standard into the IEEE 802.3 standard and modified it. Today the Ethernet has formed a series of standards, from the early 10 Mbit/s standard Ethernet, 100 Mbit/s fast Ethernet, 1 Gbit/s Ethernet, all the way to 10 Gbit/s Ethernet. With its continuous evolution, the Ethernet technology has become the mainstream of LAN technology.

In the network, if any node in a domain can receive any frame sent by other nodes in the domain, then the domain is considered as a conflict domain; similarly, if any node in a domain can receive broadcast frames from other nodes in that domain, that domain is a broadcast domain. Common network devices include hubs, switches, routers, etc., as shown in Fig. 4.9. The router is

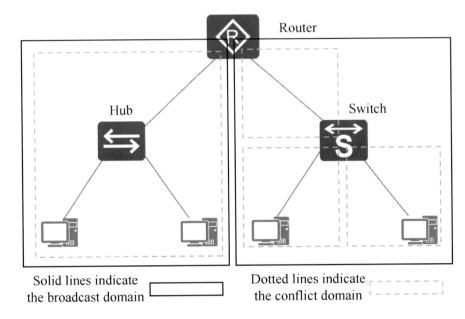

Fig. 4.9 Broadcast domain and conflict domain

used to isolate both the conflict domain and the broadcast domain. The switch can isolate the conflict domain but not the broadcast domain. The hub can isolate neither the conflict domain nor the broadcast domain.

Early Ethernets typically used hubs for networking. In such a network, all computers share a conflict domain, so the more computers there are, the more serious the conflicts is, so the network is less efficient. What's more, such a network is also a broadcast domain, where the more computers that send information in the network, the more bandwidth is consumed by the broadcast traffic. Therefore, this kind of shared Ethernet not only faces both problems of conflict domain and broadcast domain, but also fails to guarantee the security of information transmission. Today, people are using the Ethernet employing switches for networking, so it is called switched Ethernet.

2. Ethernet frame format

The frame format has evolved several times over the course of Ethernet development. To date, there are two standards for encapsulating Ethernet data frames: the Ethernet II Frame format and the IEEE 802.3 Frame format. They are explained separately in the following sections.

(a) Ethernet II Frame format is shown in Fig. 4.10.

The explanations of the fields are as follows.

(i) DMAC (Destination MAC): Destination MAC address, used to determine the recipient of a frame.

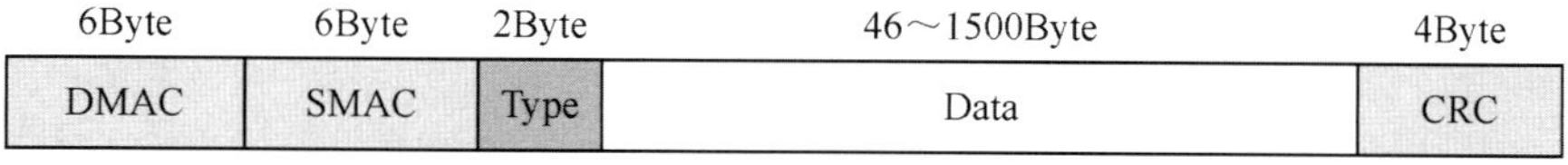

6Byte	6Byte	2Byte	46~1500Byte	4Byte
DMAC	SMAC	Type	Data	CRC

Fig. 4.10 Ethernet II Frame format

(ii) SMAC (Source MAC): Source MAC address, used to identify the sender of a frame.

(iii) Type: The 2-byte type field, used to identify the upper-layer protocol contained in the data field. That is, the field tells the receiving device how to interpret the data field. Since the Ethernet enables multiple protocols to coexist in a LAN, the hexadecimal values set in the type field of Ethernet II Frame provide a mechanism to support multi-protocol transport over the LAN.

- The frame with a type field value of "0x0800" represents the IP frame.
- The frame with a type field value of "0x0806" represents the ARP frame.

(iv) Data: Indicates the specific data encapsulated in the frame. The minimum length of the data field is set to 46 bytes to ensure the frame length of at least 64 bytes. This means that even if you transfer 1-byte information, you must use a 46-byte data field. If the information is less than 46 bytes, the rest of the field must be filled. The length of the data field is limited to 1500 bytes.

(v) CRC (cyclic redundancy check): Cyclic redundancy check field. It provides an error detection mechanism, where each sender calculates a CRC code containing address field, type field, and data field, and fills the calculated CRC code into a 4-byte CRC field.

(b) The IEEE 802.3 Frame format is developed from the Ethernet II Frame, and is seldom used at present. It replaces the type field of the Ethernet II Frame with the length field, and occupies 8 bytes of the data field as the LLC and SNAP fields, as shown in Fig. 4.11.

The explanations of the fields are as follows.

(i) Length: Defines the number of bytes contained in the data field. This field has a value of 1500 or less (that greater than 1500 is identified as the Ethernet II Frame format).

(ii) LLC (logical link control): Consists of destination service access point (DSAP), source service access point (SSAP), and control field.

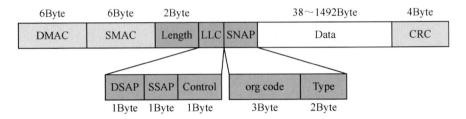

Fig. 4.11 IEEE 802.3 Frame format

(iii) SNAP (sub-network access protocol): Composed of org code and type field. All three bytes of the org code are "0"; the type field holds the same meaning as the type field in an Ethernet II Frame.
(iv) For other fields, please refer to the field description of Ethernet II Frame.

IEEE 802.3 Frames can be divided into different types by the values of the DSAP and SSAP fields. Interested readers may consult the relevant information.

3. How a switch works

The switch port that detects the bit stream in the network first restores the bit stream to the data frame of the data link layer, and then conducts corresponding operation on the data frame. Similarly, the switch port converts data frame into bit stream before sending data. So the switch is a device that operates at the data link layer and controls data forwarding through information in the frame. The switch addresses through the destination MAC address in the data frame, and builds its own MAC address table after learning the source MAC address of the data frame, which stores the mapping relationship between the MAC addresses and the switch port. There are three kinds of actions by the switch on frames: flooding, forwarding and discarding, as shown in Fig. 4.12.

(a) Flooding: The switch forwards the frame coming in from a certain port through all other ports.
(b) Forwarding: The switch forwards the frame coming from a certain port through another port.
(c) Discarding: The switch discards the frame coming in from a certain port.

The following is a general description of the basic workings of a switch.

(a) When a unicast frame enters the switch, the switch queries the MAC address table about the destination MAC address.

(i) If the MAC address cannot be found, the switch performs flooding.
(ii) If it is found, the switch checks whether the corresponding port recorded in the MAC address table is the same as the port via which the frame entered the switch. If not the same, the switch performs forwarding; otherwise, it performs discarding.

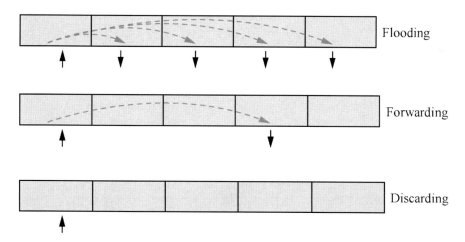

Fig. 4.12 Actions by the switch on frames

(b) When a broadcast frame enters the switch, the switch performs flooding directly, instead of querying the MAC address table.

(c) If it is a multicast frame that enters the switch, the switch has to perform more complex operations, which are beyond the scope of study here, so it will not be described here.

In addition, switches are capable of learning. When a frame enters the switch, the switch checks the source MAC address of the frame, maps the source MAC address to the port where the frame enters, and stores this mapping in the MAC address table.

Here is how the switch works.

(a) In the initial state, the switch does not know the MAC address of the host it connects to, so the MAC address table is empty. As shown in Fig. 4.13, SW1 is in the initial state, and there is no table entry in the MAC address table until the data frame sent by PC1 is received.

(b) When PC1 sends data to PC3, it usually sends ARP request to get the MAC address of PC3 first. The destination MAC address in this ARP request frame is the broadcast address and the source MAC address is the host MAC address. When SW1 receives this frame, it adds the mapping between the source MAC address and the receiver port to the MAC address table. The aging time of MAC address table entry learned by the S Series Switches defaults to 300 s. If the data frame sent by PC1 is received again during the aging time, the aging time of the mapping between the MAC address of PC1 and Port1 stored in SW1 will be refreshed. Thereafter, when the switch receives a data frame with the source MAC address "00-01-02-03-04-AA", it forwards it through Port1, as shown in Fig. 4.14.

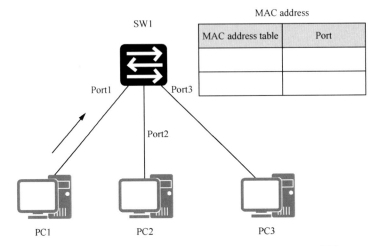

Fig. 4.13 Initial state of the switch

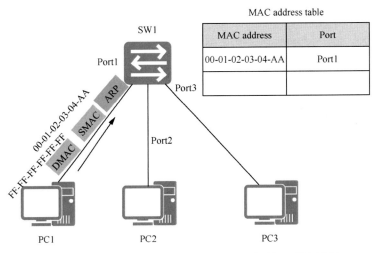

Fig. 4.14 Learn the MAC address

(c) As shown in Fig. 4.15, the destination MAC address of the data frame sent by PC1 is the broadcast address, so SW1 forward this data frame to PC2 and PC3 through Port2 and Port3.

(d) After PC2 and PC3 receive this data frame, they view this ARP data frame, but PC2 sends no reply to this frame, while PC3 processes it and send an ARP

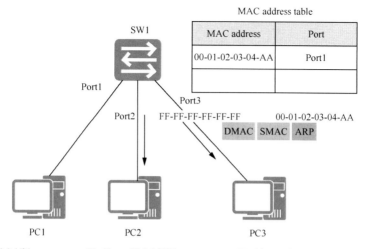

Fig. 4.15 Forward the data frame

reply. The destination MAC address of this reply data frame is the MAC address of PC1, and the source MAC address is the MAC address of PC3. When SW1 receives the reply data frame, it adds the mapping between the frame and the port to the MAC address table. If this mapping already exists in the MAC address table, it is refreshed. SW1 queries the MAC address table, confirms the corresponding forwarding port according to the destination MAC address of the frame, and then forwards this data frame through Port1. As shown in Fig. 4.16, reply to complete the communication process from PC1 to PC3.

After receiving the data frame, the switch learns the frame's source MAC address to maintain its own MAC address table, and query the MAC address table about the frame's destination MAC address, then forwards the frame from the corresponding port. Also, the MAC table will continue to record and update the correspondence between the MAC address of other devices communicating through the switch and the ports, in order to guarantee information transmission.

4.3.2 VLAN Technology

In order to extend the traditional LAN while avoiding the aggravation of the conflicts as more computers are connected, we chose the switch that effectively isolates the conflict domain. The switch uses the switching method that forwards the information from the incoming port to the outgoing port, which overcomes the problem of access conflicts on the shared medium and demotes the conflict domain to the port level.

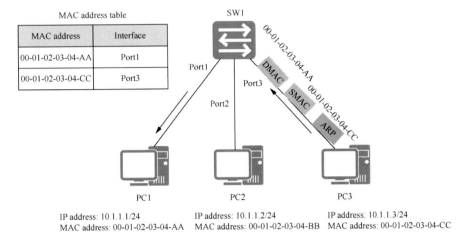

Fig. 4.16 Reply

The problem of conflict domain is solved by the two-layer fast switching realized by the networking through switches, but the problems of broadcast domain and information security still exist.

To reduce the number of broadcast domains, isolation is required between hosts that do not need to visit each other. The router selects the route based on the three-layer IP address information. When connecting two network segments, it effectively suppresses the forwarding of broadcast messages, but costs high. Therefore, people put forward the solution of constructing multiple logic LANs in a physical LAN, namely VLAN.

The solution logically divides a physical LAN into multiple broadcast domains (i.e., multiple VLANs). Hosts within each VLAN can communicate directly with each other, but the communication between VLANs is not supported. In this way, network security is improved by restraining broadcast messaging within a VLAN.

For example, if different enterprises in the same office building establish independent LANs respectively, they must bear high network investment costs; however, if they share the existing LAN in the building, it is difficult the ensure the information security of the enterprises. VLAN allows the enterprises to share LAN facilities, while taking into account their own network information security.

A typical application of a VLAN is shown in Fig. 4.17, where each dotted box represents a VLAN. Three switches are placed in different locations, such as different floors of an office building; each switch is connected to three computers belonging to three different VLANs, respectively, such as different enterprises.

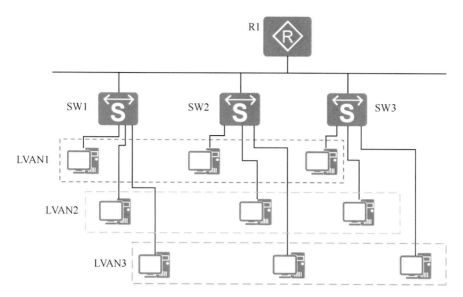

Fig. 4.17 Typical application of a VLAN

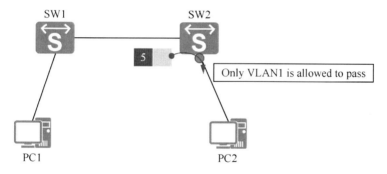

Fig. 4.18 A VLAN communication scenario

4.3.3 Principle of VLAN Technology

In order to realize forwarding control, VLAN tags are added to the Ethernet frames
to be forwarded, and then the switch port is set up to deal with the tags and frames,
for example discarding or forwarding the frames, or adding or removing labels.

When forwarding a frame, the switch checks whether the Ethernet frame can be
forwarded from a port by checking whether the VLAN label carried by the Ethernet
frame is a label that is allowed to pass through a certain port. In the scenario shown in
Fig. 4.18, given that there is a way to label all Ethernet frames sent by PC1 with
"VLAN5", SW1 can query the Layer Two Forwarding table and forward the frame
to the port to which PC2 is connected based on the destination MAC address. Since

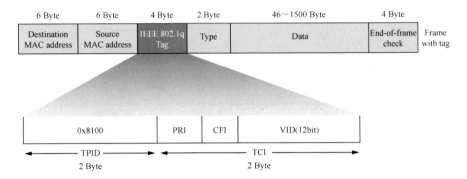

Fig. 4.19 IEEE 802.1q-based Ethernet frame format

"VLAN1 only" is configured on the SW2 port, frames sent by PC1 will be discarded by SW2. This means that the switch supporting VLAN technology does not only rely on the destination MAC address, but also consider the VLAN configuration of the port when forwarding Ethernet frames, thus realizing the control of the Layer Two Forwarding. The following is an in-depth discussion of VLAN technology.

1. Frame format of VLAN

   The IEEE 802.1q standard modifies the format of Ethernet frames by adding a 4-byte IEEE 802.1q Tag between the source MAC address field and the type field, as shown in Fig. 4.19.

   IEEE 802.1q Tag contains four fields, which have the following meanings.

   (a) TPID: 2 bytes long, representing the frame type. A value of 0x8100 indicates an IEEE 802.1q Tag frame. If received by a device that does not support the IEEE 802.1q, it will be discarded.
   (b) PRI: Priority, 3 bits long, representing the priority of the frame. The value ranges from 0 to 7. The higher the value is, the higher the priority is. When congestion occurs to the switch, data frames with higher priority are sent first.
   (c) CFI: Canonical format indicator with a length of 1 bit, indicating whether the MAC address is in a classic format. A CFI of 0 indicates classic format and a CFI of 1 indicates non-classic format. It is used to distinguish between Ethernet frames, FDDI frames, and Toking Ring frames. In the Ethernet, the CFI has a value of 0.
   (d) VID: VLAN ID, with a length of 12 bits, representing the VLAN that the frame operates on. The configurable VID value ranges from 0 to 4095, but the values "0" and "4095" are reserved as specified in the protocol, so unavailable to the user.

      With regard to VLAN tags, Ethernet frames come in the following two formats in a switched network environment.

      (i) Ethernet frames without 4-byte tags are called standard Ethernet frames, which are untagged data frames.

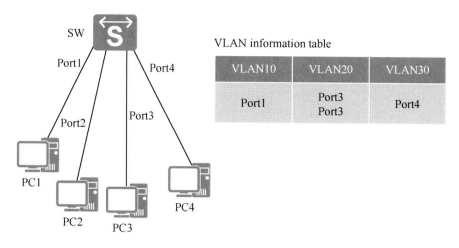

VLAN10	VLAN20	VLAN30
Port1	Port3 Port3	Port4

Fig. 4.20 VLAN allocation based on port

(ii) Ethernet frames with 4-byte tags are called tagged Ethernet frames, which are tagged data frames.

2. Allocation of VLANs

The VLANs can be allocated via the following five approaches, Among which, the port-based approach is the most common way.

(a) Port-based approach

In the port-based approach, VLANs are allocated by the port No. of switching equipment, as shown in Fig. 4.20. The network administrator configures different port default VID (PVID) for each port of the switch. When a data frame without a VLAN tag enters the switch port, if a PVID is configured on the port, the data frame will be labeled with the PVID. If the incoming frame has VLAN tag, the switch will not add VLAN tag, even if the port is configured with a PVID. Handling VLAN frames depends on the port type.

By allocating the VLANs based on ports, the grouping members can be defined very simply, but VLANs need to be reconfigured whenever members move.

(b) MAC address-based approach

In the MAC address-based approach, VLANs are allocated based on MAC addresses of devices connected to switch ports. After the network administrator configures the mapping table of MAC address and VID, if the switch receives untagged frames (without a VLAN tag), VID will be added according to the table.

In this way, there is no need to reconfigure the VLAN when the physical location of the end user changes. This improves the security of end users and the flexibility of access.

(c) Subnet-based approach

When the switching equipment receives untagged data frame, the VID to be added is determined according to the IP address information in the packet.

The subnet-based approach reduces the workload of network administers and improves the convenience of network management by transmitting packets sent from designated network segments or IP addresses in designated VLAN.

(d) Protocol-based approach

According to the protocol (cluster) type and encapsulation format of the packets received by the port, different VIDs are assigned to the packets.

When VLANs are allocated based on protocol, the service types provided in the network can be bound with VLANs to facilitate management and maintenance.

(e) Policy-based approach

This approach allocates VLANs based on the combination of MAC address, IP address and port. To allocate VLANs in this way, the MAC address and IP address of the terminal must be configured on the switch and associated with the VLAN. Only qualified terminals can join the specified VLAN. It is forbidden to modify the IP address or MAC address after the terminal meeting the policy joins the specified VLAN, otherwise it will cause the terminal to exit from the specified VLAN.

After VLAN allocation based on policy and successful VLAN allocation, users are forbidden to change IP address or MAC address, hence the high security. Compared with other VLAN allocation methods, VLAN allocation based on policy is the approach of the highest priority.

When a device supports multiple allocation approaches, the priority of the approaches is as follows: policy-based (highest priority) -> subnet-based -> protocol-based -> MAC address-based -> port-based (lowest priority). The port-based approach is the most common way currently.

3. Forwarding process of VLAN

VLAN technology realizes the control of packet forwarding through the tags in Ethernet frames and VLAN configuration of switch ports. Suppose the switch has ports A and B, and Port A receives Ethernet frames. If the forwarding table shows that the destination MAC address exists under Port B, whether the frame can be forwarded from Port B after VLAN is introduced depends on the following two key points:

(a) whether the VID carried by the frame is created by the switch;
(b) whether the destination port allows the frame carrying the VID to pass.

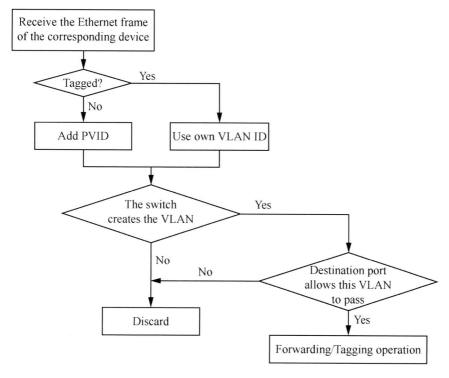

Fig. 4.21 Forwarding process

The forwarding process is shown in Fig. 4.21. In the process of forwarding, tag operation includes the following two types.

(a) Tagging: When the port receives untagged data frames, it tag the data frames with PVIDs.
(b) Untagging: VLAN tag information in the frames is deleted and sent to the opposite device in the form of untagged data frame.

Note

Under normal circumstances, the switch will not change the VID value in the tagged data frames. However, special services supported by some devices may provide the function of changing VIDs, which is beyond the scope of this book.

4.3.4   VLAN Interface Types

In order to improve the processing efficiency, the switches always use tagged data frames internally and handle them in a unified way. When an untagged data frame enters a switch port, if the port is configured with a PVID, the data frame will be marked with the PVID of the port. If the data frame is tagged, the switch will not tag the data frame with the VLAN tag even if the port is configured with a PVID. Depending on the different port types, the switch processes frames differently. The following will introduce three different VLAN port types (see Fig. 4.22).

1. Access port: Generally used to connect with user terminals (such as user hosts, servers, etc.) that cannot recognize VLAN tags, or when it is not necessary to distinguish different VLAN members. It can only send and receive untagged frames, and can only add unique VLAN tag to untagged frames.
2. Trunk port: Generally used to connect switches, routers, APS and voice terminals that can send and receive both tagged frames and untagged frames. It allows multiple data frames to pass with tags, but only one data frame without tag is allowed when the data frames are sent out from such ports (i.e., to strip the tags).
3. Hybrid port: Used to connect user terminals (such as user hosts, servers, etc.) and network equipment that cannot recognize VLAN tags, or to connect switches and routers, and voice terminals and APS that can send and receive both tagged frames and untagged frames. It allow multiple data frames to pass with tags, and allow frames sent from such ports to be configured as some with VLAN tags (i.e., not to strip the tags) and some without tags (i.e., to strip the tags) as required.

Many application scenarios support the commonality of Hybrid ports and Trunk ports, but some application scenarios only support Hybrid port. For example, in the scenario where one port is connected to different VLAN segments, Hybrid port must be used, because one port needs to add tags to multiple untagged packets.

Table 4.5 compares the above three different VLAN port types.

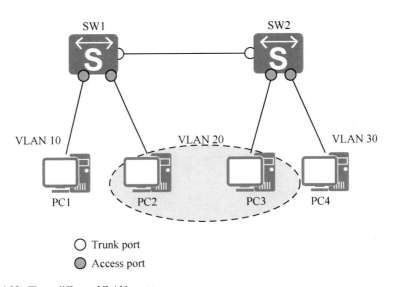

Fig. 4.22 Three different VLAN port types

Table 4.5 Comparison of the three different VLAN port types

Port type	Received frame (IN)		Sent frame (OUT)
	Untagged data frame	Tagged data frame	
Access	Receive after it is configured with the PVID of this port	Check whether the VID carried by the frame is the same as the port PVID If so, receive it; if no, discard it	Send after stripping the tag
Trunk	Configure with the port PVID and check whether the PVID is the VID allowed by the port If so, receive it; if no, discard it	Check whether the VID carried by the frame is that allowed by the port If so, receive it; If no, discard it	Check whether the VID carried by the frame is that allowed by the port
			If no, discard it. / If yes, check whether the VID carried by the frame is the same as the port PVID (If yes, send after stripping the tag; if no, send directly)
Hybrid	Same as Trunk	Same as Trunk	Check whether the VID carried by the frame is that allowed by the port
			If no, discard it. / If yes, check whether the stripping tag is configured (If yes, send after stripping the tag; if no, send directly)

4.4 IP Routing Principle

Routing is a different concept from switching, although they are very similar. Chapter 3 tells us that switching occurs in the data link layer, while routing occurs in the network layer. Although they both forward data, the information utilized and the way it is processed is different. This section will describe how routing works and routing protocols.

4.4.1 What Is Routing

Routing is an extremely interesting and complex subject, so what exactly is routing? Routing is the path information that guides an IP message from its source to its destination, as shown in Fig. 4.23. Alternatively, routing can be understood as the process of sending packets from a source to a destination.

As shown in Fig. 4.24, the transmission of packets in the network is like a relay race in sports, where each router is only responsible for forwarding packets through the optimal path at this site, and relaying packets through the optimal path to the destination by multiple routers one stop at a time. Of course, there are some exceptions. Due to the implementation of some routing policies, the path through

Fig. 4.23 Routing

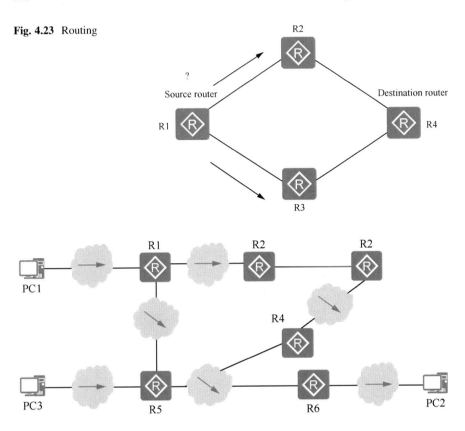

Fig. 4.24 Packet transmission in the network

which packets pass is not necessarily optimal. It should be added that if a router is connected to another router through a network, the two routers, which are one network segment apart, are considered to be adjacent in the Internet. The arrows shown in Fig. 4.24 indicate the network segments. As for which physical links each segment consists of, it is not a matter of concern for the router.

The above simple explanation shows that routers deliver packets on a hop-by-hop basis. Each router sends out the packets it receives according to certain rules, and does not bother about the subsequent sending of packets. This model can be simply understood as the devices are independent of each other for data forwarding and do not interfere with each other.

4.4.2   *How Routing Works*

We already know the concept of routing and routers. The following two aspects will explain how routing works.

1. Routing table

Routers work by relying on routing tables for forwarding data. The routing table is like a map containing information about the paths (routing entries) to each destination network, and each entry should contain at least the following information.

(a) Destination network: Indicates the address of the network that can be reached by the router.
(b) Next hop: Usually, the next hop generally points to the interface address of the next router to the destination network, which is called the next-hop router.
(c) Outgoing interface: Indicates from which interface of this router the packet is sent out.

In the router, you can view the routing table by executing the [display ip routing-table] command, the result of which is shown in Fig. 4.25.

The routing table contains the following key items.

(a) Destination: Destination address, used to identify the destination address or destination network of IP packets.
(b) Mask: Network mask, used to identify the address of the network segment where the destination host or router is located together with the destination address.
(c) Proto: Protocol, used to generate and maintain the routing protocol or way, such as Static, OSPF, IS-IS, BGP, etc.
(d) Pre: Preference, the priority of this route to join the IP routing table. For the same destination, there may be several routes with different next hops and outgoing interfaces, and these different routes may be discovered by different

[Huawei]**display ip routing-table**

Route Flags: R - relay, D - download to fib

Routing Tables: Public

Destinations : 6   Routes : 6

Destination/Mask	Proto	Pre	Cost	Flags	NextHop	Interface
1.1.1.1/32	Direct	0	0	D	127.0.0.1	InLoopBack0
192.168.1.0/24	Direct	0	0	D	192.168.1.1	Ethernet1/0/0
192.168.1.1/32	Direct	0	0	D	127.0.0.1	InLoopBack0
192.168.2.0/24	Static	60	0	RD	192.168.1.254	Ethernet1/0/0
192.168.1.255/32	Direct	0	0	D	127.0.0.1	InLoopBack0

.....

Fig. 4.25 View the results of the routing table

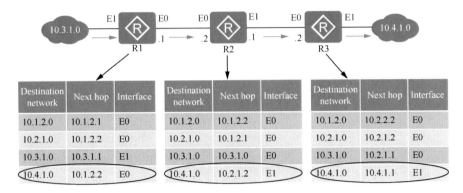

Fig. 4.26 Process of IP routing

routing protocols, or may be manually configured static routes. The one with higher priority (smaller value) will become the current optimal route.

(e) Cost: Routing overhead. When multiple routes to the same destination have the same priority, the one with the lowest routing overhead will be the current optimal route. Preference is used to compare the routing priorities between different routing protocols, and Cost is used to compare the priorities of different routes within the same routing protocol.

(f) NextHop: Next-hop IP address, indicating the next device through which the IP packet is routed.

(g) Interface: Output interface, indicating the interface on which the IP packet will be forwarded by the router.

In the subsequent content, we will explain the establishment, update, application and optimization of the routing table in more depth.

2. Routing process

After introducing the routing table, the next step is to deepen the understanding of the routing process through an example. As shown in Fig. 4.26, the left side of R1 is connected to the 10.3.1.0 network, and the right side of R3 is connected to the 10.4.1.0 network. When there is a packet in the 10.3.1.0 network to be sent to the 10.4.1.0 network, the IP routing process is as follows.

First, the packet from the 10.3.1.0 network is sent to the E1 interface of R1, which is directly connected to the network. After receiving the packet, the E1 interface looks up its own routing table and finds that the next hop to the destination address is 10.1.2.2, and the outgoing interface is E0, so the packet is sent from the E0 interface to the next hop, 10.1.2.2.

Second, the 10.1.2.2 (E0) interface of R2 receives the packet and also looks up its own routing table based on the destination address of the packet and finds that the next hop to the destination address is 10.2.1.2 and the outgoing interface is E1, so the packet is sent out from the E1 interface and handed over to the next hop 10.2.1.2.

Finally, the 10.2.1.2 (E0) interface of R3 receives the data, still looks up its own routing table according to the destination address of the packet, finds that the destination address is its own directly connected segment, and the next hop to the destination address is 10.4.1.1, and the interface is E1, so the packet is sent out from the E1 interface and handed over to the destination address.

4.4.3   Sources of Routing

There are three main sources of routing, which are direct routing, dynamic routing and static routing, and they are described below.

1. Direct routing

   A directly connected route is a routing entry for a network segment that is directly connected to the router. Directly connected routes do not require special configuration, but only need to set the IP address on the router interface, and then discovered by the data link layer (when the data link layer protocol is UP, the corresponding route entry appear in the routing table; when the data link layer protocol is DOWN, the corresponding route entry disappears).

   In the routing table, the Proto field of the direct routing is displayed as Direct, as shown in Fig. 4.27.

   When an IP address is configured for interface Ethernet1/0/0 (data link layer is UP), the corresponding route entry appears in the routing table.

2. Static routing

   Static routing involves routes that are manually configured by the administrator. Although network interoperability can be achieved by configuring static

```
[Huawei-Ethernet1/0/0]ip address 192.168.1.1 24

[Huawei]display ip routing-table
Route Flags: R - relay, D - download to fib
------------------------------------------------------------------------------
Routing Tables: Public
Destinations : 7      Routes : 7
Destination/Mask    Proto  Pre   Cost  Flags NextHop      Interface
127.0.0.0/8         Direct 0     0     D     127.0.0.1    InLoopBack0
127.0.0.1/32        Direct 0     0     D     127.0.0.1    InLoopBack0
127.255.255.255/32  Direct 0     0     D     127.0.0.1    InLoopBack0
192.168.1.0/24      Direct 0     0     D     192.168.1.1  Ethernet1/0/0
192.168.1.1/32      Direct 0     0     D     127.0.0.1    InLoopBack0
192.168.1.255/32    Direct 0     0     D     127.0.0.1    InLoopBack0
255.255.255.255/32  Direct 0     0     D     127.0.0.1    InLoopBack0
```

Fig. 4.27 Direct routing

[Huawei]display ip routing-table

Route Flags: R - relay, D - download to fib

Routing Tables: Public

Destinations : 7   Routes : 7

Destination/Mask	Proto	Pre	Cost	Flags	NextHop	Interface
127.0.0.0/8	Direct	0	0	D	127.0.0.1	InLoopBack0
127.0.0.1/32	Direct	0	0	D	127.0.0.1	InLoopBack0
127.255.255.255/32	Direct	0	0	D	127.0.0.1	InLoopBack0
192.168.1.0/24	Direct	0	0	D	192.168.1.1	Ethernet1/0/0
192.168.1.1/32	Direct	0	0	D	127.0.0.1	InLoopBack0
192.168.2.0/24	**Static**	60	0	RD	192.168.1.254	Ethernet1/0/0
192.168.1.255/32	Direct	0	0	D	127.0.0.1	InLoopBack0
255.255.255.255/32	Direct	0	0	D	127.0.0.1	InLoopBack0

Fig. 4.28 Static routing

routes as well, this configuration is prone to problems. When a network failure occurs, static routes are not automatically corrected, and the administrator must modify their configuration again. Therefore, static routes are generally used in small-scale networks.

In the routing table, the Proto field of the static routing is displayed as Static, as shown in Fig. 4.28.

The advantages and disadvantages of static routing are as follows.

(a) Advantages

    (i) Simple to use and easy to implement.
    (ii) Precise control on routing direction for optimal adjustment of network.
    (iii) Lower performance requirements for equipment and no extra link bandwidth consumption.

(b) Disadvantages

    (i) Whether the network is smooth and optimized depends entirely on the administrator's configuration.

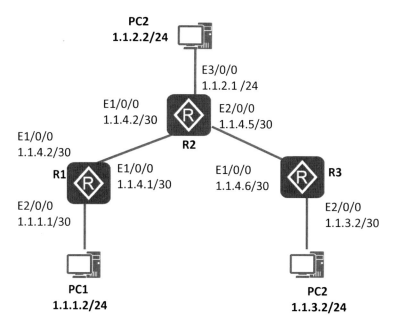

Fig. 4.29 Network topology of static routing

(ii) When the network is expanded, the complexity of configuration and the workload of the administrator will be increased due to the increase of routing table entries.

(iii) When the network topology is changed, it cannot be automatically adapted and requires the administrator to perform the correction.

Therefore, static routing is generally used in small-scale networks. In addition, static routing is also often used for path selection control, i.e., controlling the routing direction of certain destination networks.

Assume that the IP addresses and masks of each interface and host of the router are shown in Fig. 4.29. A static route is required so that any two hosts in the figure can interoperate with each other. At this time, it is necessary to configure the IPv4 static route on the router to reach the destination address, such as a static route with a destination address of 1.1.1.0 and a next hop of 1.1.4.1 for R2, and a static route with a destination address of 1.1.3.0 and a next hop of 1.1.4.6 for R2. As a result, the network belonging to R1 is connected to the network belonging to R3 by the above static route, and the specific configuration and verification process can be referred to Chap. 5.

3. Dynamic routing

Dynamic routing refers to the route discovered by dynamic routing protocol. When the network topology is very complex, the manual configuration of static routing is very laborious and prone to errors, then dynamic routing protocols can be used to automatically discover and modify routes without manual maintenance, but dynamic routing protocols are overhead and complex to configure. A comparison of static routing and dynamic routing is shown in Fig. 4.30.

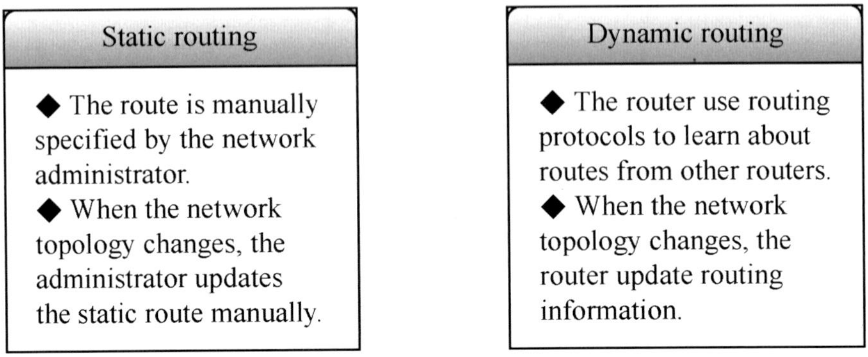

Static routing	Dynamic routing
◆ The route is manually specified by the network administrator. ◆ When the network topology changes, the administrator updates the static route manually.	◆ The router use routing protocols to learn about routes from other routers. ◆ When the network topology changes, the router update routing information.

Fig. 4.30 Static vs. dynamic routing

```
[Huawei]display ip routing-table
Route Flags: R - relay, D - download to fib
------------------------------------------------------------------------------
Routing Tables: Public
Destinations : 10    Routes : 10
Destination/Mask    Proto    Pre  Cost   Flags NextHop      Interface
1.1.1.1/32          RIP      100  1      D     12.12.12.1   Serial1/0/0
11.11.11.11/32      OSPF     10   1562   D     12.12.12.1   Serial1/0/0
12.12.12.0/24       Direct   0    0      D     12.12.12.2   Serial1/0/0
12.12.12.1/32       Direct   0    0      D     12.12.12.1   Serial1/0/0
12.12.12.2/32       Direct   0    0      D     127.0.0.1    InLoopBack0
12.12.12.255/32     Direct   0    0      D     127.0.0.1    InLoopBack0
127.0.0.0/8         Direct   0    0      D     127.0.0.1    InLoopBack0
127.0.0.1/32        Direct   0    0      D     127.0.0.1    InLoopBack0
127.255.255.255/32  Direct   0    0      D     127.0.0.1    InLoopBack0
255.255.255.255/32  Direct   0    0      D     127.0.0.1    InLoopBack0
```

Fig. 4.31 Dynamic routing

There are multiple routing protocols in the network, such as OSPF protocol, IS-IS protocol, BGP, etc. Each routing protocol has its own characteristics and application environment.

In the routing table, the Proto field of the dynamic routing is displayed as a specific kind of dynamic routing protocol, as shown in Fig. 4.31.

4.5 Summary

This chapter introduces the basics of network systems, focusing on the basics of communication networks, network addresses, VLAN technology, and the principles of IP routing. Through the study of this chapter, readers can understand the basic

concepts of network systems, understand network addressing, master the principles
of VLAN technology and IP routing, laying a solid theoretical foundation for the
subsequent study of specific network operations and maintenance.

4.6 Exercise

1. [Multiple Choice] The following options () are network topologies.

   A. Bus topology
   B. Mesh topology
   C. Star topology
   D. Tree topology
   E. Fan topology

2. [Multiple Choice] IP hierarchical structure consists of () two parts.

   A. Host
   B. Subnet
   C. Network
   D. Mask

3. [Multiple Choice] Huawei sets the interface type of VLAN ().

   A. Access
   B. Trunk
   C. Hybrid
   D. QinQ

4. [Multiple Choice] The sources of routing are ().

   A. Direct routing
   B. Cross routing
   C. Static routing
   D. Dynamic routing

5. [Multiple Choice] The advantages static routing are ().

   A. Simple to use, easy to implement
   B. Precise control on routing direction for optimal adjustment of network.
   C. When the network topology is changed, can be automatically adapted and
      requires no administrator to perform the correction.
   D. Lower performance requirements for equipment and no extra link bandwidth
      consumption.

Chapter 5
Basic Operation of Network Systems

Network operation and maintenance refers to the production organization and management activities taken to ensure the normal, safe and effective operation of communication network and business, also known as operation administration and maintenance (OAM). As the term "OAM" implies, the network operation and maintenance mainly includes the basic operation, administration and maintenance of the network system. The administration and maintenance will be introduced in Chap. 6. This chapter will focus on the basic operation of the network system, specifically, the login management, basic configuration and user management for the network equipment.

Today's mainstream network equipment manufacturers include Huawei, Cisco, Juniper, ZTE, Ruijie, H3C and so on. Their equipment operates mainly on three network operating systems: Huawei's Veritable Routing Platform (VRP), Cisco's Internetwork Operating System (IOS) and Juniper Operating System (Junos). Among them, both Huawei's VRP and Juniper's Junos adopt a single system for distribution, while Cisco adopts multiple platforms for distribution. Single distribution refers to the adoption of a single network operating system for different network devices, while multi-distribution refers to the distribution of different network operating systems for different network devices. Compared to the multi-distribution approach, a single network operating system is easier to use and can simplify network operations and management.

In order to enable readers to better grasp the ability to operate the network system, this chapter will start from the introduction of the network system, take Huawei devices and its operating system VRP as examples to illustrate how to quickly get familiar with the command-line interface (CLI) of the operating system, and then introduce the management modes, basic configuration and network configuration of various devices.

© The Author(s) 2023
Huawei Technologies Co., Ltd., *Construction, Operation and Maintenance of Network System(Junior Level)*, https://doi.org/10.1007/978-981-19-3069-0_5

By the end of this chapter, you will

(1) Understand the VRP version and structure	(4) Master basic configuration of devices
(2) Get familiar with the CLI	(5) Master basic networks configuration of devices
(3) Master login management of devices	(6) Master construction of remote login environment

5.1   What Is VRP and CLI

A complete network system, in addition to including the hardware described in Chap. 3, also carry the corresponding software, including communication protocols and network operating system. The network operating system is the system software on which the communication devices operate, providing network access and interconnection services.

This section will introduce Huawei's network operating system VRP and its CLI, so that readers can understand Huawei VRP and its characteristics, and master how to use the CLI.

5.1.1   What Is Huawei VRP

VRP is Huawei's network operating system with fully independent intellectual property rights. With IP services as its core, VRP implements a componentized architecture that carries over 300 features. It not only provides rich functional features, but also enables application-based tailoring ability and scalability ability.

As the core software engine for Huawei's whole series of routers, Ethernet switches, business gateways and other products, no matter low-end or core products, VRP delivers unified user interface and management interface; provides the control plane functions, defining the interface specification of the forwarding plane and realizing the interaction between the forwarding plane and the VRP control plane; and develops the network interface layer to shield the difference between the data link layer and the network layer.

In order to make a single software platform compatible with all kinds of routers and switches, VRP uses a componentized architecture for its software modules, which provides open standard interfaces between various protocols and modules. VRP is composed of five planes: general control plane (GCP), service control plane (SCP), data forwarding plane (DFP), system management plane (SMP) and system service plane (SSP).

1. GCP: Supports network protocol cluster, including IPv4 and IPv6. The protocols and functions it supports include socket, TCP/IP, routing management, various

routing protocols, VPN, interface management, data link layer, MPLS, security performance, and QoS support for IPv4 and IPv6.

2. SCP: Based on GCP, supports value-added services, including connection management, user authentication and billing, user policy management, VPN, multicast business management and maintenance of forwarding information base (FIB) related to business control.

3. DFP: Composed of forwarding engine and FIB maintenance, to provide forwarding service for the system. The forwarding engine can be implemented by software or hardware according to the forwarding mode of different products. Data forwarding supports high-speed switching, secure forwarding and QoS, and enables the extension of the forwarding module through open interfaces.

4. SMP: Delivers system management function to provide an interfaces for interaction with external devices and unified management of the output information of the system. As for the configuration and management of the platform, VRP can introduce some network management mechanisms in a flexible manner, such as the command line, NMP and the Web.

5. SSP: Supports common system services such as memory management, timers, IPC, load, transformation, task/process management and component management.

VRP also supports product license files, which allow the user to adjust the scope of features and performance as needed without breaking the original services.

VRP continues to evolve in terms of processing mechanisms, business capabilities, and product support with the great strides of network technology and application. As shown in the VRP version evolution in Fig. 5.1, more than a decade of development and validation brought about the VRP 1.x, VRP 3.x, VRP 5.x, VRP 8.x and more, bringing us different business capabilities and product support capabilities, respectively.

The versions of Huawei VRP system software fall into two categories: core version (or kernel version) and distribution version. The core version is the fundamental version used to develop VRP system for specific switches, namely VRP 1.x,

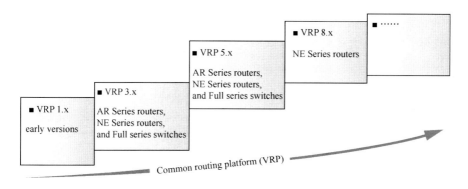

Fig. 5.1 VRP version evolution

VRP 2.x, VRP 3.x, and now VRP 5.x and VRP 8.x; the distribution version, based on the core version, is the VRP system software released for specific product series, such as S Series Switches, AR/NE Series Routers, etc.

The core version number of the VRP system is a decimal. The digit before the decimal point represents the major version number, which is updated only when a comprehensive functional or architectural change occurs. The first digit after the decimal point indicates the minor version number, only to be updated when there are major or many functional changes. The second and third digits after the decimal point make up the revision number that is issued whenever a change occurs. For example, in the software version VRP 5.120, the major and minor version numbers are 5 and 1, respectively, and 20 is the revision number.

The distribution version of Huawei VRP system is marked by the letters "V", "R" and "C" (representing three different version numbers), and the basic format is "VxxxRxxxCxx", where "X" is some specific digits. Parts "V" and "R" are necessary; "C" is determined by the property of the version and is unnecessary.

The letters "V", "R", and "C" are defined as follows.

1. "V" refers to the software or hardware platform version on which the product is based.

   "Vxxx", known as the V version number, identifies changes to the backbone platform of a product/solution. Where, "xxx" starts at 100, with increments of 100. The "V" version number changes only with the changes of the product platform.

2. "R" refers a set of general features released to the customer, as a specific manifestation of the product at a specific time.

   "Rxxx" identifies a common release for all customers, known as the R version number. Where, "xxx" starts at 001, with increments of 1.

3. "C" is a customized version developed based on "R" version to quickly meet the needs of different customer groups, known as C version number.

Under the same R version, "xx" in the C version number starts at 00, with increments of 1. In case of the change to the R version number, the "xx" in the C version number will be renumbered from 00, such as V100R001C01, V100R001C02, and V100R002C01.

On a device, you can view the device version by executing the [display version] command. Example 5.1 shows how to view the device version on the S5700 Switch.

[Example 5.1]
View the device version

When the command [display version] is executed on the S5700 Switch, the following output will be displayed. "Version 5.120" refers to the VRP core version that the switch runs on; "S5700 V200R002C00" in brackets refers to the VRP distribution version of the S5700 Series Switch; "V200" refers to the V version "2"; "R002", R version "2"; and "C00", C version "1". It also shows the corresponding BootROM software version. For example, "Basic Bootrom Version: 100" indicates that the BOOTROM software version is 100. You can also view other version information, such as PCB version, complex programmable logic device version (CPLD version), and so on.

```
<Huawei>display version
Huawei Versatile Routing Platform Software
VRP (R) software, Version 5.120 (S5700 V200R002C00)
Copyright (C) 2000-2012 Huawei TECH CO., LTD
Huawei S5700-52C-EI Routing Switch uptime is 0 week, 2 days, 1 hour,
24 minutes
EMGE 0 (Master) : uptime is 0 week, 2 days, 1 hour, 23 minutes
512M bytes DDR Memory
64M bytes FLASH
Pcb    Version : VER B
Basic BOOTROM Version : 100 Compiled at Mar 1 2011, 20:27:16
CPLD  Version : 74
Software Version : VRP (R) Software, Version 5.120 (S5700
V200R002C00)
FANCARD information
Pcb    Version : FAN VER B
PWRCARD I information
Pcb    Version : PWR VER A
```

5.1.2 What Is CLI and How to Use

CLI is a human-machine interface provided by network devices such as switches and routers. Compared with the graphical user interface (GUI), the CLI requires less system resources, and is easy to use and expand functions.

1. Go to the CLI

VRP provides the CLI as shown in Fig. 5.2.

The initial login takes the user to the user view by default. In the VRP, the user view is expressed by "< >", for instance, <Huawei>. In the user view, the user can only execute commands for such operations as file management, view and debugging, and have no right to execute commands for device maintenance, configuration modification or things like that. If you need to configure a network device, you must do that in the corresponding view. For example, the IP address of the interface can only be created under the interface view; only through the system view can you access other subviews.

You can switch to system view by executing the [system-view] command in the user view, and execute the [quit] command in the system view to switch to the user view. The commands for view switching under VRP are shown in Table 5.1.

Executing a service command in the system view can navigate you to a relevant service view. The commands can be executed varies with the view.

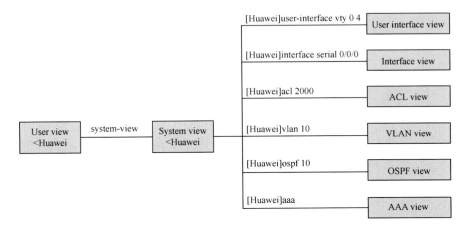

Fig. 5.2 VRP CLI

Table 5.1 Commands for view switching under VRP

Action	Command
Switch to system view from user view	system-view
Switch to user view from system view	quit
Switch to user view from any non-user view	Return; or press the Ctrl + Z shortcut

For example, to configure Interface ge0/0/0 in the system view, you can execute the [interface GigabitEthernet0/0/0] command to enter the interface view.

2. Set the command level

The commands in the VRP system are divided into four levels, from 0 to 3, as shown in Fig. 5.3.

(a) Visit level: Network diagnosis commands (such as ping, tracert), commands to access external devices from this device (such as Telnet, SSH, Rlogin), etc.

(b) Monitoring level: commands used for system maintenance and service fault diagnosis, such as display, debugging, etc.

(c) Configuration level: Service configuration commands, including commands for routing, at each network level, and offering direct network services to users.

(d) Management level: Commands used for the basic operations of the system and providing support for the services, including file system, FTP, TFTP, XMODEM download, configuration file switching command, standby board control command, user management command, command level setting command, command for system internal parameter setting, etc.

The system also restricts the access rights of different users to the device through the hierarchical management of users. The user level corresponds to the command level. Users of a level can only use commands at or below their level. By default,

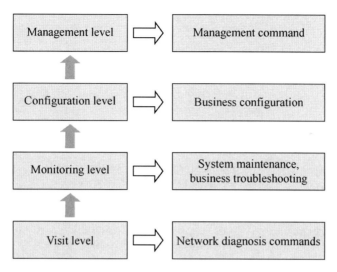

Fig. 5.3 Command level in the VRP

Table 5.2 Correspondence between user level and command level

User level	Command level	Level name
0	0	Visit level
1	0, 1	Monitoring level
2	0, 1, 2	Configuration level
3 to 15	0, 1, 2, 3	Management level

the commands register at levels 0 to 3 and users register at levels 0 to 15. The correspondence between the user level and the command level is shown in Table 5.2.

In addition, the system also supports command level customization, which allows low-level users to be authorized to use high-level commands as needed. For example, authorizing a level 0 user to use the [save] command can be done with the following configuration.

```
<Huawei>system-view
[Huawei]command-privilege level 0 view user save
```

3. Edit the command line

The CLI of VRP provides basic editing functions of the command line, and supports multi-line editing. Each command has a maximum length of 510 characters, command keywords are not case sensitive, and command parameters are

Table 5.3 Commonly used editing functions

Function key	Function
Common key	If the edit buffer is not full, insert to the current cursor position, the cursor will move right; otherwise, the alarm rings
Backspace key	Delete the character before the cursor position, then the cursor moves left; if the head of the command is reached, the alarm rings
← key or Ctrl + B shortcut key	Move the cursor one character position to the left; if the head of the command is reached, the alarm rings
→ key or Ctrl + F shortcut key	Move the cursor one character position to the right; if the end of the command is reached, the alarm rings
Ctrl + A shortcut	Move the cursor to the head of the current line
Ctrl + E shortcut	Move the cursor to the end of the current line

case sensitive depending on the parameters defined by each command. The commonly used editing functions are shown in Table 5.3.

To improve the efficiency of editing the command line, VRP provides completion function via the Tab key and supports the entry of incomplete keywords. The detailed steps are as follows. It is recommended that the user practices to familiarize themselves with these two functions, so as to improve the efficiency of command-line editing.

(a) Use of the Tab key

When editing commands, enter incomplete keyword and press Tab, then the system will automatically complete the keyword, as follows.

(i) If the matching keyword is unique, the system replaces the original input content with this complete keyword and the newline displays. The cursor is one space away from the end of the word.

(ii) If the matching keyword is not unique, press Tab repeatedly to display all the keywords starting with the input character string in turn. No space between the cursor and the end of the word.

(iii) If there is no matching keyword, press Tab key and then the newline displays, the input keyword keeps unchanged.

(b) Incomplete keyword input

The device supports input of incomplete keyword, that is, you can match the input character with a unique keyword in the current view without entering the full keyword. This feature provides a quick way to input and helps improve operational efficiency. For example, when the user needs to view the current configuration, and the full command is [display current-configuration], the user can execute this command by typing "dcu", "di cu" or "dis cu", but cannot execute by typing "dc" or "dis c", etc., because the command starting with "dc" or "dis c" is not unique.

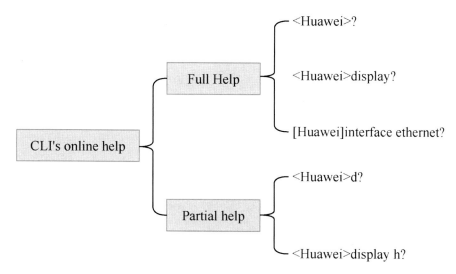

Fig. 5.4 CLI's online help

4. CLI's online help

When using the CLI, the user can utilize the online help feature to get real-time help without having to memorize a large number of complex commands. During the input, the user can type "?" at any time for online help, either full help or partial help, as shown in Fig. 5.4. Uses of the full help and partial help are described in detail below, respectively.

(a) Full help

When typing a command, the user can use the full help feature on the command line to get hints for the complete keyword or parameter. Here are some examples of full help for reference.

[Example 5.2]
Full help

(i) Under any command view, type "?" to display all the commands under this command view and their brief descriptions. An example is as follows.

```
<Huawei>?
User view commands:
backup      Backup electronic elabel
cd          Change current directory
```

(continued)

```
check       Check information
clear       Clear information
clock       Specify the system clock
compare     Compare function
. . .
```

(ii) Input a command keyword, followed by a space separated "?" If the position is for a keyword, all keywords and their brief descriptions are listed. An example is as follows.

```
<Huawei>system-view
[Huawei]user-interface vty 0 4
[Huawei-ui-vty0-4]authentication-mode ?
aaa     AAA authentication
password Authentication through the password of a user terminal
interface
[Huawei-ui-vty0-4]authentication-mode aaa ?
<cr>
[Huawei-ui-vty0-4]authentication-mode aaa
```

Among them, "aaa" and "password" are keywords, and "AAA authentication" and "Authentication through the password of a user terminal interface"are the descriptions of the keywords; "<cr>" indicates that the position has no keyword or parameter, and the command will be repeated on the next command line, so just press Enter key to execute it.

(iii) Input a command keyword, followed by a space separated "?" If the position is for a parameter, the names and brief descriptions of all relevant parameters are listed. An example is as follows.

```
<Huawei>system-view
[Huawei]ftp timeout ?
  INTEGER<1-35791> The value of FTP timeout, the default value is
30 minutes
[Huawei]ftp timeout 35 ?
<cr>
[Huawei]ftp timeout 35
```

"INTEGER <1–35791>" is the description of the value of the parameter, and "The value of FTP timeout, the default value is 30 minutes" is a brief description of the function of the parameter.

(b) Partial help

When a user types a command, if he/she remembers only the first one or several characters of the command keyword, he/she can resort to the partial help feature of the CLI to get hints for all keywords beginning with that character string. Here are some examples of partial help for reference.

[Example 5.3]
Partial help

(i) Enter a character string, followed by "?", and then all keywords that begin with the string are listed.

```
<Huawei>d?
   debugging             delete
   dir                   display
<Huawei>d
```

(ii) Enter a command, followed by a character string and "?", and then all keywords that begin with the string are listed.

```
<Huawei>display b?
bootrom                  bpdu
bpdu-tunnel              bridge
buffer
```

5. Interpret error messages of the CLI

Commands entered by the user under the CLI will be executed correctly if they pass the syntax check; otherwise the system will report an error message to the user. The common error messages are shown in Table 5.4, which allows users to check and correct command input.

Table 5.4 Common error messages

Error message in English	Error reason
Error: Unrecognized command found at '^' position	The command is not found at '^' position
Error: Wrong parameter found at '^' position	The parameter is not found at '^' position
Error: Incomplete command found at '^' position	Wrong parameter type with value out of bounds is found at '^' position
Error: Too many parameters found at '^' position	Too many parameters are found at '^' position
Error: Ambiguous command found at '^' position	Incomplete command is found at '^' position

6. Use the undo command line

Under the CLI, a command prefixed with the keyword **undo** is the **undo** command line, which is used to restore the default configuration, disable a feature, or delete a configuration. Almost every configuration command has an **undo** command line, as illustrated below.

[Example 5.4]

Use the undo command line

    (a) The [undo] command is used to restore the default configuration.

The [sysname] command is used to set the hostname of the device, as shown below.

```
<Huawei>system-view        //Enter the system view
[Huawei] sysname Server    //Set the device name to "Server"
[Server] undo sysname      //Restore the device default name
                             to "HUAWEI"

[Huawei]
```

    (b) The [undo] command is used to disable a feature.

```
<Huawei>system-view        //Enter the system view
[Huawei] undo stp enable   //Disable STP
```

    (c) The [undo] command is used to delete a configuration.

```
<Huawei>system-view        //Enter the system view
[Huawei] interface
GigabitEthernet0/0/0       //Enter the interface view
[Huawei-GigabitEthernet0/0/0] ip
address 10.1.1.1 255.255.255.0
                             //Configure the interface IP address
[Huawei-GigabitEthernet0/0/0]
undo ip address            //Delete the interface IP address
```

7. Query the history command

The CLI automatically save the history commands entered by a user for he/she to invoke them and repeat the execution at any time. By default, the CLI saves up to 10 history commands per user. The query and invocation methods of the history command are shown in Table 5.5.

Table 5.5 Query and invocation methods of the history command

Command or function Key	Function
display history-command	Display the history command
↑ key or Ctrl + P shortcut	Access the previous history command
↓ key or Ctrl + N shortcut	Access the next history command

The following points need to be noted when using the history command feature.

(a) The history commands saved by the VRP are in the same format as the commands entered by the user. For a command of an incomplete form, the saved historical command is also in an incomplete form.

(b) If the user executes the same command for many times, the VRP only saves the earliest command as the historical command; but if the same command is executed twice in different forms, the command will be saved as two commands. For example, if you execute [display ip routing-table] multiple times, only one command is saved; but if you execute [display ip routing] and [display ip routing-table] respectively, they will be saved as two historical commands.

8. Use command-line shortcuts

To simplify operations, the user can use shortcuts to quickly enter commands. The shortcut keys in the system are divided into custom shortcut keys and system shortcut keys. There are four custom shortcuts as follows.

(a) Ctrl + G: [display current-configuration] by default.
(b) Ctrl + L: [undo idle-timeout] by default.
(c) Ctrl + O: [undo debugging all] by default.
(d) Ctrl + U: No default command.

The user can also associate these four shortcuts with any command as desired. For example, set the command corresponding to the Ctrl + U shortcut to [save] by executing as follows.

```
<Huawei>system-view          //Enter the system view
[Huawei]hot-key CTRL_U save  //Set the CTRL +U shortcut to
                               execute the [save] command
```

In addition, the CLI also has some system shortcuts, which are fixed in the system and cannot be specified by the user. Common system shortcuts are shown in Table 5.6.

Table 5.6 Common system shortcuts

Shortcut	Function
Ctrl + A	Move the cursor to the head of the current line
Ctrl + B	Move the cursor one character position to the left
Ctrl + C	Stop the currently executing function
Ctrl + D	Delete the character at the current cursor position
Ctrl + E	Move the cursor to the end of the current line
Ctrl + F	Move the cursor one character position to the right
Ctrl + H	Delete the character to the left of the cursor
Ctrl + W	Delete the character string (word) to the left of the cursor
Ctrl + X	Delete all characters to the left of the cursor
Ctrl + Y	Delete all characters at and to the right of the cursor
Ctrl + K	Terminate the outgoing connection during the connection establishment phase
Ctrl + T	Enter the question mark (?)
Ctrl + Z	Return to the user view
Ctrl +]	Terminate the incoming connection or redirect the connection
Esc + B	Move the cursor one character string (word) to the left
Esc + D	Delete the character string (word) to the right of the cursor
Esc + F	Move the cursor one character string (word) to the right

9. Batch execution feature

In the actual operation and maintenance of the device, the user often needs to execute multiple commands continuously. For this reason, these commands can be defined in advance as command lines to be batch-executed, so as to simplify the input of common commands and improve efficiency.

The CLI of VRP supports automatic batch execution of a specified command line with a timer set by the Maintenance Assistant. With this feature enabled, the device can perform certain operations or configurations without being attended, mainly for timed upgrades or timed configurations of the system. The specific operations are as follows.

(a) Execute the [system-view] command to enter the system view.

(b) Execute the [assistant task *task-name*] command to create up to 5 Maintenance Assistant tasks.

(c) Execute the [if-match timer cron *seconds minutes hours days-of-month months days-of-week* [*years*]] command to configure the Maintenance Assistant task to be performed at the specified time.

(d) Execute the [perform priority batch-file filename] command to set the processing actions of the Maintenance Assistant.

5.1.3 Query the Display Information of the Command Line

1. Query the configuration information of the command line

   After completing a series of configurations, the user can execute the corresponding [display] command to view the configuration and operation information of the device.

   VRP supports querying the configuration information of a protocol or application from the command line. For example, after completing the configuration of the FTP server, the command [display ftp-server] can be executed to see the parameters of the current FTP server.

   ```
   [Huawei]display ftp-server
   ```

   The system also supports viewing the currently active configuration information and the configuration information in the current view. The applicable commands are as follows.

   (a) View the currently active configuration information.

   ```
   [Huawei]display current-configuration
   ```

   Active configuration parameters are not displayed if they are the same as the default parameters.

   (b) View the active configuration information in the current view.

   ```
   [Huawei]display this
   ```

   Active configuration parameters are not displayed if they are the same as the default parameters.

2. Configure users at different levels to view the specified configuration information

   Network devices provide capabilities that allow users at different levels to view specified configuration information, enabling users to view the information displayed by specified command lines. The specific operations are as follows.

   (a) The administrator user executes the [command-privilege level] command to set the command available to a low-level user.

   (b) The administrator user executes the [set current-configuration display] command to set the configuration information that the specified low-level user needs to display.

[Example 5.5]
Configure users at different levels to view the specified configuration information

For example, the following configuration procedure: the administrator needs to enable a low-level user (such as a Level-0 user) to execute the [display current-configuration] command, but the user at that level can only view the IP address configuration information of the interface.

```
<Huawei>system-view
[Huawei] command-privilege level 0 view cli_8f display current-
configuration
[Huawei] set current-configuration display level 0 ip address
```

At this point, the Level-0 user logs in to the device and executes the command [display current-configuration] to view the configuration information. It will generally display the following results, that only the configuration information of the interface and the corresponding IP address are displayed.

```
<Huawei>display current-configuration
#
interface GigabitEthernet0/0/0
 ip address 192.168.200.183 255.255.255.0
#
interface LoopBack0
 ip address 10.168.1.1 255.255.255.0
#
return
```

3. Control how the command line is displayed

All command lines feature common display mode, which can be flexibly controlled as needed. When too much information is displayed on the terminal screen, the PageUp key and PageDown key can be used to display the previous page information and the next page information, respectively. When a command is executed, if more than one screen of information should be displayed, the system will automatically pause for the convenience of the user. At this point, the user can control the display mode of the command line through the function keys, as shown in Table 5.7.

4. Filter the display information of the command line

The function of filtering the display information of the command line helps the user quickly find the information needed. For example, when the [display] command is executed to view the display information, a regular expression (that is, specify display rules) can be used to filter the display information. When more than one screen of information is displayed at a time of execution, the CLI activates the pause function, in which state the user is given three options, as shown in Table 5.8.

Table 5.7 Control how the command line is displayed

Function Key	Function
Press the Ctrl + C or Ctrl + Z shortcut	Stop displaying or executing a command Note: It is also available to press a key other than space and enter (which can be a numeric key or an alphabetic key) to stop displaying or executing a command
Press the Space key	Continue to display the next screen of information
Press the Enter key	Continue to display the next line of information

Table 5.8 Filter the display information of the command line

Command	Function
+*regular-expression*	Equivalent to the pipe |include *regular-expression*
-*regular-expression*	Equivalent to the pipe |exclude *regular-expression*
/*regular-expression*	Equivalent to the pipe |begin *regular-expression*

The three alternative filtering options in Table 5.8 are described below.

(a) | **begin** *regular-expression*: Output all lines starting with a line that matches the specified regular expression, that is, filter all strings to be output until the specified string (which is case sensitive) is present, and all subsequent strings will be displayed on the screen.

(b) | **exclude** *regular-expression*: Output all lines that do not match the specified regular expression, that is, if a string to be output does not contain the specified string (which is case sensitive), it will be displayed on the screen, otherwise it will be filtered and not displayed.

(c) | **include** *regular-expression*: Only output all lines that match the specified regular expression, that is, if a string to be output contains the specified string (which is case sensitive), it will be displayed on the screen, otherwise it will be filtered and not displayed.

The following is an example of a way to specify the filtering mode in a command.

[Example 5.6]

A way to specify the filtering mode in a command

Execute the [display interface brief] command to display all lines that do not match the regular expression "10GE|40GE". "10GE|40GE" means to match "10GE" or "40GE", where the command and the result of execution are as follows. Due to the filtering mode "exclude 10GE|40GE" adopted by the command, the result of the display does not contain all 10GE and 40GE interfaces.

```
<Huawei>display interface brief | exclude 10GE|40GE
PHY: Physical
*down: administratively down
^down: standby
(l): loopback
(s): spoofing
(b): BFD down
(e): EFM down
(d): Dampening Suppressed
(p): port alarm down
(dl): DLDP down
InUti/OutUti: input utility rate/output utility rate
Interface         PHY   Protocol InUti OutUti  inErrors outErrors
Eth-Trunk2        down  down       0%     0%        0        0
Eth-Trunk27       up    up       0.01%  0.01%       0        0
MEth0/0/0         up    up       0.01%  0.01%       0        0
NULL0             up    up(s)      0%     0%        0        0
Vlanif2           down  down      --     --         0        0
Vlanif10          down  down      --     --         0        0
Vlanif20          down  down      --     --         0        0
Vlanif200         up    up        --     --         0        0
```

Execute the [display current-configuration] command to only display all lines that match the regular expression "vlan" as follows.

```
<Huawei>display current-configuration | include vlan
vlan batch 2 9 to 20 77 99 200 222 4091
vlan 19
mux-vlan
vlan 222
aggregate-vlan
access-vlan 1
instance 2 vlan 2
carrier-vlan 100
ce-vlan 10
port trunk allow-pass vlan 99 200
igmp-snooping static-router-port vlan 99
port trunk allow-pass vlan 20
port default vlan 77
port trunk allow-pass vlan 20
```

Execute the [display current-configuration] command to display the number of the lines that match the regular expression "vlan" as follows.

```
<Huawei>display current-configuration | include vlan | count
Total lines: 14.
```

5.2   Device Login Management

Unlike terminals such as computers, phones and tablets, network communication devices such as switches, routers and firewalls do not have dedicated input/output (I/O) devices. Therefore, to use the operating system of these network devices, it is necessary to connect the network operating system to the computer in a specific way, and then use the network operating system and conduct OAM of the device with the help of the computer's I/O devices (that is, keyboard, mouse, monitor and other devices). This process of connecting the operating system of a network device to a computer in a specific way is called login management for the device.

This section will introduce the common login management methods, and combined with examples, elaborate on various login management methods, so that readers can understand and master how to manage the device login through different ways.

5.2.1   Common Device Login Management Methods

The operation and management of network devices by the user is called network management. By the user's configuration management mode, the common network management modes can be divided into the CLI mode and Web mode. The CLI mode means that the user logs in to the device through the Console port (also known as serial port), Telnet or STelnet, and then uses the command line provided by the device to manage and configure the device. The following will go deep into the login management through CLI and Web, respectively.

1. Log in through the Console port

   Use a dedicated Console communication cable (also known as a serial cable) to connect the device's Console port, as shown in Fig. 5.5.

   Local login via the Console port is the most basic way to log in to a device and is the basis for all other login methods. By default, the user can log in locally through the Console port, as a Level-15 user. This approach, however, is only

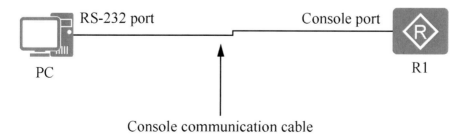

Fig. 5.5 Log in through the Console port

effective in case of local login and generally works for the following three scenarios.

(a) When the device is to be configured for the first time, it can be logged in through the Console port for configuration.
(b) When the user is unable to log in to the device remotely, he/she can log in locally through the Console port.
(c) When the device fails to start, the user can access the BootLoader through the Console port for diagnosis or system upgrade.

2. Login via Telnet

Telnet, which originated in ARPANET, is one of the oldest Internet applications that provides a way for the user to log in to a server remotely from a terminal on a network.

The traditional way of computer operation is to use a special hardware terminal directly connected to the computer for command line operations. But when using Telnet, the user can log in to another computer remotely from his/her own computer through the network to carry out operations, thus eliminating the distance and the equipment limitation. Similarly, the user can use Telnet to log in remotely to any network device that supports Telnet service, so as to realize remote configuration, maintenance, etc. Because this method can save the cost of network management and maintenance, it is widely used.

Using the TCP as the transport layer protocol, Telnet adopts Port 23 as well as the client/server mode. When a user logs in to a remote computer via Telnet, there are actually two programs enabled: one is the Telnet client program that runs on the local computer; the other is the Telnet server program that runs on the remote device to be logged. Therefore, during the remote login, the user's local computer acts as a client, while the remote computer providing the service is a server.

The remote login of Telnet between the client and server involves the following interaction process.

(a) The Telnet client establishes a connection with the remote Telnet server program through IP address or domain name. In fact, a TCP connection is established between the client and the server. The port that the server program monitors is Port 23.
(b) The system transmits the commands or characters input on the client to the server in the format of network virtual terminal (NVT). The user name, password, and any subsequent commands or characters input are transmitted as IP data units.
(c) The server converts the output data in the NVT format into a format available to the client and sends it back to the client, including the command outputs and the execution result of the commands.
(d) The client sends the command to disconnect and end the remote login.

By default, the user cannot log in to the device directly via Telnet. If necessary, the user can log locally through the Console port to complete the configuration (see Sect. 5.3.3 for details).

3. Login via STelnet

Telnet lacks a secure authentication mode and uses TCP for plaintext transmission, hence the great security risks. The single support of the Telnet service is also prone to deny of service (DOS), host IP address spoofing, routing spoofing and other malicious attacks. As people attach more importance to network security, the traditional way of sending passwords and data in a plaintext manner by Telnet has been gradually not accepted by the user.

SSH is short for Secure Shell, running in the standard Protocol Port 22. The SSH is a network security protocol, which provides secure remote login and other secure network services in an insecure network environment by encrypting network data, thus solving the security problems of the remote Telnet. The SSH relies on the TCP for data interaction, that is, building a secure channel on the TCP. In addition, the SSH supports other service ports in addition to the standard Port 22, so it is more secure and protected against illegal attacks.

It also supports password authentication and RSA authentication, and exerts encryption on the data based on DES, 3DES, AES, etc., thus effectively preventing the eavesdropping of the password, protecting the integrity and reliability of the data, and ensuring the safe transmission of data. In particular, through the support of RSA authentication, the mixed application of symmetric encryption and asymmetric encryption, and the secure exchange of keys, the SSH finally realizes the secure session process. Thanks to encrypted data transmission and more secure authentication mechanism, it is widely used and has become one of the most important network protocols.

The SSH protocol comes in two different and incompatible versions: the SSH1 (SSH 1.5) protocol and the SSH2 (SSH 2.0) protocol. The SSH 2.0 is superior to SSH 1.5 in terms of security, functionality, and performance. STelnet, short for Secure Telnet, enables the user to log in securely to devices from a remote end, and provides an interactive configuration interface, where all interactive data is encrypted thus ensuring a secure session. Huawei network equipment supports both client and server side of STelnet, as well as SSH1 (SSH 1.5) and SSH2 (SSH 2.0) protocols.

The SSH adopts the traditional client/server application model, whose security features are guaranteed in the following ways.

(a) Data encryption: Encryption Key is generated through client/server negotiation and exchange to realize symmetric Encryption of data packets and ensure the confidentiality of data in the process of transmission.

(b) Data integrity: Integrity keys are generated through client/server negotiation and exchange to uniquely identify a session link, so that the interactive messages of all sessions are identified by the integrity keys. In this way, the receiver can detect any data that has been modified by a third party and discard the data unit, ensuring the integrity of the data during transmission.

(c) Authority authentication: By providing a variety of authentication methods to ensure that only the authenticated legitimate users can have a conversation with the server, it improves the security of the system, while protecting the rights and interests of legitimate users.

4. Login via Web

Web mode refers to that the user logs in to the device through HTTP or HTTPS, where with the device as the server, the graphical operation interface is provided through the built-in Web server to facilitate the user's intuitive and convenient management and maintenance of the device.

HTTP is the most widely used network protocol on the Internet. It was originally designed to make browsers more efficient by providing a way to publish and receive HTML pages. The work of HTTP consists of two processes.

(a) The browser of the client first needs to establish a connection with the server through the network, which is completed through the TCP running on Port 80. Once the connection is established, the client sends a request to the server in the form of the uniform resource locater (URL), protocol version number, followed by MIME information, including the request modifier, client information, and license content.

(b) After receiving the request, the server will reply the corresponding response information in the form of a status line, including the protocol version number of the information, a successful or incorrect code, followed by MIME information, including server information, entity information and other possible contents.

HTTP sends information in plaintext. If a hacker intercepts a transmission between a Web browser and a server, the information in it can be accessed directly. In view of the inherent security hazards of HTTP, the security-oriented HTTP channel "HTTPS" emerges, which guarantees the security of the transmission process through transmission encryption and identity authentication on the basis of HTTP. HTTPS adds a secure socket layer (SSL) on top of HTTP to provide the security infrastructure that the SSL provides, so the encrypted details require the SSL. HTTPS uses a different default port (Port 443) than HTTP and an encryption/authentication layer (between HTTP and TCP) to provide authentication and encrypted communication. HTTPS is widely used for security-sensitive communications over the Internet, such as transactions, payments, etc.

HTTPS focuses on the following three aspects of its security design.

(a) Data confidentiality: It guarantees that the data contents will not be disclosed to a third party in the process of transmission, just like the encapsulated parcel delivered by the courier that others cannot learn the contents inside.

(b) Data integrity: It detects the transmitted content tampered with by a third party in a timely manner. Similarly, taking the parcel as an example, although the courier does not know what is in the parcel, but it may be stealthily substituted midway. The data integrity just makes it easy for the user to get aware of and reject the stealthily substituted parcel.

(c) Authentication security: It ensures that the data arrives at the desired destination of the user, that the parcel not stealthily substituted must be delivered to the correct destination. That is to say, authentication is used to ensure this correct delivery.

HTTPS has the following three advantages over HTTP.

(a) HTTPS authenticates the user and server to ensure that data is sent to the correct client and server.

(b) HTTPS, which is built by SSL + HTTP, supports the network protocol of encrypted transmission and identity authentication. It achieves higher security than HTTP, and it prevent data from being stolen and tampered in the process of transmission, so as to ensure the integrity of data.

(c) As the most secure solution under the current architecture, HTTPS, although not absolutely secure, significantly increases the cost of man-in-the-middle attacks.

Of course, HTTPS comes with some costs for improved security. On the same network, HTTPS increases page load time by nearly 50% and power consumption by 10% to 20%; affects the cache, thus increasing data overhead and power consumption; in addition, increases the consumption of computing resources. For example, a certain amount of computing resources and server costs will be occupied by the SSL protocol encryption algorithm and the intensified SSL interactions. In the case of large-scale user access to the application, the server needs to encrypt and decrypt frequently, and almost every byte needs to be encrypted and decrypted, which naturally leads to the server cost.

Huawei's data communication equipment supports device login using HTTP/HTTPS, but this Web mode can only realize the management and maintenance of partial functions of the device. The CLI mode is still needed if the device requests more complex or delicate management.

5.2.2 Common Cases of Device Login Management

[Example 5.7]
Login through the Console port

1. Topological structure
    Figure 5.6 shows the login through the Console port All network devices have the Console port, and the first time a network device is used, the Console port is usually used for local login.

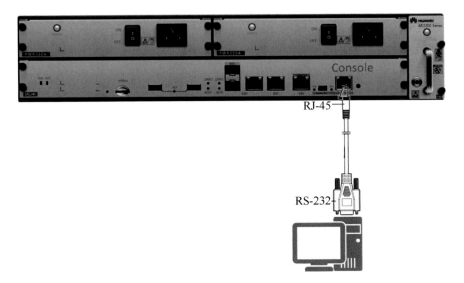

Fig. 5.6 Topological structure subject to the login through the Console port

2. Preparations

Before login to the device through the Console port, there are two things needed to do.

(a) Install a terminal emulation program on PC (such as HyperTerminal for Windows).

(b) Prepare the Console cable.

3. Steps

(a) After the preparation work is completed, follow the following 5 steps to complete the device login.

(i) Make physical connection as shown in Fig. 5.6. Insert the DB9 plug of the Console cable into the PC serial port (COM), and then plug the RJ-45 plug into the Console port of the device. It needs to be noted that if there is no DB9 serial port on the maintenance terminal (PC), a DB9 serial port to USB transfer cable can be purchased separately to connect the USB port to the maintenance terminal.

(ii) Open the terminal simulation program (such as HyperTerminal) on the PC, and create a new connection, as shown in Fig. 5.7, and then click "OK".

(iii) Set the serial port for connection according to the serial port's actual connection to the maintenance terminal. In this example, set the serial port to "COM4", as shown in Fig. 5.8, and click "OK".

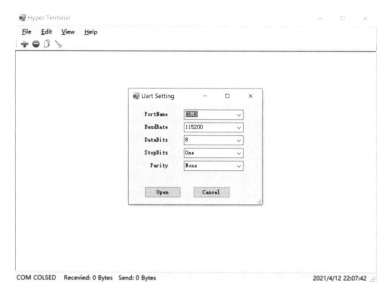

Fig. 5.7 Create a new connection

Fig. 5.8 Set the serial port

(iv) Set the serial port's communication parameters: set the baud rate to "9600", data bit "8bits", parity bit "None", stop bit "1 bit", flow control "None", as shown in Fig. 5.9, and then click "OK".

Fig. 5.9 Set the serial port's communication parameters

(v) Press "Enter" repeatedly until the system prompts the user to configure the authentication password in the following message. Then the system automatically saves the password configuration.

```
Please configure the login password (maximum length 16)
Enter Password:
Confirm Password:
```

(b) Since the Windows operating system is no longer equipped with HyperTerminal since Windows 7, it is recommended to use PuTTY, a free 32-bit Telnet, Rlogin and SSH client.

To log in to the device with PuTTY via the Console port, go through the following four steps.

(i) Make physical connections in the same way as when using HyperTerminal.
(ii) Open PuTTY on PC, as shown in Fig. 5.10, and then select "Serial Port" option.
(iii) Select the right serial port for connection and set the serial port parameters, as shown in Fig. 5.11. Connect to serial port "COM1", with speed/baud rate at "9600", data bit of "8", stop bit of "1", parity bit "none", and flow control "none".

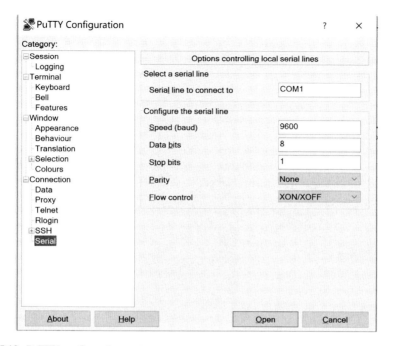

Fig. 5.10 PuTTY configuration

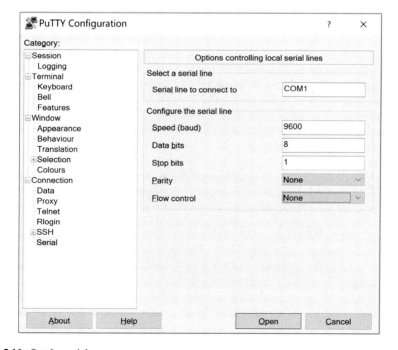

Fig. 5.11 Set the serial port parameters

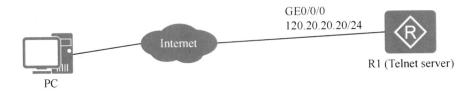

Fig. 5.12 Topological structure of Telnet login management

(iv) Click the "Open" button until the system prompts the user to configure the authentication password. The prompt message is as follows. After that, the system automatically saves this password configuration.

```
Please configure the login password (maximum length 16)
Enter Password:
Confirm Password:
```

[Example 5.8]
Telnet login management

1. Topological structure
   Figure 5.12 shows the topology of Telnet login management. In a real network environment, any network device configured with Telnet remote login can be used as a Telnet server.
2. Preparations
   Before Telnet login, it is necessary to ensure that the three-layer network of PC and Telnet server maintenance interface is accessible. The IP address of the maintenance interface can be configured as per actual requirements, which is assumed to be 120.20.20.20/24 here. With an authorized PC, login management of the device can be performed on the LAN or Internet. See Sect. 5.3.4 for the specific configuration.
3. Steps
   This example introduces the steps of Telnet login management using the built-in client of Windows. The user name for Telnet remote login is "HUAWEI" and the password is "Huawei@123".

   (a) To install he built-in client of Windows, select "Control Panel" -> "Programs and Features", click the "Turn Windows features on or off" hyperlinks to bring up the Windows features window, and then check "Telnet client", and click "OK" button, as shown in Fig. 5.13.
   (b) Log in to the device using a command prompt on the PC. As shown in Fig. 5.14, enter "telnet 120.20.20.20" at the command prompt, then press

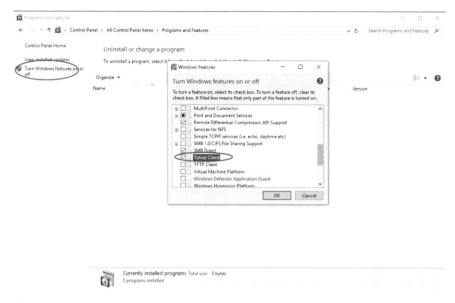

Fig. 5.13   Install the Telnet client that comes with Windows

Fig. 5.14   Log in to the device using a command prompt

"Enter" key, and then enter user name "HUAWEI" and password "Huawei@123" to successfully log in to the device, as shown in Fig. 5.15.

[Example 5.9]
STelnet login management

1. Topological structure

   Figure 5.16 shows the topology of STelnet login management. In a real network environment, any network device configured with Telnet remote login can be used as a STelnet server.

Fig. 5.15 Log in to the device with Telnet

GE0/0/0
120.20.20.20/24

R1 (Stelnet server)

PC

Fig. 5.16 Topological structure of STelnet login management

2. Preparations

Before STelnet login, it is necessary to ensure that the three-layer network of PC and STelnet server maintenance interface is accessible. With an authorized PC, login management of the device can be performed on the LAN or Internet. See Sect. 5.3.4 for the specific configuration.

3. Steps

This example introduces the steps of STelnet login management using the third-party client of Windows. The user name for STelnet remote login is "HUAWEI" and the password is "Huawei@123".

(a) Open STelnet client.Take PuTTY as an example here. After opening the PuTTY client, set "Connection Type" to "SSH", as shown in Fig. 5.17.

(b) Set the STelnet login parameters, as shown in Fig. 5.18. Set "Host Name (or IP Address)" as "120.20.20" and "Port" as "22". The SSH protocol version adopted by default is SSH 2.0. And then click "Open".

(c) As shown in Fig. 5.19, enter the user name "HUAWEI" and the password "Huawei@123" in the pop-up login window to successfully log in to the device.

[Example 5.10]

Web login management

1. Topological structure

Figure 5.20 shows the topological structure of Web login management.

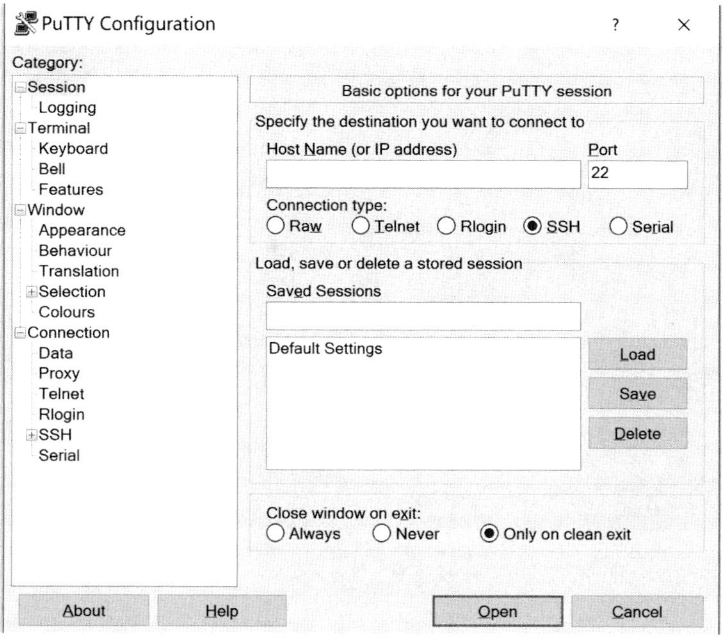

Fig. 5.17 Log in to STelnet through the PuTTY client

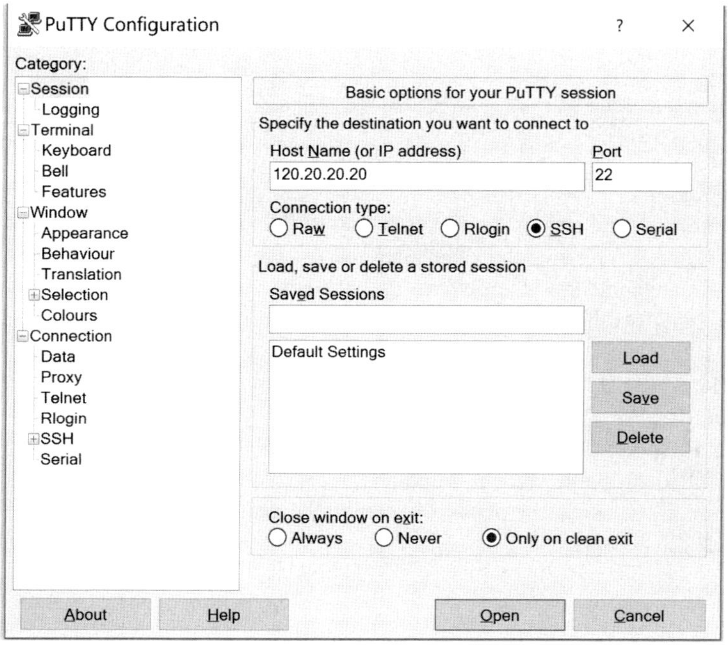

Fig. 5.18 Set the STelnet login parameters

```
120.20.20.20 - PuTTY                                    —   □   ×
login as: huawei
huawei@120.20.20.20's password:


User last login information:

Access Type: SSH
IP-Address : 192.168.0.11 ssh
Time        : 2020-03-04 15:27:45-08:00

<Huawei>█
```

Fig. 5.19 Log in to the device with STelnet

Fig. 5.20 Topological structure of Web login management

2. Preparations

Before Web login, it is necessary to ensure that the three-layer network of PC and Telnet server maintenance interface is accessible. With an authorized PC, login management of the device can be performed on the LAN or Internet. See Sect. 5.3.4 for the specific configuration.

3. Steps

Here, take Huawei USG6000V Firewall as an example to explain the steps of login over HTTPS. Note that for HTTPS, if the default port is "443", there is no need to specify a port to access the URL. In this case, the URL is "https:// 120.20.20.20", and Huawei USG6000V Firewall opens Port 8443 for HTTPS by default, so the user needs to specify the port in the URL, that is, "https:// 120.20.20.20:8443".

Fig. 5.21 Interface of Web login management

Fig. 5.22 Log in to the device via Web

(a) Open the browser (Firefox Browser and Google Chrome is recommended).
(b) As shown in Fig. 5.21, enter the URL "https://120.20.20.20:8443" of the firewall in the address bar to display the interface of Web login management.
(c) Enter the user name "HUAWEI" and the password "Huawei@123" in the interface to log in to the device, as shown in Fig. 5.22.

5.3 Basic Configuration of the Network System

In order to meet the requirements and for convenience of operation and maintenance, the network system must complete the necessary basic configuration of the device before configuring the service, including the basic configuration of the device environment, the management of the device configuration file, the configuration of the basic network and the relevant configuration of the remote login, etc.

5.3.1 Basic Configuration of Device Environment

The user can set the device environment in order to adapt to the usage habit or the demand of the actual operating environment. Device environment configuration can be divided into basic system environment configuration and basic user environment configuration. Each will be explained in detail below.

1. Basic system environment configuration

   The basic environment of the system mainly covers language mode, device name, system clock, title text, command level, etc., among which the more common are the setting of language mode, host name and system clock.

   (a) Switching of language modes

   In consideration of the language habits of the Chinese user, Huawei VRP provides help information in English and Chinese respectively, and the user can switch between them according to their needs. It is important to note that VRP help information is displayed in English by default, and some VRPs do not support language switching.

[Example 5.11]
Switch the language mode with the [language-mode] command

By default, VRP displays help information in English. In the user view, execute the command [language-mode Chinese] to switch to Chinese mode; similarly, to switch back to English mode, execute the [language-mode English] command in the user view.

```
<Huawei>language-mode Chinese
Change language mode, confirm? [Y/N]y
Jan 31 2020 12:07:00-08:00 Huawei %%01CMD/4/LAN_MODE(l)[50]:The
user chose Y when deciding whether to change the language mode.
提示:改变语言模式成功。
<Huawei>language-mode English
改变当前语言环境，确认切换? [Y/N]y
 Info: Succeeded to change language mode.
```

(b) Setting of device name

In practice, network device names can be configured according to user requirements. In order to facilitate future operation and maintenance, all network devices must be subject to uniform, clear naming specifications. It is generally recommended that the name of a network device include the information such as the equipment room and rack where it is deployed, and the function, layer, model, and serial No. of the device. The specific naming specification can be specified according to the actual requirements during the network scheme design.

[Example 5.12]
Set the device name

A certain device is located in Rack 03 in the core equipment room, and is at the convergence layer within the network structure, used for gathering the traffic of the production department; the device model adopted is Huawei S5700, so it can be named as "Core03-SC-HJ-S5700". The specific configuration steps are as follows.

(i) Execute the [system-view] command to enter the system view.

```
<Huawei>system-view
Enter system view, return user view with Ctrl+Z.
```

(ii) Execute the command [sysname Core03-SC-HJ-S5700] to set the device name, which takes effect immediately.

```
[Huawei] sysname Core03-SC-HJ-S5700
```

(c) Setting of system clock

The system clock is the time displayed by the system timestamp, which is required to be set accurately by the user in order to ensure normal coordination with other devices. For network devices, the system clock is converted with the formula "UTC + time zone offset + daylight saving time offset." UTC is short for Universal Time Coordinated.

In view of regional differences, in order to set the system clock, the user should first understand the regulations of the country or the region, and obtain the parameters of time zone offset and daylight saving time offset. The system clock is set in the user view, including time zone setting, current time setting and daylight saving time setting. The relevant parameters are shown in Table 5.9.

The following two examples illustrate the steps for setting up the system clock.

Table 5.9 Setting of relevant parameters of system clock

Function	Parameter
Set the current time zone	clock timezone
Sets the current time and date	clock datetime
Set adoption of the daylight saving time (not adopted by default)	clock daylight-saving-time

[Example 5.13]

Clock setting (not adopting daylight saving time)

Assuming the device is in use in China (UTC + 8), the current date and time is 17:00:00 on January 31, 2020, and daylight saving time is not adopted in China, the configuration process is as follows.

(i) Set the current time zone, named "BeiJing", and the time zone is UTC + 8.

```
<Huawei>clock timezone BeiJing minus 8:00:00
//"minus" is used here for UTC+8, meaning it is earlier than UTC; if
in UTC-12, "add" should be used to indicate time later than UTC
```

(ii) Set the current date and time.

```
<Huawei>clock datetime 17:00:00 2020-01-31
```

Execute the [display clock] command to check the system clock after the setting is complete.

```
<Huawei>display clock
2020-01-31 17:00:02
Friday
Time Zone(BeiJing) : UTC-08:00
```

[Example 5.14]

Clock setting (adopting daylight saving time)

Assuming the device is in use in Sydney, Australia (UTC + 10), the current date and time is 17:00:00 on January 31, 2020 (not adopting daylight saving time), and daylight saving time in Australia (starting at 2:00 a.m. on the first Sunday in October and ending at 3:00 a.m. on the first Sunday in April) is one hour ahead of the original system time, the configuration process is as follows.

(i) Set the current time zone, named "Sydney", and the time zone is GMT + 10.

```
<Huawei>clock timezone Sydney minus 10:00:00
```

(ii) Set the current date and time.

```
<Huawei>clock datetime 17:00:00 2020-01-31
```

Execute the [display clock] command to check that the system clock shows 17: 00:00 on January 31, 2020.

```
<Huawei>display clock
2020-01-31 17:00:01
Friday
Time Zone(Sydney) : UTC-10:00
```

(iii) Set adoption of the daylight saving time.

```
<Huawei>clock daylight-saving-time Australia repeating 02:00
first Sun OCT 03:00 first Sun Apr 1
```

Execute the [display clock] command to check the system clock after the setting is complete. Now the system adopts daylight saving time, which is an hour earlier than the original time.

```
<Huawei>display clock
2020-01-31 18:01:11 DST
Friday
Time Zone(Australia)  : UTC-10:00
Daylight saving time  :
        Name        : Australia
        Repeat mode : repeat
        Start year  : 2000
        End year    : 2099
        Start time  : first Sunday October 02:00:00
        End time    : first Sunday April 03:00:00
        Saving time : 01:00:00
```

2. Basic user environment configuration

In VRP, the user can configure the basic user environment and manage the device's basic files by switching user levels and locking the user interface.

Switching from a higher level to a lower level requires no password; switching from a lower level to a higher level requires the correct level switching password. The switch of the environment configuration of an user level consists of two steps: configuring the password used to switch the user level and switching the user level.

Here is an example of how to do this.

[Example 5.15]
Switch of Telnet user level

Assuming that the Telnet user is at Level 0 by default, the user can only execute commands applicable to Level 0 by default after logging in to the device in the Telnet mode, having no right to enter the system view by executing the [system-view] command, as shown below.

```
<Huawei>system-view
        ^
Error: Unrecognized command found at '^' position.
```

In order to execute high-level commands, the user must execute the [super password] command in the system view to configure the password for switching the user level. For example, the [super password level 3 cipher Huawei] command means that the password for switching from a lower level (Level 0–2) to Level 3 is "HUAWEI".

After the configuration is completed, execute the [super] command on the device to switch the user level, and then enter the password "huawei" as prompted by the system to switch the user level from 0 to 3. At this point the user can execute all the commands, as shown below.

```
<Huawei>super
  Password:
  Now user privilege is level 3, and only those commands whose level
is
     equal to or less than this level can be used.
     Privilege note: 0-VISIT, 1-MONITOR, 2-SYSTEM, 3-MANAGE
  <Huawei>system-view
  Enter system view, return user view with Ctrl+Z.
```

In addition, users who need to temporarily leave the operating terminal can be locked to prevent unauthorized users from manipulating the terminal interface. The operation is very simple, execute the [lock] command in the user view. Once the lock is successful, the screen will display "locked!". It should be noted that to lock the user interface, the user needs to enter and confirm a password. To release the lock, the password set at the time of the lock must be correctly entered.

5.3.2 Management of Device Configuration Files

VRP manages programs and configuration files through file system. File system represents the management of files and directories in storage devices, including the creation of file systems, the creation, deletion, modification and renaming of files and directories, and the display of file contents. File system can realize two kinds of functions: managing storage devices; and managing files stored in storage devices. A storage device is a hardware device for storing information. The storage devices currently supported by routers include flash memory, hard disk and memory card. The types of device actually supported by different products are not static. File is a mechanism for the system to store and manage information. System directory is a mechanism to organize the whole file collection. A directory is a logical container of files. Next, we will introduce the operation of directories and files, the management of storage devices and the management of configuration files.

1. Operation of directories and files

   For the file system, the common directory and file operations are shown in Table 5.10, including displaying, copying, moving and deleting files. Assuming that the device has been saved, that is, the configuration file "vrpcfg.zip" exists in the device, the common directory and file operations for the device are shown in the following Table 5.10.

Table 5.10 Common directory and file operations

Operation	Command
Show the current directory	pwd
Change the current directory	cd
Display a list of files under the current directory	dir
Create a directory	mkdir
Delete a directory	rmdir
Compress a file	zip
Uncompress a file	unzip
Display the file contents	more
Copy a file	copy
Move a files	move
Rename a file	rename
Delete a file	delete
Completely delete the files in the recycle bin	reset recycle-bin
Recover a deleted file	undelete

[Example 5.16]

Directory and file operations

(a) Display the current directory.

```
<Huawei>pwd
flash:
```

(b) Create a directory and name it "backup".

```
<Huawei>mkdir backup
Info: Create directory flash:/backup......Done.
```

(c) Delete the directory "backup".

```
<Huawei>rmdir backup
Remove directory flash:/backup? [Y/N] :y
%Removing directory flash:/backup...Done!
```

(d) Display the file list under the current directory.

```
<Huawei>dir
Directory of flash:/

Idx   Attr   Size(Byte)   Date          Time       FileName
  0   drw-         -       Jan 29 2020   11:19:01   src
  1   -rw-       447       Jan 29 2020   11:20:06   vrpcfg.zip
  2   -rw-     1,343       Jan 29 2020   11:24:28   vrpconfig.cfg
  3   -rw-     1,343       Jan 29 2020   11:31:10   vrpcfg.txt
  4   -rw-     1,343       Jan 29 2020   11:55:09   backup
  5   drw-         -       Jan 29 2020   11:55:28   backup1
```

(e) Decompress the configuration file.

```
<Huawei>unzip vrpcfg.zip flash:/vrpcfg.txt
Extract flash:/vrpcfg.zip to flash:/vrpcfg.txt? [Y/N] :
```

Type "Y" and press Enter to unzip the file.

```
<Huawei>unzip vrpcfg.zip flash:/vrpcfg.txt
Extract flash:/vrpcfg.zip to flash:/vrpcfg.txt? [Y/N] :y

100% complete
%Decompressed file flash:/vrpcfg.zip to flash:/vrpcfg.txt.
```

(f) Display the file contents.

```
<Huawei>more vrpcfg.txt
#
sysname Huawei
#
cluster enable
ntdp enable
ndp enable
#
drop illegal-mac alarm
#
diffserv domain default
#
drop-profile default
#
aaa
 authentication-scheme default
 authorization-scheme default
 accounting-scheme default
 domain default
 domain default_admin
 local-user admin password simple admin
 local-user admin service-type http
#
interface Vlanif1
 ---- More ----
```

(g) Copy the file, before which create the directory "backup" first.

```
<Huawei>copy vrpcfg.txt flash:/ backup/
Copy flash:/vrpcfg.txt to flash:/backup/vrpcfg.txt?? [Y/N] :
```

Type "Y" and press Enter to complete the copy operation.

```
<Huawei>copy vrpcfg.txt flash:/backup
Copy flash:/vrpcfg.txt to flash:/backup? [Y/N]:y

100% complete
Info: Copied file flash:/vrpcfg.txt to flash:/backup...Done.
```

(h) Delete the file.

```
<Huawei>delete vrpcfg.txt
Delete flash:/vrpcfg.txt? [Y/N]:
Info: Deleting file flash:/vrpcfg.txt...succeeded.
```

At this point, execute the [dir] command to view the file list under the current directory, and you can find that the file "vrpcfg.txt" has been deleted.

(i) Recover the deleted file.

```
<Huawei>undelet vrpcfg.txt
Undelete flash:/vrpcfg.txt? [Y/N]:y
%Undeleted file flash:/vrpcfg.txt.
```

At this point, execute the [dir] command to view the file list under the current directory, and you can find that the file "vrpcfg.txt" has been recovered.

(j) Completely delete the files in the recycle bin.

```
<Huawei>reset recycle-bin
Squeeze flash:/backup? [Y/N]:y
%Cleared file flash:/backup.
```

2. Management of storage devices

VRP supports some basic management of storage devices, including formatting and repairing of storage devices, as shown in Table 5.11.

[Example 5.17]
Management of storage devices

Table 5.11 Management of storage devices

Operation	Command
Format a storage device	format
Repair a storage device with abnormal file system	fixdisk

The operation of formatting a storage device is as follows.

```
<Huawei>format flash:
All data (include configuration and system startup file) on flash: will
be lost ,
proceed with format ? [Y/N] :y.
%Format flash: completed.
```

For storage devices with abnormal file system, VRP can try to repair them. The operation is shown as follows.

```
<Huawei>fixdisk flash:
Fix disk flash: will take long time if needed.
% Fix disk flash: completed.
```

Readers are advised to use the commands for managing storage devices carefully, especially the [format] command, because once used, all files in the storage devices will be deleted.

3. Management of configuration files

(a) Initial configuration and current configuration

When the router is powered on, the configuration file is read from the default storage device to initialize the router, so the configuration in the configuration file is called the saved-configuration. If there is no configuration file in the default storage device, the router is initialized with default parameters. Corresponding to the initial configuration, the configuration that is in effect during router operation is called the current-configuration. Table 5.12 lists the common operations involving the configuration file.

[Example 5.18]
Common operations involving the configuration file

As we already know, the user can configure network devices through CLI. In order to make the current configuration the initial configuration when the router is powered on next time, it is necessary to execute the [save] command

Table 5.12 Common operations involving the configuration file

Operation	Command
Check the initial configuration of the device	display saved-configuration
View the current configuration of the device	display current-configuration
Save the configuration	save
Erase the configuration file in the storage device	reset saved-configuration
Compare the initial configuration and current configuration	compare configuration

to save the current configuration to the default storage device to generate the initial configuration file. The operation steps are as follows.

```
<Huawei>save
The current configuration will be written to the device.
Are you sure to continue? [Y/N] Y
 Info: Please input the file name ( *.cfg, *.zip ) [vrpcfg.zip]:
Jan 29 2020 12:48:52-08:00 Huawei %%01CFM/4/SAVE(1)[0]:The user
chose Y when dec
iding whether to save the configuration to the device.
Now saving the current configuration to the slot 0.
Save the configuration successfully.
```

Execute the command [display saved-configuration] to view the initial configuration of the network device.

```
[Huawei]display saved-configuration
#
sysname r1
#
undo info-center enable
#
aaa
 authentication-scheme default
 authorization-scheme default
 accounting-scheme default
 domain default
 domain default_admin
 local-user admin password cipher OOCM4m($F4ajUn1vMEIBNUw#
 local-user admin service-type http
#
   ---- More ----
```

Execute the command [display current-configuration] to view the current configuration of the network device.

```
[Huawei]display current-configuration
#
sysname Huawei
#
undo info-center enable
#
 aaa
   authentication-scheme default
   authorization-scheme default
```

(continued)

```
    accounting-scheme default
    domain default
    domain default_admin
     local-user admin password cipher -$[1(P>3t>]@13D+mKgUFM@#
     local-user admin service-type http
  #
---- More ----
```

Execute the [reset saved-configuration] command to erase the configuration file in the storage device.

```
<Huawei>reset saved-configuration
Warning: The action will delete the saved configuration in the
device.
The configuration will be erased to reconfigure. Continue? [Y/N]:y
Warning: Now clearing the configuration in the device.
Jan 29 2020 12:51:56-08:00 Huawei %%01CFM/4/RST_CFG(1)[1]:The
user chose Y when
deciding whether to reset the saved configuration.
 Info: Succeeded in clearing the configuration in the device.
```

Execute the [compare configuration] command to compare whether the current configuration file is consistent with the initial configuration file stored in the storage device. For example, after modifying the device name to "Test-difference", VRP will display the inconsistency between the two files in the output information, as shown below.

```
<Test-difference>compare configuration
Warning: The current configuration is not the same as the next
startup configura tion file. There may be several differences, and
the following are some configurations beginning from the first:
    ====== Current configuration line 2 ======
sysname Test-difference
#
cluster enable
ntdp enable
ndp enable
#
drop illegal-mac alarm
#
diffserv domain default

====== Configuration file line 2 ======
    sysname Huawei
```

(continued)

```
#
 cluster enable
 ntdp enable
 ndp enable
 #
 drop illegal-mac alarm
 #
 diffserv domain default
 #
 drop-profile default
```

(b) Management of the startup configuration files

System software and configuration files need to be loaded when the system starts. Before managing the startup configuration files, it is necessary to clarify three related concepts, namely, the startup saved-configuration file, the next startup saved-configuration file and the next startup configuration file. In the device, you can check the startup configuration of the current system by executing the [display startup] command, as shown below.

```
<Huawei>display startup
MainBoard:
   Configed startup system software:          flash:/sup.bin
   Startup system software:                     flash:/sup.bin
   Next startup system software:                flash:/sup.bin
   Startup saved-configuration file:          flash:/vrpcfg.zip
    Next startup saved-configuration file:      flash:/vrpcfg.zip
   Next startup configuration:                 backup-configuration
```

Among them, the startup saved-configuration file is the configuration file used in this startup, the next startup saved-configuration file is the configuration file to be loaded in the next startup, and the next startup configuration file is the disaster recovery configuration file to be loaded in the next startup.

It should be noted that only network security products generally support the configuration management of next startup configuration, such as USG firewall, AntiDDoS and other products. In case of failure of these safety devices, only when the original current configuration or initial configuration cannot meet the expected requirements, it is necessary to load next startup configuration files on the devices to realize configuration recovery. That is to say, under normal circumstances, the next startup configuration file will not be configured.

Next, two examples are given to explain how to manage the next startup saved-configuration file and next startup configuration file at the next startup through VRP.

[Example 5.19]

Management of the next startup saved-configuration file

Execute the command [startup saved-configuration *configuration-filename*] to configure the configuration file to be loaded when the device starts next time. The operation steps are as follows.

(i) Execute the [dir] command in the user view to view the file name of the configuration file, as shown below. At this time, there are two configuration files in the device: "vrpcfg.zip" and "vrpcfg1.zip".

```
<Huawei>dir
Directory of flash:/
Idx  Attr  Size(Byte)    Date          Time(LMT)   FileName
  0  drw-           -    Feb 03 2020   03:15:00    dhcp
  1  -rw-     121,802    May 26 2014   09:20:58    poR11page.zip
  2  -rw-       2,263    Feb 03 2020   03:14:55    statemach.efs
  3  -rw-     828,482    May 26 2014   09:20:58    sslvpn.zip
  4  -rw-         656    Feb 03 2020   03:47:42    vrpcfg1.zip
  5  -rw-         656    Feb 03 2020   03:14:53    vrpcfg.zip
```

(ii) Execute the [display startup] command in the user view to view the list of current startup configuration files.

```
<Huawei>display startup
MainBoard:
  Startup system software:                null
  Next startup system software:           null
  Backup system software for next startup: null
  Startup saved-configuration file:       flash:/vrpcfg.zip
  Next startup saved-configuration file:  flash:/vrpcfg.zip
```

(iii) Configure the next startup saved-configuration file as "vrpcfg.zip". Execute Step B again, and then you can see that the configuration file to be loaded at the next startup has been modified to "vrpcfg1.zip".

```
<Huawei>startup saved-configuration vrpcfg1.zip
This operation will take several minutes, please wait....
 Info: Succeeded in setting the file for booting system
<Huawei>disp startup
MainBoard:
   Startup system software:                    null
   Next startup system software:               null
   Backup system software for next startup:    null
   Startup saved-configuration file:           flash:/vrpcfg.zip
   Next startup saved-configuration file:      flash:/vrpcfg1.zip
```

[Example 5.20]

Management of the next startup configuration file

The next startup configuration file is a backup file generated by the system in flash memory, which cannot be deleted, modified or renamed, and cannot be designated as the configuration file for the next startup by the [startup saved-configuration] command. The next startup configuration file will be lost only after the flash memory is formatted.

Operation steps for managing the next startup configuration file are as follows.

(i) Execute the [dir] command in the user view to view the available configuration file. During actual operation and maintenance, the configuration files previously backed up can be uploaded to the device in advance for standby.

```
<SRG>dir
13:45:28 2020/02/03
Directory of flash:/
   0  -rw-        61  Feb 03 2020 13:33:50  private-data.txt
   1  -rw-       986  Feb 03 2020 13:33:50  vrpcfg.zip
   2  -rw-       986  Feb 03 2020 13:36:19  backupcfg.zip
```

(ii) Execute the [backup-configuration backupcfg.zip] command in the user view to designate "backupcfg.zip" as the next startup configuration file.

```
<SRG>backup-configuration backupcfg.zip
```

(iii) Execute the [startup backup-configuration] command to set the next startup configuration file as the next startup configuration file.

```
<SRG>startup backup-configuration
```

(iv) Execute the [display startup] command in the user view and view the list of current startup configuration files, to confirm the next startup configuration file is set.

```
<Huawei>startup saved-configuration vrpcfg1.zip
This operation will take several minutes, please wait....
 Info: Succeeded in setting the file for booting system
<Huawei>disp startup
MainBoard:
   Startup system software:                      null
   Next startup system software:                 null
   Backup system software for next startup:      null
   Startup saved-configuration file:       flash:/vrpcfg.zip
   Next startup saved-configuration file:  flash:/vrpcfg1.zip
   Next startup configuration:             backup-configuration
```

In addition, after setting the next startup configuration file to be started next time, you can cancel the next startup configuration file to be started next time in the following two ways.

 (i) After modifying the configuration, execute the [save] command without parameters in the user view, and the system will use the saved configuration file as the configuration file for next startup, that is, cancel the next startup configuration file.
(ii) Execute the [undo startup backup-configuration] command to cancel the next startup configuration file as the next startup configuration file.

5.3.3   Configuration of Basic Network

Basic network configuration includes some simple service configurations, including IP address configuration, VLAN creation and configuration, static route configuration and so on. Next, the specific configuration process will be illustrated by cases.

1. Configuration of IP address
    IP address is a unique 32-bit address assigned to a host or interface connected to the Internet, which is the basis of network connection. In order to make the interface run IP service, it is necessary to configure IP address for the interface. IP address of interface can be configured manually; when IP addresses are scarce or used only occasionally, address borrowing can also be adopted.
    A layer 3 interface can be directly configured with IP address. For network devices without layer 3 interfaces, if they need to run IP services, they need to create VLAN virtual interface (VLANIF), and then configure IP address in

VLAN virtual interface. In addition, on the same device, IP addresses of different interfaces cannot be configured in the same network segment.

IP address configuration includes the following three steps.

(a) Execute the [system-view] command to enter the system view.
(b) Execute the [interface *interface-type interface-number*] command to enter the interface view.
(c) Execute the [ip address *ip-address* { *mask* | *mask-length* }] command to configure the IP address of the interface.

[Example 5.21]

IP address configuration

To configure the IP address of interface GE0/0/3 as "10.1.1.1/24", the example is as follows.

```
<Huawei>system-view
[Huawei] interface GigabitEthernet0/0/3
[Huawei-GigabitEthernet0/0/3] ip address 10.1.1.1 24
```

When IP addresses are scarce or an IP address is only used occasionally, the interface can be configured to borrow other existing IP addresses to save IP address resources. It should be noted that this configuration of borrowing IP addresses must comply with the following restrictions.

(a) Loopback interface and Ethernet interface can lent their IP addresses to other interfaces, but cannot borrow addresses from other interfaces.
(b) The borrowed interface itself cannot use the borrowed IP address.
(c) Borrowed IP addresses can be lent to multiple interfaces.
(d) If the borrowed interface has multiple IP addresses, only the main IP address can be lent.

The command to configure the borrowing of IP address is [ip address unnumbered interface interface-type *interface-number*].

[Example 5.22]

Configuration of IP address borrowing

For the tunnel interface, in order to save the IP address, the IP address of physical interface GE0/0/3 is borrowed here, and the operation steps are as follows.

a. execute the command [display ip interface brief] to display the IP addresses of all layer 3 interfaces.

```
[USG-GigabitEthernet0/0/3]display ip interface brief
*down: administratively down
(s) : spoofing
Interface                 IP Address      Physical    Protocol
Description
 GigabitEthernet0/0/3     10.2.1.1          up           up          USG
 LoopBack1                unassigned        up           up(s)       USG
 Tunnel0                  unassigned        up           down        USG
```

b. Configure the tunnel interface Tunnel 0 to borrow the IP address of GE0/0/3.

```
[USG] interface Tunnel 0
 [USG-Tunnel0] ip address unnumbered interface GigabitEthernet0/
 0/3
```

c. Display the borrowed interface IP address.

```
[USG-Tunnel0]display ip interface brief
*down: administratively down
(s) : spoofing
Interface                 IP Address      Physical      Protocol
Description
GigabitEthernet0/0/3      10.2.1.1          up     up      USG
LoopBack1                 unassigned        up     up(s)   USG
Tunnel0                   10.2.1.1          up     up      USG
```

2. Establishment and configuration of VLAN

The port-based approach is the simplest, most effective and most common way to divide VLAN. The following describes the basic configuration of VLAN in this way. Table 5.13 lists common VLAN-related commands.

[Example 5.23]
Basic configuration of VLAN

(a) Network topology

Figure 5.23 shows the topology of VLAN's basic configuration. Interface E0/0/24 of switch SW1 is connected with Interface E0/0/24 of switch SW2. Complete port-based VLAN configuration according to the networking topology is shown in Fig. 5.23.

Table 5.13 Common VLAN-related commands

Common command	View	Function
vlan *vlan-id*	System	Create a VLAN and enter the VLAN view
vlan batch {*vlan-id1* [to *vlan-id2*]} &<1-10>	System	Create VLANs in batch
interface interface-type *interface-number*	System	Enter the specified interface view
port link-type {access I hybrid I trunk I dot1q-tunnel}	System	Configure the link type of the interfaces
port default vlan *vlan-id*	Interface	Configure the default VLAN of the interface and join the VLAN
port interface-type {*interface-number1* [to *interface-number2*]}	VLAN	Add multiple specified interfaces to the specified VLAN in batch
port trunk allow-pass vlan {{*vlan-id1* [to *vlan-id2*]} &<1-10>Iall}	Interface	Configure VLANs to which Trunk interfaces join
port trunk pvid vlan *vlan-id*	Interface	Configure the default VLAN for Trunk interfaces
port hybrid untagged vlan {{*vlan-id1* [to *vlan-id2*]} &<1-10>Iall}	Interface	Configure VLANs to which Hybrid interfaces join, and the frames of these VLANs pass through the interface in untagged mode
port hybrid tagged vlan {{*vlan-id1* [to *vlan-id2*]} &<1-10>Iall}	Interface	Configure VLANs to which Hybrid interfaces join, and the frames of these VLANs pass through the interface in tagged mode
undo port hybrid vlan {{*vlan-id1* [to *vlan-id2*]} &<1-10>Iall}	Interface	Delete the VLANs for Hybrid interfaces
port hybrid pvid vlan *vlan-id*	Interface	Configure the default VLAN ID for Hybrid interfaces
display vlan [*vlan-id* [verbose]]	All	View information about all VLANs
display interface [interface-type [*interface-number*]]	All	View interface information
display port vlan [interface-type [*interface-number*]]	All	Check the interface information contained in the VLANs
display this	All	View the related configuration under the current view

(b) Networking requirements

    (i) The two downlink interfaces of SW1 are connected to VLAN 10 and VLAN 20 respectively.

    (ii) A downlink interface of SW2 accesses VLAN 20.

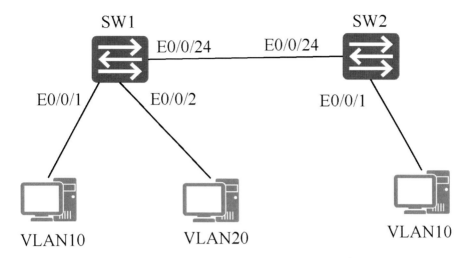

Fig. 5.23 Topology of VLAN's basic configuration

PCs in VLAN 10 need to be able to access each other, but PCs in VLAN 10 cannot access those in VLAN 20.

(c) Configuration ideas

The VLAN should be configured using the following ideas.

   (i) Create VLANs and plan the VLAN each employee should join.

  (ii) Configure the port attributes and determine the device connection objects.

 (iii) Associate ports and VLANs.

(d) Configuration steps

   (i) Configure SW1.

     • Create VLAN 10 and VLAN 20.

```
[SW1]vlan batch 10 20
```

     • Configure the port attributes.

```
[SW1]interface Ethernet0/0/1
[SW1-Ethernet0/0/1]port link-type access
[SW1-Ethernet0/0/1]port default vlan 10
[SW1-Ethernet0/0/1]quit
[SW1]interface Ethernet0/0/2
[SW1-Ethernet0/0/2]port link-type access
[SW1-Ethernet0/0/2]port default vlan 20
[SW1-Ethernet0/0/2]quit
[SW1]interface Ethernet0/0/24
[SW1-Ethernet0/0/24]port link-type trunk
[SW1-Ethernet0/0/24]port trunk allow-pass vlan 10 20
```

(ii) Configure SW2.

Refer to the configuration of SW1.

After completing the above configuration on the device, configure the IP address for each PC, just ensure that all IP addresses are in the same network segment. At this time, PCs in VLAN 10 can communicate with each other, but PCs in VLAN 10 cannot communicate with those in VLAN 20.

3. Static routing configuration

Common commands related to static routing are shown in Table 5.14.

[Example 5.24]

Static routing configuration

(a) Network topology

Figure 5.24 shows the topology of static routing configuration. The IP addresses and masks of each interface and host of the router are marked in the topology. In this example, static routing configuration is required, so that any two nodes in the graph can communicate with each other.

Table 5.14 Common commands related to static routing

Common Command	View	Function
ip route-static ip-address {mask|mask-length} {nexthop-address|interface-type interface-number [nexthop-address]} [preference preference|tag tag]	System	Configure unicast static routing
display ip interface [brief] [interface-type interface-number]	All	View the IP-related configuration and statistical information or brief information of the interface
display ip routing-table	All	View the routing table

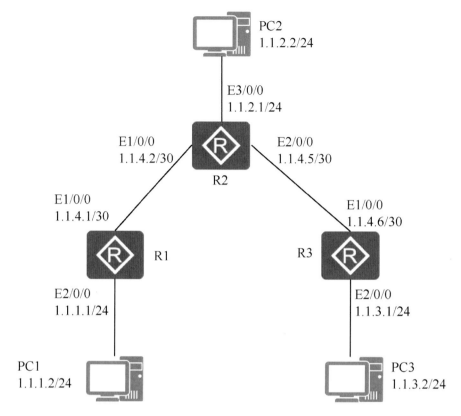

Fig. 5.24 Topology of static routing configuration

(b) Configuration ideas
    The configuration idea of this example is as follows

   (i) Configure the IPv4 address of each interface of each router to make the
      networks communicate with each other.
  (ii) Configure IPv4 static routing and default routing to destination address
      on router.
 (iii) Configure IPv4 default gateway on each host, so that any two hosts can
      communicate with each other.

(c) Data preparation
    To complete this configuration case, it is necessary to combine the work-
ing principle of static routing explained in Chap. 4, and understand and
prepare the following data.

   (i) The default route where the next hop of R1 is the 1.1.4.2.
  (ii) The static route where the destination address of R2 is 1.1.1.0 and the
      next hop is 1.1.4.1.

(iii) The static route where the destination address of R2 is 1.1.3.0 and the next hop is 1.1.4.6.
(iv) The default route where the next hop of R3 is the 1.1.4.5.
(v) The default gateways of hosts PC1, PC2 and PC3 are 1.1.1.1, 1.1.2.1 and 1.1.3.1, respectively.

(d) Configuration steps
   The specific reference configuration steps are as follows.

(i) Configure the IP address of each interface (refer to the IP address configuration above).
(ii) Configure the static routing.

   • Configure the default route for IPv4 on R1.

```
[R1] ip route-static 0.0.0.0 0.0.0.0 1.1.4.2
```

   • Configure the two default routes for IPv4 on R2.

```
[R2] ip route-static 1.1.1.0 255.255.255.0 1.1.4.1
[R2] ip route-static 1.1.3.0 255.255.255.0 1.1.4.6
```

   • Configure the default route for IPv4 on R3.

```
[R3] ip route-static 0.0.0.0 0.0.0.0 1.1.4.5
```

(iii) Configure the host. Configure the default gateways of hosts PC1, PC2 and PC3 as 1.1.1.1, 1.1.2.1 and 1.1.3.1 respectively.

After the configuration is completed, you can execute the command [display ip routing-table] to check the static routing configuration result.
(e) Result verification
(f) After the configuration is completed, you can execute the command [display ip routing-table] to view the IP routing table and check that the configured static routes are correctly added to the routing table.

```
[R1] display ip routing-table
Route Flags: R - relay, D - download to fib
------------------------
Routing Tables: Public
         Destinations : 8      Routes : 8
Destination/
Mask              Proto    Pre Cost Flags NextHop      Interface
0.0.0.0/0         Static   60   0    RD   1.1.4.2      Ethernet1/0/0
1.1.1.0/24        Direct   0    0    D    1.1.1.1      Ethernet2/0/0
1.1.1.1/32        Direct   0    0    D    127.0.0.1    InLoopBack0
1.1.4.0/30        Direct   0    0    D    1.1.4.1      Ethernet1/0/0
1.1.4.1/32        Direct   0    0    D    127.0.0.1    InLoopBack0
1.1.4.2/32        Direct   0    0    D    1.1.4.2      Ethernet1/0/0
127.0.0.0/8       Direct   0    0    D    127.0.0.1    InLoopBack0
127.0.0.1/32      Direct   0    0    D    127.0.0.1    InLoopBack0
```

After confirming that the static route is configured correctly, use the [ping] command to verify connectivity.

```
[R1] ping 1.1.3.1
PING 1.1.3.1: 56  data bytes, press CTRL_C to break
    Reply from 1.1.3.1: bytes=56 Sequence=1 ttl=254 time=62 ms
    Reply from 1.1.3.1: bytes=56 Sequence=2 ttl=254 time=63 ms
    Reply from 1.1.3.1: bytes=56 Sequence=3 ttl=254 time=63 ms
    Reply from 1.1.3.1: bytes=56 Sequence=4 ttl=254 time=62 ms
    Reply from 1.1.3.1: bytes=56 Sequence=5 ttl=254 time=62 ms
--- 1.1.3.1 ping statistics ---
    5 packet(s) transmitted
    5 packet(s) received
    0.00% packet loss
round-trip min/avg/max = 62/62/63 ms
```

You can also use the [ping] command on the PC to verify the connectivity to the router, and the operation method is similar to that on the router.

5.3.4 Configuration Related to Remote Login

As mentioned in Sect. 5.2.1, network device supports multiple login management modes, including login through Console port, through Telnet, through STelnet, through Web, etc. Among them, login through Console port is the most basic configuration mode, and it is also the basis of several other login management modes. That is to say, other login management methods must be completed after the necessary configuration is completed on the basis of logging in through the

Console port. This section mainly introduces the configuration of Telnet-based remote login and STelnet-based remote login.

1. Configuration related to Telnet-based remote login

   According to the topology structure of Telnet login management shown in Fig. 5.12, it is necessary to ensure the normal communication between the terminal PC and the Telnet server, that is, the IP address of the maintenance port of Telnet server can be pinged from the configured terminal. And then set the parameters used by the user when logging in, including the authentication method of the logged-in user, the level of the logged-in user, etc.

   There are three authentication methods for logged-in users, including none, password and AAA authentication. By default, the system adopts the method of non-authentication, that is, after Telnet login to the server, no information needs to be entered. When password authentication is used, the logged-in user needs to enter the correct password to complete the login. When AAA authentication is used, the logged-in user needs to enter the correct username and password to complete the login.

[Example 5.25]

Configuration related to Telnet-based remote login

   Because Telnet remote login only supports AAA authentication, this example uses password authentication when explaining Telnet related configuration, and the AAA authentication is explained in Telnet remote login below. The logged-in user is at Level 0 by default, and the login password is "Huawei@123". The detailed configuration process is given below.

   (a) Execute the [system-view] command to enter the system view.

```
<Huawei>system-view
```

   (b) Execute the command [user-interface vty *first-ui-number last-ui-number*] to enter the VTY user interface view.

```
[Huawei]user-interface vty 0 4
```

   (c) Execute the [protocol inbound telnet] command to configure the protocol for the VTY user interface to support Telnet.

```
[Huawei-ui-vty0-4]protocol inbound telnet
```

(d) Execute the command [authentication-mode password] to set the authentication mode as password authentication.

```
[Huawei-ui-vty0-4]authentication-mode password
```

(e) Execute the command [set password cipher|simple Huawei@123] to set the login password.

```
[Huawei-ui-vty0-4]set authentication password cipher Huawei@123
```

(f) Execute the command [user privilege level 0] to set the default level of the logged-in user.

```
[Huawei-ui-vty0-4]user privilege level 0
```

2. Configuration related to STelnet-based remote login

   To log in to the device through STelnet, it needs to be configured that the protocol supported by the user interface is SSH, so the authentication mode of VTY user interface must be set to AAA authentication; otherwise, the VTY user interface cannot be successfully configured to support SSH protocol when executing the [protocol inbound ssh] command.

   In addition, SSH users are used for STelnet login. On the basis of configuring AAA authentication as the authentication mode of VTY user interface, it is also necessary to configure authentication mode of SSH users. SSH user authentication supports password authentication, RSA (Rivest-Shamir-Adleman) authentication, elliptic curves cryptography (ECC) authentication, password-RSA authentication, password-ECC authentication and ALL authentication.

   (a) Password authentication: an authentication method based on "user name + password". Configure the corresponding password for each SSH user through AAA. When logging in through SSH, you can log in by entering the correct username and password.
   (b) RSA algorithm authentication: a verification method based on the client's private key. RSA is a public key encryption system based on asymmetric encryption algorithm. RSA key consists of public key and private key. During configuration, the public key generated by the client needs to be copied to the server, and the server uses this public key to encrypt data. A device as an SSH client can only store up to 20 keys.
   (c) ECC authentication: An elliptic curve algorithm, compared with RSA, featuring shorter key length, less computation, faster processing speed, smaller

storage space and lower bandwidth requirements under the same security performance.

(d) Password-RSA authentication: The SSH server performs password authentication and RSA authentication on the logged-in user at the same time, and only when both are met can the authentication pass.

(e) Password-ECC authentication: The SSH server performs password authentication and ECC authentication on the logged-in user at the same time, and only when both are met can the authentication pass.

(f) ALL authentication: The SSH server performs RSA authentication, ECC authentication or password authentication on the logged-in user, and the authentication can pass as long as any one of them is met.

[Example 5.26]
Configuration related to STelnet-based remote login

Assume that the STelnet login user name is "Huawei", the password is "Huawei@123", the authentication method of SSH user is password authentication, and the default level of login user is Level 0, the detailed configuration process is given below.

(a) Enter AAA view and create a remote login user.

```
[Huawei]aaa
[Huawei-aaa]local-user Huawei password cipher Huawei@123
[Huawei-aaa]local-user Huawei privilege level 0
[Huawei-aaa]local-user Huawei service-type telnet ssh
```

(b) Enter the user interface view, configure the authentication mode as AAA authentication, the user level as Level 0, and the SSH protocol to be supported.

```
[Huawei]user-interface vty 0 4
[Huawei-ui-vty0-4]authentication-mode aaa
[Huawei-ui-vty0-4]user privilege level 0
[Huawei-ui-vty0-4]protocol inbound ssh
```

(c) Configure the SSH user authentication mode. Here, for simplicity, it is configured as password authentication, and the RSA authentication involves key creation, so interested readers can consult the product manual by themselves.

```
[Huawei] ssh user Huawei authentication-type password
```

(d) Configure SSH server functions.

```
[Huawei] stelnet server enable
[Huawei] rsa local-key-pair create
The key name will be: Host
% RSA keys defined for Host already exist.
Confirm to replace them? (y/n) [n] :y
The range of public key size is (512 ~ 2048).
NOTES: If the key modulus is greater than 512,
           It will take a few minutes.
Input the bits in the modulus [default = 512]:
Generating keys...
....................++++++++++++
...............++++++++++++
....++++++++
...............................++++++++
```

3. Configuration related to Web login

Generally, the device supports login via HTTP or HTTPS, but for security reasons, it is recommended to turn off HTTP and adopt HTTPS-based login.

Generally, configuring the Web login management includes the following three steps.

(a) Configure the maintenance interface.
(b) Configure the user for Web login.
(c) Open HTTPS and configure protocol parameters.

Next, the detailed processes of configuring Web login on AR router and USG6000V firewall are illustrated by cases.

[Example 5.27]
Configuration of Web login on AR router

The topology of Web login on AR router is shown in Fig. 5.25.

After logging in the device through the Console port, use CLI to complete the configuration related to Web login as follows.

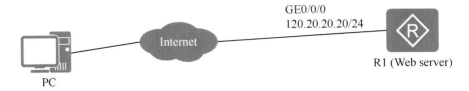

GE0/0/0
120.20.20.20/24

R1 (Web server)

PC

Fig. 5.25 Topology of Web login on AR router

(a) Configure the maintenance interface IP address.

```
<Huawei>system-view
[Huawei]interface GigabitEthernet0/0/0
[Huawei-GigabitEthernet0/0/0]ip add 120.20.20.20 24
```

(b) Configure the Web login user, whose username is "Huawei" and password is "Huawei@123".

```
[Huawei]aaa
[Huawei-aaa]local-user Huawei password cipher Huawei@123
[Huawei-aaa]local-user Huawei service-type web
```

(c) Turn on HTTPS and configure relevant parameters. HTTPS on AR router uses Port 443 by default.

```
[Huawei]http server enable
[Huawei]http secure-server port 8443
```

After the above configuration is completed, open the browser on the PC and use the URL "https://120.20.20.20:8443" to log in to the router.

[Example 5.28]
Configuration of Web login on the USG6000V Fireware

The topology of Web login on the USG6000V Fireware is shown in Fig. 5.26.
After logging in the device through the Console port, use CLI to complete the configuration related to Web login as follows.

GE0/0/0
120.20.20.20/24

Firewall1 (Web server)

Fig. 5.26 Topology of Web login on the USG6000V Fireware

(a) Configure the maintenance interface, and designate the interface to a safe area (such as trust area).

```
<USG6000V>system-view
[USG6000V]interface GigabitEthernet 0/0/0
[USG6000V-GigabitEthernet0/0/0]ip add 120.20.20.20 24
[USG6000V1]firewall zone trust
[USG6000V-zone-trust]add interface GigabitEthernet 0/0/0
```

(b) Configure the Web login user, whose username is "Huawei" and password is "Huawei@123".

```
[USG6000V]aaa
[USG6000V-aaa]local-user Huawei password cipher Huawei@123
[USG6000V-aaa]local-user Huawei service-type web
```

(c) Turn on HTTPS and configure relevant parameters. HTTPS on the USG6000V Fireware uses Port 8443 by default.

```
<USG6000V>system-view
[USG6000V]interface GigabitEthernet 0/0/0
[USG6000V1-GigabitEthernet0/0/0]service-manage https permit
```

After the above configuration is completed, open the browser on the PC and use the URL "https://120.20.20.20:8443" to log in to the fireware.

5.4 Summary

The basic operation of network is one of the important components of network operation and maintenance. This chapter takes Huawei's network devices as examples to introduce the common basic operations of network devices. Section 5.1 first introduces the network operating system VRP for Huawei's data communication products, and then focuses on some skills of using CLI; Section 5.2 introduces the common login management modes of network devices, including the CLI mode and Web mode, among which the CLI mode can be subdivided into Console port, Telnet and STelnet modes; Section 5.3 introduces how to perform some basic operations on devices through CLI, including device environment configuration, operation and management of configuration files, basic network configuration, configuration related to remote login, etc.

Through the study in this chapter, readers should understand the network operating system, master the use of Huawei VRP and its CLI, get familiar with and master the login management modes of network devices, master some basic operations in network operation and maintenance, and be able to make necessary configuration for devices according to design requirements or usage habits.

5.5 Exercise

1. VRP is the abbreviation of ().

   A. Versatile Routine Platform
   B. Virtual Routing Platform
   C. Virtual Routing Plane
   D. Versatile Routing Platform

2. [Multi-choice] VRP supports Telnet users of ().

   A. Visiting class
   B. Monitoring level
   C. Configuration level
   D. Management level

3. For Huawei routers, the user needs to input the command () to enter the system view from the user view.

   A. system-view
   B. enable
   C. configure terminal
   D. interface system

4. [Multi-choice] When logging in to the router by Telnet, you can choose ().

   A. Password authentication
   B. AAA authentication
   C. MD5 authentication
   D. Non-authentication

5. [Multi-choice] Compared with Telnet, SSH has the advantage of ().

    A. Encrypting all transmitted data to avoid man-in-the-middle attacks
    B. Preventing DNS and IP spoofing
    C. Accelerating the transmission because the transmitted data is compressed
    D. Being suitable for large-scale use based on UDP connection

Chapter 6
Basic Operation and Maintenance of Network System

During the operation of the network system, the operation and maintenance personnel need to manage the hardware and software resources in the network system according to the service requirements, and at the same time, monitor and regularly maintain the switches, routers, wireless AC/AP, firewalls, servers and other equipment in the network system, so as to quickly and effectively collect fault information, analyze the cause of the fault and recover the equipment in time.

This chapter will first introduce the resource management in network operation and maintenance, including hardware resource management and software resource management. Among them, hardware resource management includes the management of electronic labels, CPU, memory, single board and other resources of network equipment, while software resource management includes the management of license, system software, configuration files and other resources. Then, the routine maintenance and fault handling of network system will be introduced, in which the purpose of routine maintenance is to find and eliminate the hidden trouble of network equipment, while the purpose of fault handling is to quickly analyze and locate the fault and repair it after the fault occurs, so as to resume service.

By the end of this chapter, you will

(1) Understand the management of network system	(4) Master how to manage software resources.
(2) Understand the maintenance of network system	(5) Familiar with routine maintenance of the equipment room
(3) Master how to manage hardware resources	(6) Acquire the ability to handle common faults

© The Author(s) 2023
Huawei Technologies Co., Ltd., *Construction, Operation and Maintenance of Network System(Junior Level)*, https://doi.org/10.1007/978-981-19-3069-0_6

6.1 Network System Resource Management

Before the management and maintenance of the network system, the operation and maintenance personnel should first collect the planning and data information of the whole network system, including network topology, data planning, user name and password of remote login, etc., so as to query, compare and maintain at any time in the later period.

The resource management of network system includes the management and maintenance of hardware and software resources of equipment in the whole network system. The management of hardware resources mainly refers to the management of equipment system resources (CPU and memory), cables, boards, fans, etc., while the management of software resources includes equipment license management, system software and patch management, backup and recovery of configuration files, user information management, etc.

6.1.1 Hardware Resource Management and Maintenance

Hardware resource management refers to the operation and management of hardware resources of equipment through command line, such as resetting boards, backing up electronic labels, turning on or off power supply, etc. In the process of equipment operation, the necessary management of hardware resources can reduce the actual plugging, unplugging or loading/unloading of equipment hardware resources, which is convenient and fast, and can improve the reliability of hardware resources. Common hardware resource management will be described in detail below.

1. Electronic label backup

    Electronic labels, also known as radio frequency tags, which are commonly called equipment serial numbers, play a very important role in dealing with network failures and replacing hardware in batches.

    When the network breaks down, the related hardware information can be obtained conveniently and accurately through the electronic labels, which improves the efficiency of maintenance work. At the same time, through the statistical analysis of the electronic label information of the faulty hardware, the hardware defect can be analyzed more accurately and efficiently. In addition, when replacing hardware in batches, the distribution of hardware in the whole network can be accurately learned through the electronic label information established in the file system of customer equipment, which is convenient to evaluate the impact of replacement and formulate corresponding strategies, thus improving the efficiency of replacing hardware in batches.

    Huawei's network equipment supports backing up electronic labels to file servers or device storage media. When backing up the electronic labels to the file server, it is necessary to ensure that the device and the file server communicates with each other with accessible routes. The currently supported file servers are FTP server and TFTP server.

To execute the [backup elabel] command to back up the electronic label, there are three methods.

(a) Execute the [backup elabel *filename* [*slot-id*]] command to back up the electronic label to the device storage medium.
(b) Execute the command [backup elabel ftp *ftp-server-address filename username password* [*slot-id*]] to back up the electronic label to the FTP server.
(c) Execute the command [backup elabel tftp *tftp-server-address filename* [*slot-id*]] to back up the electronic label to the TFTP server.

Then, taking router AR3260 as an example, the specific process of backing up electronic labels is shown as follows.

[Example 6.1]
Backup of electronic label

Method (1): Back up to a storage device, which is the simplest method. Assuming that the file name of the electronic label is "ar3260_elabel", execute the command [backup elabel ar3260_elabel] directly, as detailed below.

```
<Huawei>backup elabel ar3260_elabel
It is executing, please wait...
Backup elabel successfully!
```

Method (2): Back up to the FTP server. The network topology is shown in Fig. 6.1. The FTP server's IP address is 192.168.0.11, the user name is "user1", and the password is "pass1". Ensure that the user has the permission to upload files. The command and execution results are as follows.

```
<Huawei>backup elabel ftp 192.168.0.11 ar3260_elabel user1 pass1
It is executing, please wait...
Backup elabel successfully!
```

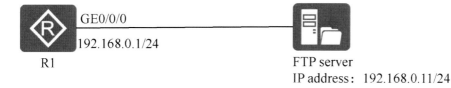

Fig. 6.1 Network topology of backup to the FTP server

GE0/0/0

192.168.0.1/24

R1

TFTP server

IP address: 192.168.0.11/24

Fig. 6.2 Network topology of backup to the TFTP server

After the above operation, the backup file "ar3260_elabel" can be found in the root directory of the FTP server, indicating that the electronic label was successfully backed up.

Method (3): Back up to the TFTP server. The network topology is shown in Fig. 6.2. The command and execution results are as follows.

```
<Huawei>backup elabel tftp 192.168.0.11 ar3260_elabel
  It is executing, please wait...
Info: Transfer file in binary mode.
Uploading the file to the remote TFTP server. Please wait...
TFTP: Uploading the file successfully.
     915 bytes send in 1 second.
```

After the above operation, the file transfer process can be queried in the TFTP server, and the backup file "ar3260_elabel" can be found in the root directory of the TFTP server, indicating that the electronic label was successfully backed up (Fig. 6.3).

2. Configuration of the alarm of CPU usage threshold

CPU is the core part of the equipment. When there is a lot of routing information in the system, it will take up a lot of CPU resources, which will greatly affect the system performance, resulting in data processing delay or high packet loss rate. In the process of data processing, if we get an alarm to the CPU with high usage rate in time, we can more effectively monitor the CPU usage and optimize the system performance, so as to ensure that the system is always in a benign operation state.

The alarm threshold of CPU usage includes usage threshold and restore threshold, whose configuration calls for the following three steps.

(a) Execute the command [display cpu-usage configuration] to view the configuration information of CPU usage rate of the equipment.
(b) Execute the [system-view] command to display the system view.
(c) Execute the command [set cpu-usage threshold *threshold-value* [**restore** *restore-threshold-value*] [**slot** *slot-id*]] to configure the CPU usage threshold alarm and restore threshold.

By default, the CPU usage threshold is 80%, and the restore threshold is 75%.

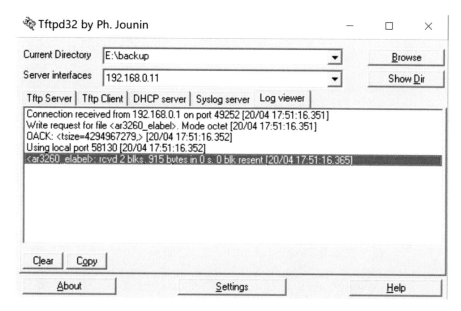

Fig. 6.3 File transfer process in the TFTP server

3. Configuration of the alarm of memory usage threshold

Memory usage rate is one of the important indicators to measure equipment performance. In the process of network equipment running, too high memory usage rate will lead to abnormal service. During the process of data processing, if we get an alarm to the memory with high usage rate in time, we can more effectively monitor the memory usage and optimize the system performance, so as to ensure that the system is always in a benign operation state. So how to configure the alarm of memory usage threshold? The steps are as follows.

(a) Execute the command [display memory-usage threshold] to view the configuration information of the device memory usage rate.
(b) Execute the [system-view] command to display the system view.
(c) Execute the [set memory-usage threshold *threshold-value*] command to configure the alarm of memory usage threshold.

4. Board management

There are many slots in the frame equipment, which can be used to carry many redundant network interface cards, including system bus, power supply, security module, etc. The so-called board management refers to the operation management of the board in a single slot. In the process of equipment operation, board management allows maintenance or troubleshooting of equipment with as little disruption to service as possible. Huawei network equipment supports the operation management of a single board, including board reset, power-on and power-off of the board, and the active/standby switchover of the master control board.

(a) Board reset

In the actual operation and maintenance process, in order to provide better services, a single board may need to be upgraded. During the upgrade, the board may fail. At this time, we can repair the failure by resetting the board. Execute the command [reset slot *slot-id*] to reset the board in the slot corresponding to "slot-id". In the following, taking router AR3260 as an example, the operation steps of resetting a board are introduced.

[Example 6.2]

Reset a board

(i) Execute the [display device] command to view the status information of the board. The execution results are as follows.

```
[Huawei]display device
AR3260's Device status:
Slot Sub Type      Online    Power      Register      Alarm    Primary
- - - - - - - - - - - - - - - - - - - - - - - - - - - - - - - - - - - -
2   -  2E1/T1-F    Present   PowerOn    Registered    Normal   NA
3   -  2E1/T1-F    Present   PowerOn    Registered    Normal   NA
4   -  1GEC        Present   PowerOn    Registered    Normal   NA
6   -  8FE1GE      Present   PowerOn    Registered    Normal   NA
15  -  SRU80       Present   PowerOn    Registered    Normal   Master
16  -  FAN         Present   PowerOn    Registered    Normal   NA
```

(ii) Reset the board, for example, resetting the board "2E1/T1-F" in the slot "2". The command and execution results are as follows.

```
<Huawei>reset slot 2
Are you sure you want to reset board in slot 2 ? [y/n]:y
Feb 7 2020 14:56:40-08:00 Huawei %%01DEV/4/ENTRESET(1)[0]:Board
[2] is reset, The reason is: Reset by user command.
INFO: Resetting board[2] succeeded.
```

In addition, for equipment supporting dual master control boards, the standby master control board can also be reset without affecting the normal operation of the equipment. At this time, just execute the [slave restart] command in the system view.

(b) Power-on and power-off of the board

The actual network has certain service redundancy, including network-level redundancy, equipment-level redundancy and board-level redundancy. That is to say, in the actual network, some boards on the equipment may be idle. Therefore, the designated idle board can be powered off without interfering the service, which is beneficial to the stable operation of the system and saves energy. When the board is needed for later service expansion, it can be powered on in real time without impeding service expansion. In the following, taking router AR3260 as an example, the operation steps of power-on and power-off of the board are introduced.

(i) Power-off of the board

  Execute the [power off] command to power off the board. Example 6.3 shows the process of powering off an idle board.

[Example 6.3]
Power-off of the board

  Taking router AR3260 as an example, the operation steps of powering off the board are as follows.

- Execute the [display device] command to view the status information of the board. There are many slots in the network equipment, especially the frame equipment, which can be used to carry many redundant network interface cards, including system bus, power supply, security module, etc.

```
<Huawei>disp device
AR3260's Device status:
Slot Sub Type        Online    Power      Register    Alarm    Primary
- - - - - - - - - - - - - - - - - - - - - - - - - - - - - - - - - - - - - -
2    -  2E1/T1-F     Present   PowerOn    Registered  Normal   NA
3    -  2E1/T1-F     Present   PowerOn    Registered  Normal   NA
4    -  1GEC         Present   PowerOn    Registered  Normal   NA
6    -  8FE1GE       Present   PowerOn    Registered  Normal   NA
15   -  SRU80        Present   PowerOn    Registered  Normal   Master
16   -  FAN          Present   PowerOn    Registered  Normal   NA
```

- Assume that the board in Slot 3 is idle, not hosting any service. Enter the user view and execute the command [power off slot 3] to power off the board.

```
<Huawei>power off slot 3
Feb 7 2020 15:56:02-08:00 Huawei %%01DEV/4/ENTPOWER
OFF(1)[0]:Board[3] is power off, The reason is: Power off by user
command.
```

(ii) Power-on of the board

As power-off of the board, the power-on is also supported. When the powered off board is needed for later service expansion, just execute the command [power on] to power on the board.

[Example 6.4]

Power-on of the board

Also taking router AR3260 as an example, the operation steps of powering on the board are as follows.

- Execute the [disp device] command to view the status information of the board.

```
<Huawei>disp device
AR3260's Device status:
Slot Sub Type      Online   Power    Register    Alarm    Primary
- - - - - - - - - - - - - - - - - - - - - - - - - - - - - - - - - - - -
2    -  2E1/T1-F   Present  PowerOn  Registered  Normal   NA
3    -  2E1/T1-F   Present  PowerOff Registered  Normal   NA
4    -  1GEC       Present  PowerOn  Registered  Normal   NA
6    -  8FE1GE     Present  PowerOn  Registered  Normal   NA
15   -  SRU80      Present  PowerOn  Registered  Normal   Master
16   -  FAN        Present  PowerOn  Registered  Normal   NA
```

- Enter the user view and execute the command [power on slot 3] to power on the board in Slot 3.

```
<Huawei>power on slot 3
Info: Power on slot [3] successfully.
Feb 7 2020 16:02:42-08:00 Huawei %%01DEV/4/ENTPOWERON(1)[8]:
Board[3] is power on.
```

(c) Active/Standby switchover of the master control board

For some equipment supporting hot backup by dual master control boards, during software upgrade or system maintenance, operation and maintenance personnel can manually switch between the active master control board and the standby master control board. This operation process is called active/ standby switchover. After active/standby switchover, the current master control board will be restarted and become the standby master control board after startup, and the current standby master control board will become the active master control board.

It is important to note that during the active/standby switchover of the equipment, it is forbidden to plug, unplug or reset all the active and standby master control boards, service interface boards, power modules or fan modules, otherwise, the whole equipment may restart or fail.

The active/standby switchover of the master control board is only applicable to some equipment supporting hot backup by dual master control boards. The specific operation steps are as follows.

(i) Execute the command [display switchover state] to check whether the active or standby master control board meets the conditions for switchover. It must be emphasized again that only when the master control boards are in the real-time backup stage, the user can perform the active/standby switchover operation.

(ii) Execute the [system-view] command to display the system view.

(iii) Execute the command [switchover enable] to enable the active/standby switchover operation. By default, the active/standby switchover function is enabled.

(iv) Execute the [slave switchover] command to perform the switchover.

5. Interface management

The interfaces in the equipment include management interface, physical interface and logical interface. A management interface mainly provides configuration management support for the user. The user can log in to the device and perform configuration and management operations through this interface. A management interface does not undertake service transmission, such as Console port, MiniUSB port and Meth. The physical interface is a real interface supported by the device, which is responsible for service transmission, such as Ethernet, Gigabit Ethernet, Serial interface, etc. A logical interface refers to the interface that can realize the data exchange function but does not exist physically, which needs to be established through configuration, such as Loopback, Eth-Trunk, VLANIF, Tunnel, etc.

Interface management includes basic parameter configuration, physical interface configuration, logical interface configuration, etc. The basic parameter configuration refers to setting interface description information, bandwidth, traffic statistics, etc. The physical interface configuration refers to the configuration of real Layer 2 and Layer 3 interfaces, including VLAN configuration and IP address configuration. The logical interface configuration refers to the configuration of Null0, Loopback, Tunnel and other interfaces, mainly for configuring IP addresses. The following mainly introduces the basic parameter configuration. For the configuration of VLAN and IP address, please refer to Chaps. 4 and 5.

(a) Configuration of interface description information

In order to facilitate the management and maintenance of equipment, the interface description information can be configured during actual operation and maintenance, describing the equipment to which the interface belongs, the interface type, the opposite network element equipment and other information.

[Example 6.5]
Configuration of interface description information

Assuming that the current interface is connected to the "GE0/0/1 interface" of Device B, the description information can be configured as "To_DeviceB_GE0/0/1″ through the following configuration.

```
[Huawei-GigabitEthernet0/0/0]description To_DeviceB_GE0/0/1
```

(b) Configuration of interface bandwidth and network management bandwidth

The Ethernet interface supports bandwidth setting and network management bandwidth setting.

The [speed] command is used to configure the speed of the Ethernet interface in non-auto-negotiation mode. By default, when an Ethernet interface works in a non-auto-negotiation mode, the speed is the maximum supported by the interface, so the auto-negotiation function must be disabled before using the [speed] command to modify the bandwidth.

The [bandwidth] command is used to set the interface bandwidth acquired by the network management device on MIB. By default, the interface bandwidth acquired by the network management device on MIB involves the interface type, and configuring the interface bandwidth acquired by the network management device does not change the actual bandwidth of the interface. For example, the actual bandwidth of the GE interface is 1000 Mbit/s, and the command [bandwidth 10] can be executed under the GE interface view to configure the interface bandwidth acquired by the network management device to 10 Mbit/s.

[Example 6.6]
Configuration of interface bandwidth

The following is a configuration example of modifying the bandwidth of the GE interface to 10Mbit/s.

```
<Huawei>system-view
[Huawei]interface GigabitEthernet0/0/0
[Huawei-GigabitEthernet0/0/0]undo negotiation auto
[Huawei-GigabitEthernet0/0/0]speed 10
```

(c) Setting of the interval of interface traffic statistics

By setting the interval of interface traffic statistics, the user can make statistics and analysis on interested packets. At the same time, network congestion and service interruption can be avoided by checking the interface traffic statistics in advance and taking timely measures of traffic control. By default, the interval of interface traffic statistics is 300 s. When the user detect network congestion, they can set the interval to less than 300 s (set to 30s when congestion intensifies) and observe the traffic distribution in a short time. For data packets that cause congestion, traffic control measures can be taken. When the network bandwidth is abundant and the service runs normally, the traffic statistics interval can be set to be greater than 300 s. Once abnormal flow parameters are found, it is necessary to modify the interval in time, so as to observe the trend of the traffic parameters in real time.

Huawei network equipment supports executing the command [set flow-stat interval *interval-time*] in system view to set the interval of interface traffic statistics. This setting in the system view is effective for all interfaces with the default interval; while the setting in the interface view only takes effect on this interface, not affecting other interfaces, with priority higher than the interval configured in system view.

[Example 6.7]
Setting of the interval of interface traffic statistics

Next, set the traffic statistics interval of interface GE0/0/0 to 100 s and other intervals to 200 s. The setting example is as follows.

```
<Huawei>system-view
[Huawei]set flow-stat interval 200
[Huawei]interface GigabitEthernet0/0/0
[Huawei-GigabitEthernet0/0/0]set flow-stat interval 100
```

(i) Configure to open or close the interface

When the working parameter configuration of the interface is modified and the new configuration fails to take effect immediately, execute the [shutdown] and [undo shutdown] commands in turn, or execute the [restart] command to shut down and restart the interface to make the new configuration take effect.

By default, all interfaces are open. When an interface is idle (i.e., no cable or optical fiber is connected), it is best to use the [shutdown] command to shut down the interface to prevent it from being abnormal due to interference. It is important to note that some logical interfaces (such as Null0 and Loopback interfaces) will remain open once they are created, and cannot be shut down or opened by command.

(ii) Clear interface statistics.

If it is necessary to conduct statistics on the traffic of the interface in a period of time, the original statistics information must be cleared before the statistics start. The [reset counters interface] command can be used to clear the statistical information of the specified interface, whose format is [reset counters interface { *interface-type* [*interface-number*] }], where "interface-type" indicates the interface type and "interface-number" indicates the interface No. If no interface type is specified, the statistics information of all types of interfaces will be cleared. If you specify an interface type without specifying an interface No., the statistics of all interfaces of that type will be cleared.

The [reset counters interface] command clears the statistics information of input and output packets of the interface, which cannot be recovered after clearing, and the packet statistics of each interface is the basis of traffic charging. Thus, clearing the statistics information of the interface will have an impact on the result of traffic charging. Therefore, in the normal application environment, do not clear the interface statistics at will.

6. Optical module alarm management

Huawei's network equipment supports both Huawei-certified optical modules and non-Huawei-certified optical modules, but it should be noted that when non-Huawei-certified optical modules are used on the device, the functions of these optical modules may not work normally, and the system will generate a large number of alarms, trying to remind the user to replace it with Huawei-certified ones for management and maintenance. In addition, the optical modules produced by Huawei in the early days may not record the manufacturer information, thus also generating the alarms to non-Huawei-certified modules.

On the device, check the general, manufacturing and alarm information of the optical module by executing the command [display transceiver]. For Huawei-certified optical modules, you can choose the most suitable optical module alarm method by configuring the optical module alarm function; for non-Huawei-certified modules, in order to make full use of resources, they can continue to service in the device, but it is recommended to turn off such alarms by command.

For Huawei-certified optical modules, the operation steps of alarm management are as follows.

(a) Execute the command [display transceiver] to check the general, manufacturing and alarm information of the optical module on the device interface.

(b) Configure the optical module alarm switch. In the system view, the power alarm switch of the optical module can be turned on by executing the command [set transceiver-monitoring enable]. Execute the command [set transceiver-monitoring disable] to turn off the power alarm switch. By default, the power alarm switch of the optical module is turned on.

(c) Configure the threshold for the transmitting power alarm to the optical module. Enter the optical interface view to be configured, and execute the commands [set transceiver transmit-power upper-threshold *upper-value*] and [set transceiver transmit-power lower-threshold *lower-value*], respectively, to set the upper and lower thresholds of the optical module's transmitting power. When the transmitting power exceeds the range defined by the upper and lower thresholds, an alarm will be generated.

(d) Configure the threshold for the receiving power alarm to the optical module. Enter the optical interface view to be configured, and execute the commands [set transceiver receive-power upper-threshold *upper-value*] and [set transceiver receive-power lower-threshold *lower-value*], respectively, to set the upper and lower thresholds of the optical module's receiving power. When the receiving power exceeds the range defined by the upper and lower thresholds, an alarm will be generated.

By default, the alarm function of non-Huawei-certified optical modules is enabled. In order to make these modules work normally on the device without generating a large number of alarms, it is recommended to disable the alarm function. To disable the function, execute the command [transceiver phony-alarm-disable] in the system view.

7. Energy saving management

With the continuous expansion of network scale, the energy consumption of equipment accounts for an increasing proportion of operating costs, and "green" and "energy saving" have become the main concerns of network construction and operation. The equipment in the network system supports the adoption of many energy-saving technologies to reduce energy consumption, so as to achieve the purpose of green energy saving.

The energy-saving management technologies supported by Huawei network equipment include automatic fan speed regulation, Automatic Laser Shutdown (ALS), Energy Efficient Ethernet (EEE), etc. The specific characteristics of these three energy-saving management technologies are described as follows.

(a) Automatic fan speed regulation

The fan adopts automatic speed regulation strategy to monitor the temperature of key components of the device. When the temperature of a sensitive device inside the equipment is higher than the set value, the fan speed is increased; and when the temperature is lower than the set value, the fan speed is reduced. Finally, the equipment is controlled in a stable temperature state, so as to save energy and reduce noise.

(b) ALS

The ALS controls the light emission of the optical module laser by detecting the loss of signal (LoS) at the optical port. It provides the user with security protection, and at the same time, reduces energy consumption by the user. If the device does not enable or support the ALS function, when the interface optical fiber is not in place or the optical fiber link fails, although the data communication is interrupted, the optical interface is not turned off and the light emitting function of the optical module laser is turned on. When the data communication is interrupted, the continuous light emission by the optical module laser will not only cause the waste of energy, but also cause certain danger, because the laser accidentally entering the human eye will also cause certain harm. On the contrary, if the equipment enables the ALS function, when the interface optical fiber is not in place or the optical fiber link fails, after the system detects the LoS signal of the optical port, it can be judged that the service has been interrupted at this time, and the system will automatically turn off the optical module laser; when the optical fiber or optical fiber link plugged into the interface is restored, the system detects that the LoS signal of the optical port is cleared, and automatically turns on the optical module laser, thereby resuming the service.

(c) EEE

EEE is an energy-saving method that dynamically adjusts the power of electrical interfaces according to network traffic. If the device is not configured with the power self-adjustment function for the electrical interfaces, the system will supply power to each interface with constant power, and even if an interface is idle, it consumes the same energy. On the contrary, if the power self-adjustment function of the electrical interfaces is configured, when an interface is idle, the system will automatically reduce the power supply to the interface, thus saving the overall energy consumption of the system; when the interface starts to transmit data normally, it will resume normal power supply without affecting normal service.

The configuration processes related to these three energy-saving management technologies are introduced below.

(a) Configuration of automatic fan speed regulation

The fan speed affects the device temperature. Reasonable adjustment of the fan speed helps keep the device in a stable temperature and state. By default, the system enables the automatic fan speed regulation, that is, the system automatically adjusts the fan speed according to the device state. Under normal circumstances, when the fan runs in the automatic state, the noise is low, the energy is saved and the normal function of the system is not affected. It is suggested to confirm the current device temperature and fan state before configuring the fan speed, and then reasonably adjust the fan speed according to the current device state, that is, if the current temperature is too high, the fan speed can be increased, otherwise, the fan speed can be reduced. Specific operation steps are as follows.

(i) Execute the command [display temperature all] to check the device temperature information.
(ii) Execute the [display fan] command to check the current state of the fan.
(iii) Execute the command [set fan-speed fan *slot-id* percent *percent*] in the system view to adjust the fan speed. For example, by executing the command [set fan-speed fan 0 percent 100], the fan speed on Slot 0 is adjusted to 100%, that is, the maximum speed. If there are multiple fans on the board, all fans will be adjusted to the maximum speed.

(b) ALS configuration

The ALS function is only applicable under the optical port, not supported by the electric port. Next come the steps of ALS configuration.

[Example 6.8]
ALS configuration

In the topology shown in Fig. 6.4, the interfaces GE1/0/0 of R1 and GE1/0/0 of R2 are interconnected by optical fiber. The user hopes that when the link fails, the optical module laser of the optical port can automatically turn off the light emission, and can resume it after the link recovers, so as to achieve the purpose of energy saving. To meet this requirement, it is necessary to configure the interfaces interconnected by two routers to enable the ALS function, so as to automatically turn off the light emission when the link fails, and at the same time, configure the laser to automatic restart mode, so that the laser will automatically resume lighting when the link is restored.

(i) Enable the ALS function of interface GE1/0/0 of R1, and configure the restart mode of the laser as automatic restart. The specific commands are as follows.

```
<Huawei> system-view
[Huawei] sysname R1
[R1] interface GigabitEthernet1/0/0
[R1-GigabitEthernet1/0/0] als
[R1-GigabitEthernet1/0/0] als restart mode automatic
[R1-GigabitEthernet1/0/0] return
```

(ii) Enable the ALS function of interface GE1/0/0 of R2, and configure the restart mode of the laser as automatic restart. The specific commands are as follows.

Fig. 6.4 Topology of ALS configuration

```
<Huawei> system-view
[Huawei] sysname R2
[R2 interface GigabitEthernet1/0/0
[R2-GigabitEthernet1/0/0] als
[R2-GigabitEthernet1/0/0] als restart mode automatic
```

(iii) [R2-GigabitEthernet1/0/0] **return**Verify the configuration results, and check the configuration of interface ALS on R1 and R2. The specific commands and execution results are as follows.

```
<R1> display als interface GigabitEthernet1/0/0
Interface                  Mode   Pulse Interval Pulse  Width
GigabitEthernet1/0/0       AUTO   100                    2
<R2> display als interface gigabitethernet 1/0/0
Interface                  Mode   Pulse Interval Pulse  Width
GigabitEthernet1/0/0       AUTO   100                    2
```

(c) EEE configuration

By default, the network equipment supplies power to each interface with constant power, and even if an interface is idle, it consumes the same energy. After configuring the EEE function of the electrical interface, the power of the electrical interface is dynamically adjusted according to the network traffic. When the interface is idle, the system automatically adjusts the power supply to the interface, which enters the low power consumption mode, that is, the sleep mode, reducing the overall energy consumption of the system and achieving the purpose of energy saving; when the interface starts to transmit data normally, the normal power supply is restored. The EEE mechanism can only be configured on electrical ports above 100 Mbit/s, not supported by optical ports, Combo ports with photoelectric multiplexing and electrical ports with negotiation rate of 10 Mbit/s. By default, the EEE function of the electrical port is not enabled. The operation steps for enabling the EEE are as follows.

(i) Execute the [system-view] command to display the system view.

(ii) Execute the command [interface *interface-type interface-number*] to display the interface view.

(iii) Execute the command [energy-efficient-ethernet enable] to enable the EEE of the electrical port.

6.1.2   Software Resource Management and Maintenance

In the process of operation and maintenance, operation and maintenance personnel should not only manage hardware resources, but also configure and manage software resources, including license management, configuration of equipment startup files, system software upgrade, software patch management, file management, interface management and so on.

1. License management

A license is a contract form in which suppliers and customers authorize/get authorization of the use scope and term of products sold/purchased. Through the license, customers can get the corresponding services promised by suppliers. After purchasing the device, the user can use the basic functions of the equipment. When the user need to use value-added features or expand equipment resources due to service expansion, he/she must purchase licenses for corresponding functions or resources of the equipment to meet service needs. Such function or resource control based on license allows the user to flexibly choose the appropriate license as needed, and to use the value-added features customized without purchasing additional devices, thus effectively reducing the cost of the user.

The license can be divided into COMM and DEMO types by the use. Under normal circumstances, the licenses purchased according to the contract are all COMM type, most of which is generally permanent. But a part of COMM licenses are subject to fixed term. Temporary licenses used for special purposes such as testing and trial use are DEMO licenses, which are generally subject to strict time limit.

The physical form of license is represented by license authorization certificate and license file. The licenses feature convenience, security and disaster tolerance. Convenience means that the installation of license is an uninterrupted process, which does not need to restart the device, nor affect other running services. Security is reflected in the binding of license file and equipment serial number (ESN), that is, the license file is unique and exclusively corresponds to the device. If the content of the license file is modified manually, the file will be invalid immediately, thus effectively preventing the license from being stolen. In addition, in case of unexpected emergencies, such as earthquake, rescue, etc., the license activated by the traditional license mechanism can also be converted into the disaster-tolerant state. In the disaster-tolerant state, the resource-based license no longer controls the size of corresponding dynamic resources, but opens up the maximum resources that the product can support, ensures the product to work fully, and satisfies the service to the maximum extent. Hence the disaster-tolerant mechanism.

In license management, the following concepts should be noted.

(a) License file

The license file is an authorization file that controls the capacity, function and time of the software version. It is generated by special encryption tools according to the contract information, and is generally distributed in the form of electronic document.

In practical application, one device can only load one license file. When the number of features or resources contained in the currently loaded license file is insufficient, it is necessary to increase the number of corresponding functions or resources, that is, license expansion. The Electronic Software Delivery Platform (ESDP) of Huawei automatically merges all license items on the same device to generate the final license file, and then the device reloads the merged license file to complete the license expansion.

(b) License authorization certificate

The license authorization certificate, also called license certificate, records the product name, authorization ID, customer name and validity period of the license. The license authorization certificate is sent to the customer by mail, or provided to the customer with the product in paper (A4 size) or CD. Only the COMM license includes a license authorization certificate.

(c) ESN

ESN is a character string used to uniquely identify a device, which is the key to ensure that the license is granted to the designated device, also known as "device fingerprint".

(d) License serial number

The license serial number (LSN) uniquely identifies the license file.

(e) Revoke code

A character string obtained after executing the revoke command on the network element is called revoke code. This character string is the certificate for self-service ESN change and adjustment after logging in to the license website. After the revoke command is executed on the network element, the license file on the network element is invalidated immediately.

(f) Expired period

The license limited by a fixed term enters the expired trial period after the running deadline, and the trial days at this time are called the expired period, which is generally 60 days. During the expired period, the features in the license file continue to run normally, and after the expiration period, the features in the license file cannot be used normally.

The management of license generally includes applying for, installing, viewing, uninstalling, upgrading or downgrading, restoring the license, etc. Next, examples are given to illustrate the common operation steps of license management.

(a) Apply for the license.

The application for the license includes the application for COMM license and for temporary license. Among them, the temporary license is applicable to temporary tests, such as POC test in the stage of market expansion, brand exhibition, and service scenarios of R&D test before product launch, etc. If the user needs to apply, he/she needs to contact Huawei technical support to obtain a temporary license. The following mainly introduces the application of COMM License.

There are two ways to apply for COMM license: authorization activation and password activation. When using the authorization activation method, you can enter query conditions (such as contract number, order number and authorization ID) to query authorization, and then select authorization according to the query results before activation; when using the password activation method, you must obtain the activation password from the license certificate and activate the license through the activation password. Currently, only the enterprise network user is eligible to the password activation method.

[Example 6.9]
Application for COMM license

There are two ways to apply for COMM license: authorization activation and password activation. The specific operation steps of application through password activation are as follows.

(i)   Obtain the authorization ID or activation password from the license certificate.The example of a license certificate is shown in Fig. 6.5.
(ii) Log in to the device and execute the command [display esn] in any view to obtain the ESN of the device.

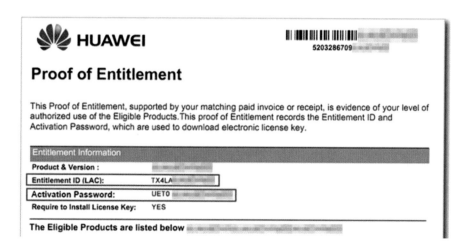

Fig. 6.5 An example of License certificate

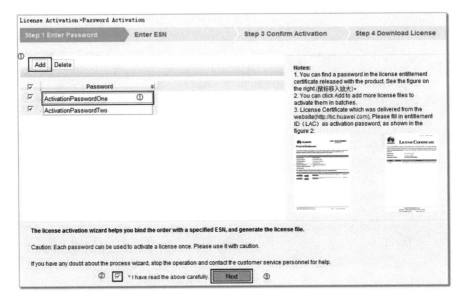

Fig. 6.6 Password activation—enter the authorization ID or activation password

Fig. 6.7 Password activation—enter the ESN of the device

(iii) Log in to ESDP website.

(iv) Activate the license.

- Select the option "License activation" -> "Password activation" in the left tree navigation bar, enter the authorization ID or activation password in the text box "Activation password", check the "I have learned the above information" check box after confirmation, and click the "Next" button, as shown in Fig. 6.6.

- Bind the ESN of the device. Enter the ESN directly, or select the added device (network element) to obtain the ESN, and click "Next", as shown in Fig. 6.7.

License Activation >Password Activation

| Step 1 Enter Password | Enter ESN | Step 3 Confirm Activation | Step 4 Download License |

	ESN	Company Name	Existing Volume	Final Volume	Product	
1	ESNofEsightForTest==		-	Part Details	eSight	

Back   Activate

Fig. 6.8   Password activation—confirm activation

Fig. 6.9   Password activation—download the license

✓   **Activated successfully.**
To download the license, click Download here or go to the
Equipment (Node) Management page.

Download   Go to Home Page

- Enter the activation confirmation interface and confirm the activation information, as shown in Fig. 6.8. If it is correct, click the "Confirm activation" button to enter the next step; otherwise, click the "Back" button to modify it.
- After successful activation, enter the license download screen, as shown in Fig. 6.9, and click the "Download" button to download the license file locally.

(b) Install the license.

After the license application is successful, it needs to be installed on the device before it can be used. Taking router AR3260 as an example, the operation steps of license installation are as follows.

[Example 6.10]
License installation.

After the license application is completed, it can be downloaded locally, assuming that the license file is named "LICAR3200all_201404110L1Q50. dat" (note that the license file name cannot contain spaces). The specific operation steps are as follows.

(i) Upload the license file to the device by FTP or TFTP.
(ii) Execute the command [license active *file-name*] to activate the license file and obtain the corresponding authorization. The command and execution results are as follows.

```
<Huawei> license active LICAR3200all_201404110L1Q50.dat
Info: The License is being activated. Please wait for a moment.
GTL Verify License passed with minor errors on MASTER board:
     This item LAR0CM00 License File value more than maximum value.
     This item LAR0CT00 License File value more than maximum value.
Warning: If this operation is performed, the trial license may
          replace the current license, and resources and functions
          in the current license may reduce. Continue? (y/n) [n]:y
Info: Succeeded in activating the License file on the master board.
```

(c) View the license.

After installing the activated license file, execute the [display license] command to view the detailed information of the activated license file in the current system, including the name, storage path, status and revoke code of the license file.

If you only need to check the license status of the master control board, you can execute the command [display license state]. The output information and description of this command are shown in Table 6.1.

In addition, you can check the usage of the resource items defined in the license file by executing the command [display license resource usage]. The output information and description of this command are shown in Table 6.2.

(d) Uninstall the license.

Table 6.1 Output information and description of the command [display license state]

Item	Description
Master board license state (Status of the master board license)	Normal: Normal activation state Demo: Demo status Trial: Expires and enters the expired trial period. The License file in this state is still valid during the trial period Emergency: State of emergency Default: Default state
The remain days (Days remaining)	Remaining valid days of the license

Table 6.2 Output information and description of the command [display license resource usage]

Item	Description
ActivatedLicense	Activated license file name and storage path
FeatureName	Feature name
ConfigureItemName	Control item name
ResourceUsage	Proportion of resource usage

For the redundant license files installed on the device, you can uninstall and delete them to save the storage space. The specific operation steps are as follows.

(i) Execute the [license revoke] command in the user view, so that the license that needs to be uninstalled at present get into a trial state.
(ii) Upload and activate a new license file. For specific operation steps, please refer to the operations of installing license.
(iii) Execute the [delete *filename*] command in the user view to delete the license file to be uninstalled, where "*filename*" is the name of the license file to be deleted.

(e) Merge the license.

In the process of operation and maintenance, if some devices need to be temporarily suspended (for example, those need maintenance, etc.), the licenses of such devices can be merged with the license of other devices, so that the existing license resources can be fully utilized and the service capability will not be affected. The operation steps are as follows.

(i) Obtain revoke codes of the disabled device and target device.

- Execute the [license revoke] command in the user view to change the current license into trial state and obtain the license's revoke code.
- Or execute the command [display license revoke-ticket] to obtain the license's revoke code after changing the current license into trial state.

(ii) Provide the revoke code to Huawei technical support personnel, who will perform the license merging operation.

2. System management

System management refers to the management of device software, configuration files and system patches.

Among them, the software of the device includes BootROM software and system software. After the device is powered on, first run the BootROM software to initialize the hardware and display the hardware parameters, and then run the system software. On the one hand, the system software provides the function of driving and adapting the hardware, on the other hand, it realizes the service characteristics. BootROM software and system software are necessary for starting and running the device, which provide support, management, service and other functions for the whole device.

A configuration file is a collection of command lines. The user saves the current configuration in the configuration file, so that these configurations can continue to take effect after the device restarts. In addition, through the configuration file, the user can conveniently consult the configuration information, and can also upload the configuration file to other devices to realize batch configuration of the device.

Patch is a kind of software compatible with the system software, which is used to deal with the problems that need to be solved urgently. During the device operation, it is sometimes necessary to modify the software of device system for adaptability and debugging, such as correcting the defects in the system and optimizing a specific function to meet the service requirements. Patches are usually released in the form of patch files. A patch file may contain one or more patches, and different patches deliver different functions. When the patch file is loaded into the memory patch area by the user from the memory, the patches in the patch file will be assigned a unique unit serial number in the memory patch area for identifying, managing and operating each patch.

In the process of operation and maintenance, for security reasons, the operation and maintenance personnel need to back up the configuration files of network device. If some new features need to be deployed on the device, the operation and maintenance personnel also need to upgrade the version of system software or install new system patches. The following will introduce the methods of software upgrade, patch management and configuration file backup and recovery.

(a) Software upgrade.

In the process of equipment operation, it may be necessary to add new features and optimize the original features based on user requirements. At this time, it is necessary to upgrade the current software version to meet user requirements. This optimizes the device performance, increase the new features, and solve the problem overdue update.

In order to ensure the smooth upgrade, the following preparations should be made before upgrading the software.

(i) The user prepares relevant hardware as required, such as clearing the memory space of the device for storing supporting files for the new version.

(ii) Confirm whether to apply for a new GTL license file. If so, do obtain it from the formal channels of Huawei.

(iii) Get the required upgrade software. Do get the new version of system software (*.cc) to be upgraded and the supporting files for the new version from the formal channels of Huawei.

(iv) In the user view, execute the [display version] command to check the current software version. If the version is consistent or better than the version to be upgraded, there is no need to upgrade.

(v) Check the running status of the device through a series of commands.

- In the user view, execute the command [display memory-usage] to check the memory usage rate of the master control board of the device, so as to ensure the normal operation of the master control board.

- In the user view, execute the command [display health] and record the displayed information. If there is any problem that cannot be located during the upgrade, send the information to Huawei technical support engineers for fault location.

(vi)   Build an upgrade environment, where Web or CLI can be used. If CLI is used, FTP, TFTP, XModem and other different ways can be used to transfer files.

(vii)   Back up the important data in the storage medium of the equipment to be upgraded.

(viii)   Check the remaining space in the storage medium of the device to be upgraded to ensure that there is enough space to store the software and supporting files to be uploaded and upgraded.

The following will take AR2220 as an example, and its topological structure is shown in Fig. 6.10, respectively introducing the operation process of upgrading system software in different ways such as Web, FTP and TFTP.

[Example 6.11]
System software upgrade (Web mode)

Web mode refers to that the user logs in to the device through HTTP or HTTPS, where with the device as the server, the graphical operation interface is provided through the built-in Web server to facilitate the user's intuitive and convenient management and maintenance of the device. Operation steps of software upgrade in Web mode are as follows.

(i)   Log in to the device by Web (refer to the corresponding parts of Sects. 5.2 and 5.3 for details).

(ii)   Select "System management" -> "Upgrade maintenance", and then "System software" tab to enter the interface of upgrade maintenance for system software, as shown in Fig. 6.11.

(iii)   Click the "Browse" button to select the system software to be uploaded, which is the new version of system software (*.cc) obtained from formal channels in the preparation stage.

(iv)   Click the "Load" button to upload the system software to the device, and designate the uploaded system software as the system software to be used when the device starts up next time.

Fig. 6.10   Software upgrade topology

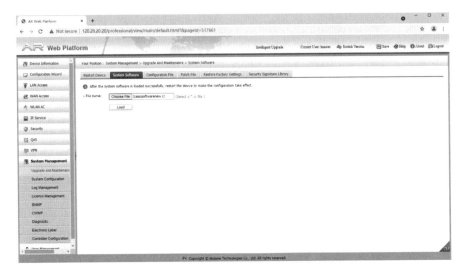

Fig. 6.11 Interface of upgrade maintenance for system software

After restarting the device, the specified system software takes effect and the upgrade process is completed.

[Example 6.12]

System software upgrade (FTP mode)

Log in to the device by Telnet or STelnet, and the system software is transmitted between the terminal and the device via FTP, where with the device as the FTP client or server.

(i) Serving as the FTP client, the device is subject to the operation steps as follows.

When the device serves as the FTP client, it is necessary to open the FTP server on the maintenance terminal (PC), and place the new version of system software (*.cc) obtained through formal channels in the root directory of the FTP server. The IP address of the maintenance terminal, that is, the FTP server, is 192.168.0.11, as shown in Fig. 6.12.

Log in to the device by Telnet or STelnet (refer to the corresponding parts of Sects. 5.2 and 5.3 for details), and perform the following operations.

- In the user view, execute the [ftp *host* [*port-number*]] command and log in to the FTP server on the PC, where "*host*" is the IP address of the maintenance terminal, and "*port-number*" is the port of FTP server. If the port is "21" by default, it can be left blank. After entering the correct user name and password, you can successfully log in to the FTP server.

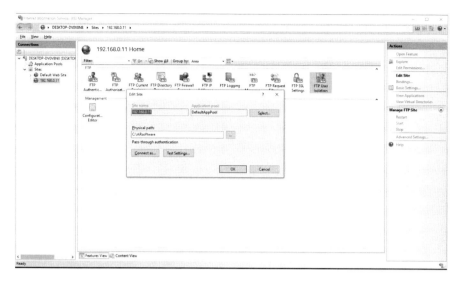

Fig. 6.12   Open the FTP Server on PC

```
<Huawei>ftp 192.168.0.11
Trying 192.168.0.11 ...
Press CTRL+K to abort
Connected to 192.168.0.11.
220 欢迎访问 Slyar FTPserver!
User(192.168.0.11:(none)):user1
331 Please specify the password.
Enter password:
230 Login successful.
```

- Execute the [binary] command to set the file transfer mode to binary mode.

```
[Huawei-ftp]binary
```

- Execute the command [get *remote-filename* [*local-filename*]] to download system files from FTP Server, where "*remote-filename*" is the file name of the new-version system software that needs to be downloaded on the FTP server, and "*local-filename*" is the file name that is downloaded locally, and it is unnecessary to specify if it does not need to modify.

```
[Huawei-ftp]get ar2200new.cc
200 Port command successful.
150 Opening BINARY mode data connection for file transfer.
1%_ 2%_ 3%_ 4%_ 5%_ 6%_ 7%_ 8%_ 9%_10%_11%_12%_13%_14%_15%_16%_
17%_18%_19%_20%_
21%_22%_23%_24%_25%_26%_27%_28%_29%_30%_31%_32%_33%_34%_35%

36%_37%_38%_39%_40%_
41%_42%_43%_44%_45%_46%_47%_48%_49%_50%_51%_52%_53%_54%_55%

56%_57%_58%_59%_60%_
61%_62%_63%_64%_65%_66%_67%_68%_69%_70%_71%_72%_73%_74%_75%

76%_77%_78%_79%_80%_
81%_82%_83%_84%_85%_86%_87%_88%_89%_90%_91%_92%_93%_94%_95%

96%_97%_98%_99%_100%
Transfer complete
FTP: 181886978 byte(s) received in 297.370 second(s) 611.66Kbyte(s)/
        sec.
```

- After downloading the system file successfully, execute the [bye] or [quit] command to terminate the connection with the server.

```
[Huawei-ftp]bye
```

- Execute the [dir] command in the user view to check that the new-version system file exists in the current storage directory of the router.
- In the user view, execute the command [startup system-software *filename*] to set the system software to be loaded at the next startup, where "*filename*" is the file name of the new-version system software on the device.

```
<Huawei>startup system-software ar2200new.cc
```

- Execute the [reboot] command in the user view to restart the device. After that, the upgrade is completed.

```
<Huawei>reboot
```

(ii) Serving as the FTP server, the device is subject to the operation steps as follows.

- Log in to the device by Telnet or STelnet (refer to the corresponding parts of Sects. 5.2 and 5.3 for details).
- In the user view, execute the [ftp server enable] command to start the FTP server.

```
[Huawei] ftp server enable
```

- Execute the [aaa] command to display the AAA view.

```
[Huawei] aaa
```

- Create an FTP user, whose username is "Huawei" and password is "Huawei@123".
- Execute the command [local-user *user-name* password cipher *password*] to configure the local user name and password. Here, the italicized "*user-name*" and "*password*" are the user name and password set by the user.
- Execute the command [local-user *user-name* privilege level *level-number*] to set the user level, where "*user-name*" is the user name created by the user, which is "huawei" here, and "*level-number*" is the number of user level, which can be set to 3 here.
- Execute the command [local-user *user-name* service-type ftp] and configure the service type of local user to FTP, where "*user-name*" is the user name created by the user, which is "huawei" here.

```
[Huawei-aaa] local-user huawei password cipher Huawei@123
[Huawei-aaa] local-user huawei privilege level 3
[Huawei-aaa] local-user huawei service-type ftp
```

- Execute the command [local-user *user-name* ftp-directory *directory*] and configure the authorized directory for the FTP user, where "*user-name*" is the user name created by the user, which is the same as that in step d; "*directory*" is the root directory of the FTP server on the device, if which is set to "flash:", it means that the FTP root directory is the root directory of the flash card.

```
[Huawei-aaa]local-user huawei ftp-directory flash:
```

- Execute the command [display ftp-server] to view the configuration information of the FTP server.

```
[Huawei]display ftp-server
    FTP server is running
    Max user number                    5
    User count                         1
    Timeout value(in minute)      30
    Listening port                     21
    Acl number                          0
    FTP server's source address    0.0.0.0
```

- Open the FTP client on the PC and log in to the FTP server on the device, as shown in Fig. 6.13. Execute the [binary] command to set the file transfer mode to binary mode. Execute the [put *remote-filename*] command to upload the acquired new-version system software to the device, where "*remote-filename*" is the storage path and file name of the new-version system software on the PC.
- In the user view, execute the command [startup system-software *filename*] to set the system software to be loaded at the next startup, where "*filename*" is the file name of the new-version system software on the device.

▪ C:\WINDOWS\system32\cmd.exe - ftp 192.168.0.1

```
C:\Users\yelb>ftp 192.168.0.1
连接到 192.168.0.1。
220 FTP service ready.
530 Please login with USER and PASS.
用户(192.168.0.1:(none)): huawei
331 Password required for huawei.
密码:
230 User logged in.
ftp> binary
200 Type set to I.
ftp> put e:/arsoftware/ar2200new.cc
200 Port command okay.
150 Opening BINARY mode data connection for ar2200new.cc.
226 Transfer complete.
```

Fig. 6.13 Upload the system software with the PC as the FTP client

```
<Huawei>startup system-software ar2200new.cc
```

- Execute the [reboot] command in the user view to restart the device.
  After that, the upgrade is completed.

```
<Huawei>reboot
```

[Example 6.13]
System software upgrade (TFTP mode)

When TFTP is used to transfer files, the device only serve as a TFTP client. The specific operation steps are as follows.

(i) Open TFTP server software on the PC and set the TFTP server root directory as the directory where the new-version system software is located, as shown in Fig. 6.14.
(ii) Log in to the device by Telnet or STelnet (refer to the corresponding parts of Sects. 5.2 and 5.3 for details).
(iii) In the user view, execute the command [tftp *tftp-server* get *source-filename* [*destination-filename*]] to download the system file from the PC. where "*tftp-server*" is the IP address of the TFTP server, "*source-filename*" is the directory and file name of the new-version system software to be downloaded, and "*destination-filename*" is the name of

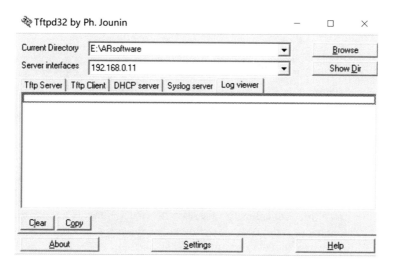

Fig. 6.14   Set the TFTP server root directory

the file downloaded to the device, which may not be specified if it needs no change.

```
<Huawei>tftp 192.168.0.11 get ar2200new.cc
```

(iv) In the user view, execute the command [startup system-software *filename*] to set the system software to be loaded at the next startup, where "*filename*" is the file name of the new-version system software on the device.

```
<Huawei>startup system-software ar2200new.cc
```

(v) Execute the [reboot] command in the user view to restart the device. After that, the upgrade is completed.

```
<Huawei>reboot
```

(b) Patch management

Patch management includes installation and uninstallation of system patches. Patches are installed to upgrade the system without interrupting the service. If the patch file does not need to take effect immediately, it can be executed after the next startup as specified. Uninstalling patches can deactivate patches that do not meet the system requirements, or delete patch files that are not needed by the system, thus releasing the memory space in the patch area of the master control board.

(i) Install the patch.

Since more than one patch files cannot run in the system simultaneously, it is necessary to execute the [display patch-information] command to check all the current patch information, including the running patch files, before installing a patch. If the running patch file is displayed in the information, the patch deletion operation should be performed to complete the uninstallation and deletion of this patch file.

Before loading a patch, the user need to obtain the patch file through Huawei support website and upload it to the device. For specific steps, please refer to the software upgrade section. To install and load the new patch file immediately, execute the [patch load *patch-name* all run] command in the user view, where "*patch-name*" is the file name of the new patch, and the system will install and activate the patch immediately. If you want to load a new patch file at the next startup, execute [startup patch *patch-name*] in the user view, where "*patch-name*" is the file name of the new patch, and the system will load the new patch file at the next startup.

(ii) Uninstall the patch.

If the patch fails to meet the system requirements, or the storage space for the patches is insufficient, the user can uninstall the patch. In the user view, execute the [patch delete all] command to delete all patches in the system.

(c) Backup and recovery of configuration files

In the process of device operation, abnormal operation may occur for various reasons, which may affect the service. In order to ensure quick repair of faults and service recovery, backup of configuration files is required during routine maintenance.

For the device running normally, there are many ways to back up the configuration files, among which the following are common.

(i) Copy them directly from the screen. In this way, the user logs in to the device through CLI, executes the command [display current-configuration] to copy all displayed information to the text file, and then saves the text file to back up the configuration file to the hard disk of the maintenance terminal.

(ii) Back up the configuration file to the flash card or other memories. The following steps are given to back up the configuration file to the flash card.

```
<HUAWEI> save config.cfg
<HUAWEI> copy config.cfg backup.cfg
```

(iii) Back up via the FTP or TFTP. Through the FTP or TFTP, the user can transfer the configuration file to the hard disk of the maintenance terminal, the specific operation mode of which is similar to that in software upgrade.

In case of device failure, you can transfer the previously backed-up configuration files to the device. Execute the [startup saved-configuration] command to specify the configuration file for restart (specified as the file name of the backup configuration file transferred to the device), and then execute the [reboot] command to restart the device, thus restoring the configuration and repairing the failure.

6.2 Routine Maintenance and Troubleshooting

Network maintenance refers to the unified and coordinated actions in management and technology for the normal operation of the network system and the improvement of its stability and security. Network maintenance mainly includes routine maintenance and troubleshooting, in which routine maintenance refers to routine inspection and maintenance of the network to eliminate hidden dangers of equipment operation when the network is in normal operation, while troubleshooting refers to the process of emergency handling of the network when the network fails.

6.2.1 Maintenance Overview

In network maintenance, network operation and maintenance personnel must be familiar with the use of various network equipment such as routers and switches, which constitute the core components of the network, and understand their performance, data configuration, command and function realization. Also, they need to follow up the configuration of main network equipment and the changes of corresponding parameters, and take corresponding technical measures to repair faults and resume services in time when faults occur.

Operation and maintenance personnel must follow the following precautions when carrying out network maintenance.

1. When a fault occurs, evaluate whether it is an emergency fault. If yes, use the pre-established emergency troubleshooting method to recover the fault module as soon as possible, and then resume the service.
2. Strictly abide by the operation regulations and industry safety regulations to ensure personal safety and equipment safety.
3. In the process of replacing and maintaining equipment parts, take ESD measures and wear the ESD wrist strap.
4. In the process of troubleshooting, if any problems are encountered, record all original information in detail.
5. All major operations, such as restarting the equipment and erasing the database, shall be ed., and the feasibility of the operation shall be carefully confirmed before the operation. Only after the corresponding backup, emergency and safety measures are taken, can them be performed by qualified operators.

6.2.2 Routine Maintenance

On the one hand, the stable operation of the network system depends on the complete network planning, on the other hand, it is necessary to discover and eliminate the hidden dangers of equipment operation through routine maintenance. Routine maintenance of network system mainly includes equipment environment check, basic equipment information check, equipment running status check, interface content check and service check, etc.

Normal operation environment is the premise to ensure the normal running of equipment. During routine maintenance, the temperature, humidity, air conditioning status and power supply status of the equipment room should be checked regularly. The Checklist for equipment operation environment is shown in Table 6.3.

The basic information check of equipment mainly involves the correctness of the operating version, patch information and system time of the equipment. The checklist for basic information of equipment is shown in Table 6.4.

In the process of equipment operation, it is also necessary to check its operation status, such as the board operation status, equipment reset status and equipment temperature. The checklist for operation status is shown in Table 6.5.

During routine maintenance, it is necessary to check the interface contents of network equipment and some basic services. Common interface content to be checked include interface configuration items, interface status and other information, while service checks involves the normality of services including IP, multicast, routing, etc. The items of interface content check and IP service check are shown in Table 6.6, and the recommended maintenance cycle is 1 week.

6.2.3 Troubleshooting

It is a challenge for network maintenance and management personnel to maintain the network correctly to prevent failure, and to ensure that the problems can be located and eliminated quickly and accurately after failure. This requires not only a deep understanding of network protocols and technologies, but also the establishment of a systematic troubleshooting idea and its rational application in practice, so as to isolate, decompose or reduce the scope of troubleshooting a complex problem and repair network faults in time.

1. Basic steps of troubleshooting

The basic steps of network troubleshooting are observing circumstance, collecting information, judging and analyzing, and identifying the causes. The basic idea is to systematically reduce or isolate all possible causes of faults into several small subsets, so that the complexity of the problems decreases rapidly. Generally speaking, the troubleshooting process can be divided into three stages, namely, the fault information collection stage, the fault location and diagnosis stage and the fault repair stage. The following paragraphs will introduce the handling and operations required in each stage.

(a) Fault information collection stage

In case of service failure, the failure-related information should be collected first, which includes the following contents.

Table 6.3 Checklist for equipment operation environment

SN	Item	Evaluation criteria and description	Check results
1	Reasonable and firm placement of the equipment	The equipment shall be placed firmly and flatly in a ventilated and dry environment where is away from the heat source. There shall be no debris accumulating around the equipment	• Passed • Not passed • N/A
2	Room temperature	Room temperature: 0–40 °C	• Passed • Not passed • N/A
3	Room humidity	Relative humidity (RH) of the equipment room: 5–90%	• Passed • Not passed • N/A
4	Air conditioning status	The air conditioning can run continuously and stably, to keep the temperature and humidity of the equipment room within the specified range	• Passed • Not passed • N/A
5	Cleanliness condition	1. The dustproof nets are cleaned or replaced in time to avoid affecting the ventilation and heat dissipation of the cabinet door and fan frame 2. The equipment itself have no obvious dust adhesion 3. Effective rat-proof measures are in place to prevent small animals (such as cockroaches) from entering the room	• Passed • Not passed • N/A
6	Compliance of grounding method and grounding resistance	1. It is generally required that the working grounding, protective grounding and building grounding for lightning protection in the equipment room are set separately, but the integrated grounding can be adopted in case of limitation of equipment room conditions 2. When the grounding cable of the equipment is connected to the terminal of the grounding bar, the grounding resistance should be less than 5 Ω 3. When the grounding cable of the equipment is connected to a grounding body, the grounding resistance should be less than 10 Ω 4. If the environment is not applicable for grounding, the grounding cables of multiple devices can be interconnected to maintain a consistent band voltage difference among the devices	• Passed • Not passed • N/A
7	Normal and reliable power connection	1. The power cable is correctly and firmly connected to the designated position of the equipment.The power indicator of the equipment is green and normally on 2. The power busbar is reliable in quality and is CCC-certified	• Passed • Not passed • N/A

(continued)

Table 6.3 (continued)

SN	Item	Evaluation criteria and description	Check results
8	Normal power supply system	The power supply system runs normally. 1. DC rated voltage range: -60 V to -48 V 2. AC rated voltage range: 100 V to 240 V	• Passed • Not passed • N/A
9	Acid-base condition	No metal rusting, PCB corrosion or connector rusting in the equipment room	• Passed • Not passed • N/A
10	Lightning protection	1. There is no outdoor routing for serial cables 2. there is no outdoor routing for ethernet cables	• Passed • Not passed • N/A
11	Normalization of installation	1. Filler panels are installed in the slots without the interface module 2. The interface modules, filler panels and cables are fixed by tightened screws 3. Insulation layers of various cables is avoided from contact with high temperature objects 4. All types of cables are classified neatly and properly bound, and are designated with certain redundant space, so as to prevent the wrong plugging and unplugging 5. The power cable is not bound with the signal cable 6. Unused light ports are installed with dust plugs	• Passed • Not passed • N/A

(i)   Time of failure, network topology structure of the failure point (upstream and downstream equipment connected by the failure equipment, network location), operation causing the failure, measures and results taken after the failure, failure symptom and affected service scope (the ports and services getting abnormal due to the failure), etc.

(ii)   Name, version, current configuration and interface information of the failed equipment.

(iii)   Log information generated in case of failure.

Failure information is generally acquired in two ways, one is through the [display] command, and the other is through viewing the equipment log and alarm information. Among them, the [display] command is an important tool for network maintenance and troubleshooting, which tells the current status of equipment, detects neighboring equipment, monitors the network as a whole, and locates network faults. The device provides several [display] commands for checking the status information of hardware, interfaces and software. The commonly used [display] commands are shown in Table 6.7. Analyzing these status information is helpful to locate network faults.

Table 6.4 Checklist for basic information of equipment

SN	Item	Check method	Evaluation criteria	Check results
1	Operating version of the equipment	Execute the [display version] command	The PCB version number and software version number of the board meet the requirements	• Passed • Not passed • N/A
2	Software package	Execute the [display startup] command	Check whether the following system file names are correct: 1. The current start package name 2. The name of the start package for the next startup 3. Backup package name 4. Current startup file name and next startup file name of configuration, license file, patch and voice	• Passed • Not passed • N/A
3	License information	Execute the [display license] and [display license state] commands in turn	1. Check whether the file name, version and configuration items of GTL license meet the requirements and confirm whether them need to be upgrade 2. Check that the item "Master board license state" is "Normal". When the item is "Demo" or "Trial", it is necessary to confirm that the license is still within the validity period	• Passed • Not passed • N/A
4	Patch information	Execute the [display patch-information] command	1. The patch file must meet the actual requirements. It is recommended to load the latest patch file corresponding to the product version issued by Huawei 2. Patches must have taken effect, that is, the total number of patches is consistent with the number of patches running	• Passed • Not passed • N/A
5	System time	Execute the [display clock] command	1. The time should be consistent with the local time (The error is no more than 5 min), so that the fault can be accurately located by time 2. If not, you can execute the [clock datetime] command in the user view to modify the system time	• Passed • Not passed • N/A

(continued)

Table 6.4 (continued)

SN	Item	Check method	Evaluation criteria	Check results
6	Flash space	Execute [dir flash:] command in user view	All files in the Flash space must be useful; otherwise, execute the [delete/unreserved] command in the user view to delete them	• Passed • Not passed • N/A
7	SD card space	Execute the [dir sd0:] or [dir sd1:] command in user view	All files in the SD card space must be useful; otherwise, execute the [delete/unreserved] command in the user view to delete them	• Passed • Not passed • N/A
8	Information center	Execute the [display info-center] command	The "Information Center" item is set to "enabled"	• Passed • Not passed • N/A
9	Configuration correctness	Execute the [display current-configuration] command	Verify that the device configuration is correct by viewing the configuration parameters currently in effect	• Passed • Not passed • N/A
10	Debug switch	Execute the [display debugging] command	When the equipment is running normally, the debug switches should all be turned off	• Passed • Not passed • N/A
11	Saving of configuration	Execute the [compare configuration] command in the user view	The current configuration is consistent with the configuration file to be started next time	• Passed • Not passed • N/A
12	Network connectivity	Execute the [ping] command and [tracert] command respectively	The devices communicate with each other normally	• Passed • Not passed • N/A

In addition, the diagnosis information of the device can be obtained with one click through the command [display diagnosis-information [*file-name*]], including the startup configuration, current configuration, interface, time and system version of the device. If the "*file-name*" parameter is not specified, the diagnosis information will be displayed on the terminal; if the "*file-name*" parameter is specified, the diagnosis information will be directly stored in the specified TXT file. It is recommended to output diagnosis information to the specified TXT file. By default, the saving path of TXT file is flash:/, and executing [dir] command in user view can confirm whether the file is generated correctly.

[Example 6.14]

Get diagnosis information with one click and output it as a TXT file

The following is an operation example of obtaining diagnosis information with one click and outputting it as a TXT file. The specific commands and execution results are as follows.

Table 6.5 Checklist for equipment operation status

SN	Item	Check method	Evaluation criteria	Check results
1	Board operation status	Execute the [display device] command	Check whether the in-place information and status information of the board are normal: The "Online" status is "Present" The "Power" status is "PowerOn" The "Register" status is "Registered" The "Alarm" status is "Normal"	• Passed • Not passed • N/A
2	Equipment reset	Execute the [display reset-reason] command in the diagnosis view	Verify that there is no abnormal reset operation by checking the reset information (including reset time and reset reason)	• Passed • Not passed • N/A
3	Equipment temperature	Execute the command [display temperature all]	The current temperature of each module is with the range from the upper to the lower limit, that is, the value of the "Temperature" is between "Upper" and "Lower"	• Passed • Not passed • N/A
4	Fan status	Execute the [display fan] command	The "Present" item is "YES", which indicates normal	• Passed • Not passed • N/A
5	Power status	Execute the [display power] command	The "State" item is "Supply", which indicates normal	• Passed • Not passed • N/A
6	FTP network service port	Execute the command [display ftp-server]	Unused FTP network service ports are closed	• Passed • Not passed • N/A
7	Alarm information	Execute the command [display alarm active]	There is no alarm. If there is an alarm, it should be recorded, and any serious alarm or at higher level should be analyzed and handled immediately	• Passed • Not passed • N/A
8	CPU status	Execute the command [display cpu-usage]	The CPU occupancy rate of each module is normal. If the CPU occupancy rate exceeds 80%, it should be followed up	• Passed • Not passed • N/A
9	Memory usage rate	Execute the command [display memory-usage]	Memory usage is normal. If the memory usage rate exceeds 60%, follow up it	• Passed • Not passed • N/A
10	Log information	Execute the [display logbuffer] and [display trapbuffer] commands	There is no abnormal information	• Passed • Not passed • N/A

Table 6.6 Items of interface content check and IP service check

Item		Check method	Evaluation criteria	Check results
Interface Content	Wrong package of interface	Execute the command [display interface]	When the service is running, check whether the interface has a wrong packet, including wrong packet of CRC, etc.	• Passed • Not passed • N/A
	Interface configuration item	Execute the command [display interface]	The configuration items of the interface are reasonable, such as interface duplex mode, negotiation mode, speed, loopback configuration, etc.	• Passed • Not passed • N/A
	Interface status	Execute the command [display interface brief]	The Up/Down state of the interface meets the planned requirements	• Passed • Not passed • N/A
	PoE	Execute the command [display poe power-state interface *interface-type interface-number*]	Interfaces supporting PoE are in normal state, with "Port power ON/OFF" being "ON" and "Port power status" being "Delivering-power"	• Passed • Not passed • N/A
	Interface statistics data	Execute the command [display ip interface]. Collect data twice every 5 min and compare the data	Under normal circumstances, the data of the second time stays non-increased, and the baseline is greater than 500	• Passed • Not passed • N/A
IP service	IP traffic statistics	Execute the [display ip statistics] command to collect data twice every 5 min and compare the data	1. The number of wrong packets and TTL time-out packets collected in a single time is less than 100 2. Under normal circumstances, the number of wrong packets and TTL time-out packets collected in the second time stays non-increased	• Passed • Not passed • N/A
	ICMP traffic statistics Information	Execute the command [display icmp statistics]	The "destination unreachable" and "redirects" items should not exceed 100	• Passed • Not passed • N/A

Table 6.7 Common-used [display] commands

Information item	Command	Description
Equipment Information	display device	Used to check the status of a board when it is not running normally.If "Status" is "Abnormal", the status is abnormal
Interface information	display interface	Used to view various information of interfaces, often for viewing statistics of equipment interface docking failures and packet loss
Version information	display version	Used to obtain version information of equipment software, BootROM, master control board, interface board and fan module, and to obtain size information of various memories
Patch information	display patch-information	Used to obtain service package information of the current system, including basic information such as service package version number and service package name
Electronic labels	display elabel	Used to check the electronic label information on the board
Equipment status information	display health	Used to check the equipment temperature, power supply, fan, power, CPU and memory usage rate, storage medium usage and other information
Current system configuration information	display cur-rent-configuration	Used to display all configuration information on the current device. You can use regular expressions to filter configuration information in order to find the information you need at present
Configuration information saved by the system	display saved-configuration	If the device fails to work properly after being powered on and entering the system, you can execute this command to view the startup configuration of it, that is, view the specified configuration file through the [startup saved-configuration] command 1. The [display saved-configuration last] command is used to view the last saved system configuration information 2. The [display saved-configuration time] command is used to view the time of the last saved system configuration
Time information	display clock	Used to display the current date and clock of the system
User log information	display logfile buffer	Execute this command in the diagnosis view to view the user log information in the log file buffer
Diagnosis log information	display diag-logfile buffer	Execute this command in the diagnosis view to view the diagnosis log information in the log file buffer
Alarm information	display trapbuffer	Used to check the information recorded in the Trap buffer of the information center
Memory usage information	display mem-ory-usage	[display memory-usage [slot *slot-id*]] command description: If the parameter "slot *slot-id*" is specified, the memory usage of the specified interface board will be displayed; If not specified, the memory usage of the master control board is displayed

(continued)

Table 6.7 (continued)

Information item	Command	Description
CPU occupancy information	display cpu-usage	[display cpu-usage [slot *slot-id*]] command description: If the parameter "slot *slot-id*" is specified, the CPU usage of the specified interface board will be displayed; If not specified, the CPU usage of the master control board is displayed

```
<Huawei>display diagnostic-information t0212.txt
This operation will take several minutes, please wait....
.................
Info: The diagnostic information was saved to the device
successfully.
<Huawei>dir
Directory of flash:/
Idx Attr   Size(Byte)      Date         Time(LMT)    FileName
0      drw-          -     Feb 12 2020   05:31:54      dhcp
1      -rw-    121,802     May 26 2014   09:20:58      portalpage.zip
2      -rw-      2,263     Feb 12 2020   05:31:49      statemach.efs
3      -rw-    828,482     May 26 2014   09:20:58      sslvpn.zip
4      -rw-    135,168     Feb 12 2020   07:39:14      t0212.txt
5      -rw-        724     Feb 12 2020   05:31:47      vrpcfg.zip
1,090,732 KB total (784,328 KB free)
```

The fault information can also be obtained by viewing the logs and alarm information of the device. When the device fails, the system automatically generates some system logs and alarm information. Collecting and analyzing these information will help the user to know what happened during the device operation and locate the failure point. The operation steps for obtaining the log and alarm information in the log file are as follows.

(i) In the user view, execute the [save logfile] command to manually save the information in the log file buffer to the log file.

(ii) Transfer all files in the directories "flash:/syslogfile/" ("flash:/logfile/" for v200r005c00 and later versions) and "flash:/resetinfo/" to the terminal by FTP/TFTP.

(b) Fault location and diagnosis stage

The purpose of fault location is to identify the cause of fault, which is the core action in troubleshooting. It depends on the fault information collected before. The more completely and accurately the information is collected, the more accurate and rapid the location can be.

There are many reasons for network failure. In the case of newly completed configuration, the causes of network failure may include the following:

(i) Incorrect or incomplete configuration;
(ii) Excessively strict rules for configuration access;
(iii) Equipment/protocol compatibility issues.

For the faults in the actual operation network, the common reasons may be as follows:

(i) Equipment changes, such as configuration modification, version upgrade, and board addition and deletion;
(ii) Link failure in the network, and the configuration modification of peripheral equipment;
(iii) Abnormal traffic, such as burst high traffic;
(iv) Hardware failure.

When a network fault actually occurs, the network management and maintenance personnel can reasonably analyze and locate the possible fault causes according to the fault information collected in the fault information collection stage, combining with appropriate network diagnosis tools, so as to lay a solid foundation for the next fault treatment.

(c) Fault repair stage

The purpose of troubleshooting is to eliminate the fault symptom and restore the normal operation of the network without causing other faults. Generally, the following three steps should be followed for troubleshooting.

(i) List the possible causes through the collected fault phenomena. This step usually requires fault handlers with high technical level and experience.
(ii) Develop a troubleshooting plan. When formulating a troubleshooting plan, the operation and maintenance personnel should comprehensively consider a variety of factors according to the network conditions and fault severity, including prioritize the troubleshooting steps, determining troubleshooting methods and tools, estimating the troubleshooting time and determining the actions after fault causes is identified, etc.
(iii) Troubleshoot according to the plan formulated in Step B. During the process of troubleshooting, before proceeding to the next scheme, it is necessary to restore the network to the state before implementing the previous scheme. If the changes made to the network by the previous scheme are saved, it may interfere with the location of fault causes and may lead to new faults.

2. Common fault cases

(a) Power module failure

Generally, there are two kinds of power module failures. One is that the device cannot be powered on, and the system indicator and power indicator fail to light at this time. The other is that the power indicator is always red.

If both "SYS" indicator and power indicator of the device are not on, the reason may be one of the following three.

(i) The power switch of the device is not turned on.

(ii) The power cable of the device is not firmly inserted.

(iii) The device's power supply module is faulty, which may be a pluggable power supply module, an external power adapter or a built-in power supply module.

Corresponding handling includes the following four steps.

(i) Confirm whether the power switch of the device is turned on.

(ii) Confirm whether the power cable of the device is plugged in.

(iii) Confirm whether the power module of the device is faulty. For the pluggable power module, it can be confirmed by replacing other pluggable power modules that works normally. If the device can power up normally, it can be confirmed that the pluggable power module is faulty. Please collect the fault information and contact technical support to replace the power module. If the device adopts an external power adapter, it can be verified by replacing another external power adapter that works normally. If the device can power up normally, it can be confirmed that the external adapter is faulty. Please collect the fault information and contact technical support to replace the power adapter.

(iv) After completing the above three steps, if the device still cannot be powered on normally, it can be confirmed that the device itself is faulty. Please collect the fault information and contact technical support to replace the device.

For the fault situation that the power indicator is always red, the reason may be one of the following three.

(i) The power module of the device is not firmly plugged in.

(ii) The pluggable power module of the device is faulty.

(iii) The external power supply module of the device is faulty.

In view of the above three fault causes, the following three steps can be taken to repair the fault correspondingly.

(i) Insert the power module firmly.

(ii) Replace the pluggable power module of the equipment.

(iii) Replace the external power module of the equipment.

(b) Fan module failure

Common fault symptoms of fan module are full-speed operation of fan, loud noise, and "STATUS" indicator in red flashing state. There are four possible fault reasons.

(i) The fan module is not fully inserted into the fan slot.

(ii) The fan blade is stuck by foreign matter, resulting in locked rotation.

(iii) The fan software is not upgraded to the latest version.

(iv) The Fan module is faulty.

Generally, the following steps can be taken to deal with fan module failures.

(i) Re-plug and unplug the fan module to ensure that the fan module is reliably inserted into the equipment backplane, and tighten the loose screws on the fan module panel.

(ii) Pull out the fan module, remove the foreign matter blocking the fan blades, and insert the fan module back into the frame.

(iii) Confirm whether the device software version corresponding to the fan is old. If so, upgrade the software version of the fan.

(iv) Replace the fan module with another one of the same model that works normally. If the fault disappears, it demonstrates that the fan module itself has a fault, and a new fan module should be replaced.

[Example 6.15]

Fan software version upgrade

When the fan module fails, one of the possible reasons is that the fan software version is too old. Taking AR3260 as an example, the operation steps of upgrading the fan software version are introduced below.

(i) When the fan operates at full Speed, execute the command [display fan] to check the status of the fan module. If the "Speed" status indicates "NA", the fan is abnormal.

```
<Huawei> display fan
FanId   FanNum   Present   Register   Speed   Mode
  16     [1-3]      YES       YES       NA     MANUAL
```

(ii) Re-plug the fan module, and execute the [display version] command to check the software version of the device. If the version is older than V200R003C01SPC300, the fan software version needs to be upgraded.

```
<Huawei> display version
Huawei Versatile Routing Platform Software VRP (R) software,
Version 5.120 (AR3200 V200R003C01SPC300)
Copyright (C) 2011-2013 HUAWEI TECH CO., LTD
Huawei AR3260 Router uptime is 1 week, 5 days, 2 hours, 40 minutes
BKP 0 version information:
1. PCB    Version : AR01BAK3A VER.B
2. If Supporting PoE : No
3. Board   Type   : AR3260
4. MPU Slot Quantity : 2
5. LPU Slot Quantity : 10
```

    (iii) Collect fault information and contact technical support to obtain the corresponding software version.

    (iv) Refer to the software upgrade steps in Sect. 6.1.2, and add the software version to the storage medium of the device by FTP or TFTP.

    (v) In the diagnosis view, execute the [upgrade fan-software startup] command to upgrade the fan software version.

```
<Huawei> system-view
Enter system view, return user view with Ctrl+Z
[Huawei] diagnose
Now you enter a diagnostic command view for developer's testing,
some commands
may affect operation by wrong use, please carefully use it with
HUAWEI engineer's direction
[Huawei-diagnose] upgrade fan-software startup
Info: Now Loading the upgrade file to fan-board, please wait a moment
Info: Upgrade the fan-board successfully. The new version is
108, while the old version is 103
```

    (vi) If the fan module is plugged or unplugged or the upgrade fails in the process of upgrading the fan software version, the following message will appear. At this time, you can re-plug the fan module, and return to Step E to upgrade the fan software version again.

```
[Huawei-diagnose] upgrade fan-software startup
Info: Now Loading the upgrade file to fan-board, please wait a moment
Load app get response fail! Index = 0xaa
Load Tx fail!
Error: Load the upgrade file to fan-board fail
```

(c) Board failure

    During the device operation, the board may fail to power on, register or reset normally.

    There are two possible reasons for the failure that the board fail to power on.

    (i) The board is not firmly inserted.

    (ii) The software version is not compatible.

Generally, the following steps can be taken to deal with board failures.

    (i) Check whether the board is firmly inserted.

    (ii) Execute the [display version] command to check the software version.

(iii) Submit the version information displayed in Step B to the technical support to check whether the board supports the software version.

During the software upgrade of the system, the original board that can be registered normally may fail to register, where if you execute the [display device] command, you will find that the "Register" status of the board is "Unregistered", meaning that the registration failed. The reasons for such failure generally include the following two.

(i) The board is not plugged firmly.
(ii) When upgrading the device software, the system software is upgraded before upgrading the board software. If the device occurs power failure during the board software upgrade after the system software upgrade, the board software update error will result.

The corresponding troubleshooting steps are as follows.

(i) Re-plug the board, and check whether there is a reverse pin in the backplane connector in the device case. If there is a reverse pin, repair the reverse pin before inserting the single board to ensure that the single board can be reliably plugged into the backplane.
(ii) Collect fault information and contact technical support to restore the corresponding software version.

In addition, the abnormal reset of the board may occur during the device operation. Generally, there are four reasons for the abnormal reset of the board.

(i) The system power supply is not connected reliably.
(ii) The board is not firmly plugged in the device backplane.
(iii) The power grid voltage is unstable.
(iv) There is a thunderstorm.

To repair the fault of abnormal board reset, the corresponding steps are as follows.

(i) Turn off the power switch of the device, and plug in the power cable and power module to re-power it on.
(ii) Re-plug the board for reliable connection between the board and the device backplane.
(iii) Observe whether the incandescent lamp is flickering to judge whether the voltage is stable. If the voltage is unstable, it is recommended to use a voltage stabilizer or an uninterruptible power supply to supply power.
(iv) Connect the grounding point on the device with the indoor equipotent connection terminal for effectively reducing the risk of abnormal board reset due to thunderstorm.

(d) Port failure

Generally, a port failure shows that the port cannot be "UP", and the indicator of the corresponding port on the device is abnormal. Common ports include Ethernet port, optical port, E1 interface, etc. Taking Ethernet port and optical port as examples, the troubleshooting steps for the occasion that the port cannot be "UP" are introduced as follows.

When the Ethernet port cannot be "UP", the port indicator is off, and the physical layer or protocol layer cannot be "UP" also. The possible reasons include the following four.

(i) There is a problem with the network cable.
(ii) There is a problem with the configuration of the network port.
(iii) There is a problem with the auto-negotiation compatibility.
(iv) The board is faulty.

The corresponding troubleshooting steps are as follows.

(i) Replace a workable network cable.
(ii) Check whether the configuration parameters (port speed, duplex or not, auto-negotiation, etc.) of the device at both ends of the network cable are consistent; if not modify them for consistence.
(iii) If the parameters at both ends are consistent and both are in auto-negotiation mode, but the fault still exists, try to set the ports at both ends to mandatory mode, because interconnection between some non-Huawei devices and Huawei devices may lead to failure of auto-negotiation.
(iv) Interconnect with another port on the same board with a workable network cable to perform the loopback test. If the loopback test works normally, it indicates that there may be a problem with the opposite device; otherwise, replace the port for the next test.
(v) If the port still fails to "UP" after the port replacement and the loopback test, it is judged that the board is faulty.
(vi) Replace a port on another board for test. If the fault is repaired, replace the original faulty board; otherwise, collect fault information and contact technical support.

After the optical fiber is connected, if the optical port fails to "UP", the "LINK" indicator corresponding to the optical port is generally off. Possible fault causes include the following four.

(i) There is a problem with the optical fiber.
(ii) There is a problem with the optical module.
(iii) Inappropriate optical attenuation is selected.
(iv) For the interface where the electrical port and the optical port are multiplexed, the fault cause may be that the interface is configured as an optical port.

For such failure, the general handling steps are as follows.

    (i) Adopt a workable optical fiber or optical module to verify whether
         there is any problem with the optical fiber or optical module.
   (ii) Confirm whether the optical module used by the port is Huawei-
         certified.
  (iii) Confirm whether the speed of the optical module is consistent with that
         of the optical port.
   (iv) Confirm whether the working wavelength of the optical module is
         consistent with that of the optical module at the opposite end.
    (v) Confirm whether the use distance of the optical module is equivalent to
         the nominal distance.
   (vi) For the interface where the electrical port and the optical port are
         multiplexed, execute the [display this] command in the corresponding
         interface view to check if the current interface is set as an optical port.
  (vii) Execute the command [display transceiver verbose] to check the infor-
         mation of the optical module, check whether there is an alarm, and take
         actions according to the alarm. For example, when it is indicated that
         the received signal is too high, the optical attenuation of the receiving
         circuit can be appropriately increased.
 (viii) After the above troubleshooting, if the fault still exists, collect fault
         information and contact technical support.

 (e) Storage failure
       Common storage failures include memory usage alarm, failure to use SD
     card, failure to use USB memory, etc.
       Memory usage rate refers to the proportion of the memory space occupied
     by the program to the total memory. It is one of the important indicators to
     measure equipment performance. By default, an alarm will be generated
     when the memory usage rate exceeds 95%. In this case, if the memory
     usage rate continues to increase, the system will eventually reset automati-
     cally, resulting in service interruption. In the process of equipment operation,
     some applications may occupy memory for a long time without releasing it,
     which leads to the cumulative increase of memory occupancy, eventually
     leading to the exhaustion of system memory. This failure is called memory
     leakage.
       In case of memory leakage, the total memory usage rate of the device, the
     size of Zone 2, the specified block, the memory usage of each PID and the
     specified PID shall be collected and delivered to technical support.
       The more common storage failure is the inability to read and write SD card
     or USB memory, which may be caused by damage or poor contact of SD card
     and USB memory. In case of such failure, it can usually be repaired by
     replacing or re-plugging the SD card or USB memory. If the failure still
     exists, you can collect fault information and contact technical support.

6.3 Summary

This chapter mainly introduces the related knowledge of network system resource management and maintenance, in which the resource management includes the management of hardware resources and software resources, while the maintenance involves routine maintenance and troubleshooting.

Through the study of this chapter, readers will have a understanding the main parts of network resource management and network system maintenance, master the common resource management methods and specific steps, and acquire familiarity with the routine maintenance of network system and certain capability to handle failures.

6.4 Exercise

1. In the frame equipment, the board on Slot 1 can be reset by executing the () command in the user view.

   A. reset system
   B. reset slot 1
   C. reset slot 2
   D. reboot

2. [Multiple choices] The energy-saving management technologies supported by Huawei network equipment include ().

   A. EEE
   B. Automatic fan speed regulation
   C. Automatic laser turn-off
   D. Frequency conversion

3. [Multiple choices] License can be divided into () by purpose.

   A. COMM
   B. DEMO
   C. Temporary License
   D. Permanent License

4. [Multiple choices] Electronic labels can be backed up by ().

   A. Backup to storage medium
   B. Backup to FTP server
   C. Copy and paste
   D. Backup to the TFTP server

5. [Multiple choices] Troubleshooting can be divided into ().

A. Fault information collection stage
B. Fault location and diagnosis stage
C. Service recovery stage
D. Fault repair stage

Index

Printed in the United States
by Baker & Taylor Publisher Services